Otherwise 181

Intro p95
47   81
53   92
          97
          98
         130
         137
         138
         144

         164, 171
         I. Story

         180
         205
         223
         229
         258
         273

Yale p269

THE MAKING OF A RANGER

Volume One in the series
INSTITUTE OF THE AMERICAN WEST BOOKS

Alvin M. Josephy, Jr., Acquiring Editor

Author, Seasonal Ranger, 1932. "Ninety-day wonder."

THE MAKING OF A RANGER

Forty Years with the National Parks

By *LEMUEL A. GARRISON*

with an introduction by Russell Dickenson
Director, National Park Service

an Institute of the American West Book

HOWE BROTHERS • SALT LAKE CITY AND CHICAGO
THE INSTITUTE OF THE AMERICAN WEST • SUN VALLEY

1983

published by
Howe Brothers — 155 Pierpont Avenue, Salt Lake City, Utah
and
The Institute of the American West — Sun Valley, Idaho

an Institute of the American West Book

manufactured in the United States of America

typography by Donald M. Henriksen

LIBRARY OF CONGRESS CATALOGING IN PUBLICATION DATA

Garrison, Lemuel A., 1903–
   The Making of a ranger.

   1. Garrison, Lemuel A., 1903–   . 2. Park rangers —
United States — Biography. 3. United States.
National Park Service — Officials and employees —
Biography. 4. National parks and reserves — United
States — History. I. Title.
SB482.A4G37   1983   333.78'3'0924   [B]   83-10841
ISBN 0-935704-19-1
ISBN 0-935704-18-3 (pbk.)

To Inger

my wife and partner in these adventures

ACKNOWLEDGMENTS

MANY THANKS TO Dr. Leslie Reid for the invitation to come to Texas A&M University, giving me the academic climate in which to work, and the opportunity to touch more young lives going into the conservation field; to Lois Beach, who crystalized the direction which this book has taken; to Peggy Lauer and her beautiful typing, whose patience was monumental; to Dr. Ed Heath, for coordinating all the extraneous material; to his wife, Dr. Kathleen Heath, who was the proofreader *par excellance*; to Mr. Alvin M. Josephy, Jr., of the Institute of the American West; to Richard Howe; and to the friends in this book without whom it could not have been written.

In addition, we wish to thank the following employees of the National Park Service for their assistance in locating photographs and maps for the book: Mary Vocelka, Research Librarian, Yosemite National Park; Edward M. Chamberlin, Curator, Grand Canyon Study Collection, Grand Canyon National Park; Joan M. Anzelmo, Public Information Officer, Yellowstone National Park; and Thomas DuRant, Picture Librarian, National Park Service Archives in Springfield, Virginia.

CONTENTS

FOREWORD

NATIONAL PARKS TODAY include some of the most scenic natural resources our continent has to offer — the wonders of Yellowstone, Yosemite Valley, seashores and lakeshores, the Everglades, and the Grand Canyon. It is somewhat miraculous that they have survived in their natural condition in the face of widespread deforestation, decimation of wildlife, exploitation of minerals and water resources, and an expanding population's voracious demands for food and fiber.

The national parks exist today because of the caring, dedicated commitment of men and women who believed in them. These have included presidents, cabinet officers, members of Congress, and leaders of the judiciary. Most important of all, however, are the thousands of Americans who have devoted their careers — their life's work — to protecting, nurturing, improving, and expanding the national parks.

Neither the lifetime nor the experience of any one individual has encompassed the history and all the experiences that culminate in the National Park System today. This autobiography by Lemuel Alonzo "Lon" Garrison describes a career which may come as close as any ever will. Lon's active years in the national parks extended from 1932 to 1973. He was seasonal ranger at Sequoia National Park; park ranger at Yosemite National Park; superintendent or assistant superintendent at Glacier, Grand Canyon, Big Bend, and Yellowstone National Parks and Hopewell Village National Historic Site; regional director in the Midwest and Northeast regions; national chief of conservation and protection; and chairman of the Mission 66 Steering Committee. Lon's experiences ranged broadly over the concerns and needs of national parks; he served at all levels of the National Park System. His lively and entertaining recounting of the highlights of an active National Park Service career provides insights we might otherwise have lost.

The Making of a Ranger is not only an autobiography. It illuminates the human devotion and dedication which has been essential, with public use and preservation, to the formation and management of national parks in America; and as Lon Garrison's contemporary in the National Park Service, I find that it reinforces our commonly-held experiences, observations, and expanding interpretations of this formative period in the history of the National Park System.

Russell Dickenson, Director
National Park Service

INTRODUCTION

THE MAKING OF A RANGER is an autobiography about my journey from ranger to National Park superintendent, with stations in some of the most beautiful scenery in America — Alaska, Arizona, California, Yellowstone, Montana, Texas, and Pennsylvania. It was also a journey into lively political, economic, and spiritual territory. The force that drove me all those years was a great sense of wonder which led first to awe and then identity with this living force we call Mother Nature. The unity of the natural world and my role in it was my message; evangelism became my purpose. I *had* to share my vision with others — and with whom more appropriately than park visitors?

This wonderful journey into the world of America's magnificent park lands led to exciting adventures: rescue missions for unfortunate park visitors; fire fighting in remote areas; wildlife observations and friendships; wilderness enjoyment; ski patrols; lost kids in campgrounds; contrary pack mules and hornets; communication with a host of inquisitive visitors and politicians; an overnight ski bivouac in a raging blizzard; the management of death under strange circumstances; and experiences with parks in other parts of our planet. These episodes are all recorded here — but there were more. They blend together with a respect and love for our environment and with a faith that my special ranger task was to cherish the resources and help visitors enjoy them. The visitors, in turn, might help with the job of caring for the parks.

I must include my youthful discovery of a natural world complete with a private glimpse of a first quarter moon, high in an August afternoon Idaho sky as my mother taught her turkey-herding son to be a good observer of nature; Alaskan adventures as a Forest Guard; and National Park beginnings for me, as well as my observations on the beginnings of the National Park Service.

I include too, meeting and courting the lovely, serene Norwegian girl, Inger Wilhelmine Larsen, and our half-century of love and growth together. The Depression years were frustrating as I pursued my degree in psychology at Stanford University and then secured a ranger appointment at Sequoia. As the years passed, we shared three youngsters, a love affair with American history as another dimension of the National Park role, ten years' residence at Grand Canyon, seven at Yellowstone, Regional Director years in Omaha and Philadelphia, and my final job as Superintendent of the National Park Service Albright Training Academy for Park Rangers at Grand Canyon. We then moved smoothly to retirement, a teaching career at Texas A&M University, and the writing of this book.

Now, as the Park years become history and assume less magnitude in our lives, Inger's career in ceramics and sculpture has also blossomed. She is committed to the selection and exhibition of Indian arts and crafts with the Arizona Arts Commission as well as her own creative ceramics and sculpture. She is a constant contributor to the quality preservation and development of native arts. She has contributed to a book on resource interpretation through a living history chapter on nature interpretation (G. W. Sharp, *Interpreting the Environment* [New York: John Wiley and Sons, 1976]).

We built and shared our careers together — first as a ranger family, then as a park official's family, and even more recently as art world participants. We freely entertained Senators, Governors, international conservationists and politicians, teachers, and artists. Many parts of the world are now home for our friends, former associates, former instructors, and former students.

Let's return for a moment to the legislation — and the people — that made my career possible. At the time of the formation of the Interior Department's Bureau of the National Park Service in 1916 there were already nineteen designated National Parks and several other categories of areas, including National Monuments, National Historical Parks, National Military Parks, National Battlefields, National Historic Sites, National Battlefield Sites, and National Cemeteries.

The legislative action year was 1916, although the drama began to develop much earlier — probably in 1913 when President Woodrow Wilson chose Franklin K. Lane as his Secretary of Interior. As I read the political realities of that situation, Lane (who was the City Attorney for San Francisco) was probably chosen for the Interior post because of *two* evident "national" problems. The *first* and the most political had to do with San Francisco's drinking water. For some years the city had focused on the Tuolumne River in Yosemite National Park as their future water supply. There were alternatives, but some way the attack was focused on the Tuolumne. This was prior to the establishment of the National Park Service, but it still required legislation to breach the protective wall of the Yosemite Act of 1890, which created Yosemite National Park. Under the leadership of Lane and San Francisco Congressman John Raker, a dam was completed across the Tuolumne at Hetch Hetchy in 1914–15 — later the site of my first permanent ranger job. The dam was a tragedy which mightily distressed John Muir and other early conservationists. But surprisingly, Raker then became a *supporter* of the *second* major program Interior must carry, and introduced legislation in the House to create a National Park Service. This is politics!

But more clout was needed, and Secretary Lane invited Professor Adolph Miller, an economist from the University of California, to come to Washington to help on Raker's National Park proposal.

Adolph Miller did not stay long. He had great ideas and major political input into policy and legislation about the Federal Reserve Board. So he moved to the Treasury Department. As he did so, President Wilson is supposed to have facetiously commented that "Lane will have to find another millionaire to work on the National Park legislation." Miller's major contribution was that he brought with him a young law student named Horace Marden Albright whom Miller called a "political reader." Albright was considerably more durable!

And most fortuitously, Secretary Lane at that same time received a letter from a National Park visitor complaining about the management of the National Parks. I have always assumed that this must have been about Yosemite. The letter was on a first-name basis to Lane and signed by Stephen Mather. They were University of California friends — as of course Miller and Albright were also! Secretary Lane is reported to have responded with equal informality:

"Dear Steve —

If you don't like the way the parks are being run why don't you come down here and run them yourself.
                                        Frank Lane."

Mather was a likely candidate. He was a successful businessman, the former Editor of the New York *Sun*, a member of the Sierra Club, a mountain climber, and a friend and admirer of John Muir (who died in 1914). But Mather did not want to be a National Park Director. He had other personal commitments. It took considerable negotiation and pressure to get Mather to come in and discuss his complaints with Lane. But he did and Lane introduced him to Horace Albright. Lane left them alone together in a private office with a wood fire to review National Park needs. They soon found an affinity of thoughts and principles which sparked a friendship and led to the great working team which exploded into both national and world conservation history.

From a sixty-six-year retrospect it is possible to recreate a comment upon a program that Mather and Albright suggested to Lane that day:

1. Establish the National Park Service. This was a real political job; Mather believed that he could lead it.

2. Create an operational unity for the National Parks within the framework of Interior. This was to be mainly Albright's task.

3. Develop public interest in parks and political support for them. This must be translated into larger appropriations. Political backing must be created, visitor facilities developed — roads, campgrounds, hotels, trails, and other facilities needed by park visitors. To get bigger appropriations, park use would be encouraged.

4. Add worthy new areas to the National Park system — purge it of unsuitable ones. This could be started promptly.

These are the major points that Mather and Albright reported to Lane, with an offer that they would both stay in Washington to get it done — their estimate of needed time was one year!

Reading between the lines, probably the clincher for Lane was the offer of this team to take it over. Ultimately they succeeded in all but the time frame. They tried, but that one year was too optimistic. It took longer.

Their first priority was for new National Park Service legislation. This became a major political campaign. Raker's bill to set up the

National Park Service was a beginning but needed more support, and after his rape of Hetch Hetchy, Raker did not have it. But Congressman William Kent, also from San Francisco, was another possible sponsor. Kent had served only briefly, but during that time he had donated a family estate, a magnificent grove of coast redwoods — *Sequoia Sempervirens* — to the National Parks. It was named for the greatest conservationist of the day — John Muir — The Muir Woods National Monument.

Kent's willingness to co-sponsor the National Park Service legislation became a great positive factor in the final enactment.

Mather was an old hand at national politicking and was confident that he could get the legislation passed. Albright was an apt student and soon adapted to the requirements of the legislative process. They were an excellent team. Mather often needed help from political laggards and his procedure was to take them to the golf course or on long pack trips or on other great journeys to create National Park enthusiasm. Albright was dependable and had a rapidly growing reputation for honesty and leadership. He had an uncanny perception of political opportunities, and his own idealism was always evident. The character of these two great men became the standard for the National Park Service. And this was the group I would join in 1932.

The vigor and enthusiasm of "the Service" was exemplified by the final successful passage of the Enabling Act on August 25, 1916, which became the foundation of the new service. There had been delays, and Mather and Albright had had to extend their own promised terms for a second year. By 1932, when I came on the scene, Mather and Albright had captured public acceptance for the idea of the preservation of our wild lands and historic heritage. It would become a very popular, exportable concept in the next fifty years. Many countries adopted the idea to their own use. And the philosophy that we as a nation should set aside areas where nature can take her own course became to many National Park Service employees and idealists a driving concept of tremendous challenge. Mather and Albright's legacy to us is immeasurable; today their ideas have become a part of our fabric of life and education. In 1932, I became a willing proponent of them.

National Park Service leadership was always supportive and compassionate, but the Parks themselves were my true lode-star. The Sherman Tree, Tokopah Falls, J O Pass, Yosemite Falls, the Grizzly Giant, The Iron Master's House, Chief Mountain, Bright Angel Creek, Boquillas Canyon, The Sierra del Carmen, and Old Faithful Geyser are still pristine and, in 1983 vernacular, the bottom line reads that these are my relict Holy Land! This is the real joy of my ranger tasks!

Other rangers with equal zeal have extended the horizon here and elsewhere. Later generations must decide if we did it well. At least the treasures remain about which to make decisions! Our vote is in — a ranger career was a great way to go!

But let's go back to the beginning, to a knobby-kneed ten-year-old youngster with big feet, called "Skinny Long Legs," a tourist as his dad drove a Studebaker touring car on a transcontinental journey in 1913. Fifty years of ranger adventures followed. Every conservation job was a ranger job. And if events from 1932 to 1933, when National Park philosophies and operational patterns were just emerging, are mixed with their blooming in the 1950s (and the 1980s dimensions of people and cities), it is just more comfortable that way.

CHAPTER I

THE TURKEY HERDER

THE MOTOR OF OUR GREAT 1913 STUDEBAKER seven-passenger touring car gave its last "chug" and died exactly astride the main track of the Union Pacific railroad about fifty yards from Wamsutter, Wyoming. We were perched on a ten-foot-high railroad embankment. Our family of six were all in the car. The self-starter was broken — we were locked in gear and couldn't even coast unless we could slide the car over the hump. It was about noon on Sunday, November 23, 1913.

I started to get the crank out of the back seat. It was under one of the jump seats. But suddenly from the east came the shrill scream of an urgent locomotive whistle — "WHOO! WHOO! WHOO! WHOOP TE DOO!" it yelled. A westbound passenger train was flying at us at high speed — possibly two miles away. Steam and smoke were flying above and behind as it demanded the right-of-way immediately! Our car doors flew open. Mother and the three kids erupted out of the tonneau with bundles of clothing and began to tumble down the embankment. Dad and I slid out of the front seat and ran — but if the train hit the car, where could we be safe?

"WHOO! WHOO! WHOO!" cried the engine. Sparks were flying from the wheels as the engineer sanded the brakes.

There were four cowboys sitting in the sunshine of the porch of the false-front Bugas hotel-store-bar that was Wamsutter's business district. As one man they rose and sprinted to the car and with a sudden *heave-ho* slid it safely away just in the nick of time. The train roared past. We were saved! The engineer probably had adrenalin shock for an hour. We did.

But we had other problems. As the big car coasted down the road embankment, the motor backfired, started, and dashed away, still in high gear, but fortunately steering in a big circle. Dad raced after it, leaped aboard, and then steered it on through the circle across the sagebrush, scattering the rest of our belongings from the open doors among the horses along the hitch rail.

This was our first meeting with cowboys. I had not expected them to wear halos, but they seemed to be more than angels that day! After the adrenalin released us from its spell, they helped us repack the car. We then had our first tin can lunch on butcher paper spread on the Bugas store counter in Wamsutter. We listened to a fervent invocation in which Dad thanked the Lord for His protection and the cowboys for their rescue. He was particularly eloquent. Lunch on the counter of the Wamsutter store was a big box of crackers, cans of corned beef, wienies (which they called Vienna Sausages), sardines, tomatoes, and peaches, plus bologna, cheese, potato chips (which we knew as Saratoga chips), a big dill pickle, a big raw onion, cookies, caramel candy, and a new beverage called soda pop. It was mostly foreign and very deluxe food to us kids. This was the rich man's way to travel! (The delightful memory has survived over six decades of similar meals. It was still an adventure in 1978 at the Castalon Trading Post store along the Rio Grande in Big Bend National Park. The only difference was one long-necked bottle of Lone Star Beer!)

Large and small, we all took part in an exhilarated gab fest following lunch. The cowboys contributed generously and responded freely. Yes, they were cowboys. Yes, they rode horses. Yes, Sunday was a day off, but only because there had been a community dance the night before. No, they were not married. They would return to bunkhouses or line camps that afternoon.

Then it was their turn. We were tourists — our car license plates said Nebraska, but where? Were we going back? Did we know a cattle buyer in Columbus, Nebraska? What would we do if it snowed? (We found out later that week. After Thanksgiving Day dinner in Ogden, Utah, it snowed heavily and we took the Union Pacific Railroad to Caldwell, Idaho. Dad returned in the spring to get the car.) Was the Studebaker car made by the same people who made Studebaker wagons? They were good wagons. Was it a good car? Why didn't the self-starter work? (One of the cowboys tinkered with it and it worked all day!) Did we need more gasoline? (We did. The Wamsutter store had a barrel of gasoline on a back porch with a little one-gallon-at-a-time pump and we filled up.)

(Forty-four years later, when I had just become Superintendent of Yellowstone National Park, I learned that Wamsutter was an important town in park history. One after another, the prolific and capable Bugas family of Wamsutter furnished seasonal rangers for Yellowstone. It surprised many people that I knew where Wamsutter was!)

In the early years before our move to Idaho I was a dedicated reader and dreamer, but alert to provocative words such as ranger, scout, pioneer, explorer, frontiersman, forester, even aviator, with adventuresome connotations.

Every evening after supper, mother would read aloud to us — my brother Firth, our three sisters, Pauline, Helen and Margaret, and me. We met the Greek tales of *Ulysses*, the *Jungle Book*, *Alice of Old Vicennes*, *Betty Zane* and other Zane Grey western dramas. I was certain that I wanted a life as full of color, adventure, travel and good deeds as these inviting tales suggested. I was less certain that I possessed the cool, unflinching, steady nerves of Zane Grey's golden heroes. With my equally youthful companions I discussed the phenomenon that these daring leaders never had to go to the bathroom! In our reading, we ignored it too.

I had become a tourist when I was ten. I had trouble spelling the word — the diphthong threw me. But suddenly I became a tourist because the family moved. We all became tourists.

Dad had had recurrent health problems — "weak lungs," the doctors called it. His own father, Alonzo Garrison, had died of tuberculosis contracted in a Confederate prison in Texas. Upon Alonzo's return to Iowa from the prison camp, no more than twenty years old, he acquired farm land, went to "Normal School," became a teacher, married Margaret Eliza Cross, and fathered two daughters. He died shortly before his third child was born. His wife made a prenatal vow that if the child were a son, he would be dedicated to both the ministry and to teaching. This was my dad, Lemuel.

He worked on his stepfather's farm, but with his mother's support he broke away to attend the Academy at the Central University of Iowa, a Baptist school in Pella. As a dedicated and inspiring young ministerial student, he "supplied" a number of nearby churches. By the exercise of great frugality he was able to help his mother with her subsequent children and still continue with his educational goals. After many years he not only graduated from Central's Academy, but also received a Bachelor's degree from the University as well, and became a permanent member of the University teaching staff. He then assisted his stepbrother and seven siblings with their higher education.

My father was a gracious and sincere, resounding minister, although not the evangelical type. He met and married the tall, hazel-eyed, blonde, English girl, Mary Firth, and together they went to Shurtliff, the Baptist Theological Seminary in Rochester, New York, where he received the degree of Doctor of Divinity. He then returned to his alma mater, Central University, and became its president. We lived in the gracious Dunn Cottage on campus. I have only vague memories of it because the drive for new adventures moved Lem and Mary to Cambridge, Massachusetts, where Dad acquired a Master's Degree in the new field of Behavioral Psychology from Harvard University.

He then moved to Grand Island, Nebraska, as President of Grand Island University, another Baptist school. Ultimately his wanderlust, his love of adventure and concern for his health, pulled him onward and in 1913 he traded Iowa and Nebraska farm land for ranch land in the Boise Valley in Idaho. Hopefully, the drier climate would be beneficial.

So our tourist adventures started from Grand Island, Nebraska. Dad signed up for an "Emigrant Car" from the Union Pacific Railroad. One summer afternoon I went with him to the railroad siding where he and a helper were packing for the move. The Emigrant Car, of course, was simply a clean box car. However, to a ten-year-old it was a magic carpet, a window into a dream world, a fabulous romantic starting point for great adventure. Our upright piano looked tiny and forlorn next to the wall in the box car. Our home furniture was a small, neat stack beside it. There was a water barrel with a lid and a dipper, a manager and bales of hay and straw for our horse and our generous milk cow, Old Cherry. There was a crate of noisy chickens in the car, and I saw my first bed rolls. Dad took all of this west, unloaded at the new farm home in Caldwell, and returned to Nebraska for the family.

He had just purchased the Studebaker. It was the cheapest transportation — educational, too. But the real reason for the purchase was Dad's love of challenge and adventure.

In September, 1913, Mother, Dad, and four youngsters (Polly, the oldest girl, stayed with friends in Grand Island to finish high school that year) packed the last of our belongings and travel gear into the car and we performed the rituals of "moving away." First, we drove east to Iowa to test the car, and for a final visit with all of our relatives. Our first stop was Pella.

Dad's stepbrother, Will Young, was on the University staff. Mother's sister, Martha Firth, was a history professor. Her brother, Nathan Firth, also lived in Pella. Pella remains a hallowed memory, as does my childhood residence in Dunn Cottage.

We visited Dad's mother in Knoxville, where she lived with her second husband. We went to every hamlet where Dad's sisters and halfbrothers and halfsisters lived, and every churchyard where his relatives were buried. We visited the small cemetery in Cascade where Mother's English parents had been laid to rest. We missed only John Firth — Mother's older brother who was a foreign missionary in Assam, India. Family relationships and pride in ancestry were important factors in social life.

Finally, we pointed our car west, ready for new adventure. It was now November, and we were suddenly in a hurry. We had a new life style. For several weeks we had been entertained in relatives' "guest rooms" and at special family farewell dinners. Now we were tourists with a routine of hotel rooms and restaurant meals — no convenient motels, no lunch supply stores, no ice suppliers, or even little refrigerators. Our days started in a hotel dining room where an impatient waitress might bawl our order through an open window to a cook we never saw, "Six on the oatmeal!"

Dad was an unskilled but optimistic driver. Our brakes were feeble, the road rugged and dusty, the springs stiff, and the car body sturdy. When Dad would see that we were about to hit a big bump or a dust pocket he would do his best with the brakes and holler "Everybody get set!" We would hang on grimly as the car bounced and rattled through the obstruction.

Helen and I took turns sharing the front seat with Dad as navigators. We had a 1913 Blue Book of the American Automobile Association with a faithful, mile-by-mile chronicle for our journey. We relied both on our speedometer and our trip odometer, keyed to the Blue Book.

For example:

CHEYENNE, WYOMING — set odometer to 0.00 at 16th and Cary. From center city go straight west on 16th Street crossing RR at 0.4 (odometer) and running under RR at 1.4 (odometer) fork in road. Avoid left hand road which leads to Denver keeping straight ahead along north side of tracks. Odometer 5.9 (now 4.5 miles past last previous reference point). Pass Orlet water tank on left shortly before commencing a long, winding upgrade.

And then,

. . . odometer 32.9 Fork — keep right, road is going over crest of divide at an elevation of over 8,000 feet.

Our self starter was an experimental device which operated by the simple expedient of yanking a wire on a recoil spring. It was usually out of order and we used the car crank frequently. If the motor was warm and not flooded I could often give it the quarter-turn flip needed to get it started. But I had to keep a loose hold on the crank handle, because sometimes it fired backwards. So usually Dad had to crank the car.

All roads were unpaved and only a few of them were graded. Tourists were curiosities to most of the local people. There were several cars a day going each way even in November, each with its separate little penumbra of dust. Occasionally we were reviled as public menaces. We frightened horses hitched to buggies or wagons, and dogs chased us. The unfortunate hound that overtook us was often unable to understand our size and speed and was run into. We scattered and sometimes killed roadside chickens. If you hit one of these creatures our advisors had counseled us — "Don't stop!" Ordinary leghorn roosters suddenly became blue-ribbon show stock. If you just kept going the farmer had no way to catch up with you and would be left shaking his fists at the empty sky and cursing! (Dad's mores would not tolerate this inhumanity, although we usually could not find anyone with whom to negotiate. And dead chickens were not frequent.)

We frightened people, too — not only because of our alarming speed, but because they rightly suspected that we were only the vanguard of what would prove to be an invading army. Heavens! Here was a college professor with a wife and four kids headed west in November, right up against the highest mountains in America.

In North Platte we had our first and only accident. A Hupmobile roadster came charging in from a side street and slammed into our right rear fender. I do not remember how the matter was adjusted or how the car was repaired, but we were not delayed. I remember the long-necked radiator fill pipe on the front end of the Hupmobile and the ragged dent in the radiator honeycomb which gushed hot water over our rear seat.

Even though we had the new-fangled "demountable tire rims," a puncture or a flat tire was at least a half-hour delay. It was a knuckle-buster performance with heavy, clanking tire irons, tube patching material, and a tire pump. Inner tubes were untrustworthy. Patches might slip off, or we might pinch another hole in a repaired tube as we remounted the tire and not discover this until we had pumped for ten minutes. The side curtains were unmanageable in a rain storm. The running board luggage carrier occasionally fell off. Light bulbs were apt to blow out, and fuses were unreliable. One day we finished driving well after dark. In a strange procession, I walked ahead carrying a kerosene lantern, illuminating the left wheel track while Dad steered slowly and cautiously behind me in low gear. Those hotel lights were mighty welcome!

Garages — pronounced "gair-age" — were infrequent, and mechanics had always just "gone fishing." Often the community blacksmith provided the first aid we needed for emergency repairs.

But when it all worked, it was wonderful. On good days we might make one hundred fifty miles. Road markers were two-foot-long oblong strip signs mounted vertically on fence posts, telephone posts, trees — any convenient location. The white face of the sign bore a three-inch blue stripe across the top and a similar red stripe across the bottom. In the middle was blazoned either a blue "L," meaning the Lincoln Highway, or a blue "30." (Our first recognizable and numbered transcontinental highway, it ran from Coit Tower in San Francisco to Atlantic City, New Jersey. The Ames Monument on top of the Con-

tinental Divide between Cheyenne and Laramie, Wyoming was a
Union Pacific Railroad tribute to the Ames brothers who located and
designed the railroad through the pass. But because it was The Lincoln Highway it was later commemorated by a huge copper colored
replica of the Lincoln penny.)

Being a tourist in 1913 did not make a very pleasant impression on
me. We were not sightseers. Dad and Mother had taken a "land-
looking" journey early in the summer and visited the Garden of the
Gods, the Royal Gorge, Pikes Peak, Manitou Land, and the usual
tourist attractions in Colorado. Now, however, it was November,
cold, windy, and dusty, and we were just interested in getting the miles
behind us.

And when we did arrive in Caldwell and our isolated farm home,
we had many adjustments to make. Farm routines were different, edu-
cationally demanding and confining. Milk cows are a terrible restric-
tion on free scheduling of time! I still spent all my free time dreaming
with books from Dad's library. I was now eleven years old.

It was not until I was fourteen that I really got acquainted with the
natural world I lived in. The daily cycle of life was right in front of
me — a calf born in our cow pasture, white leghorn roosters fully occupied in our barn yard, mule genetics and breeding, a neighbor's small
"bull service" operation, neighboring bitches, animal food supplies and
feeding tasks, milking, feeding calves and pigs, gathering eggs, and
the large kitchen garden with endless digging, planting, hoeing, daily
irrigation schedules and a personal assault on potato bugs. I remember
the great farm kitchen meals. Dad was strictly an Iowa-trained meat-
potatoes-gravy specialist and Mother was expert in preparation.

But suddenly in high school a teacher in General Science began
asking some fundamental questions. "What does sea level mean? What
is the elevation where we live? How high is Squaw Butte over there
to the north, or the dark ridge of the Boise Mountains, snow-capped
most of the year, which cut off the eastern sky? How far is it to the
Pacific Ocean? What is barometric pressure?" Youngsters from states
with sail boats would have found my barometric ignorance appalling,
but I had to learn about the weight of gravity and of air pressure,
about barometers, lenses, levels, watts and volts, decibels, velocity,
inertia, horsepower, latent energy, winds and tides, meters, foot pounds

and even gestation periods. All of this information was a headful but not a headache. I also became acquainted with concepts like life zones, environment, food chains, timberline, the balance of nature, the Pyramid of Life, the differences between political and theological concepts and the survival of the fittest.

In a short time I gloried in my new vocabulary. Someone had thought this all out and it fit together. It explained the way life is and the satisfying logic of some of its verities. I recognized which way is north, had a smattering of astronomy and an idea of how a flat surface map could describe a round world. (In fact, it is still interesting to ask new acquaintances if they can remember the exact point in geography or time at which the concept of "North" emerged for them. Almost without exception each person retains this memory. Mine is based on Squaw Butte in the Boise Valley, and a pause is needed each time to rearrange my mental furniture for the return there.)

Suddenly a lot of my reading made more sense, and I became an incurable naturalist. But at fourteen I was also a pheasant hunter and very inquisitive. I roamed our Boise Valley grain fields one August afternoon with Dad's 12 gauge, single-shot Winchester. The hypnotic marching stubble rows led my eyes to the far crest of the Boise Mountains — our eastern horizon. To my amazement I saw a thin sliver of a half-moon deep in the gray sky. There was a star with it. This was a new experience! And, as I sat on a ditch bank, I heard the melodious echoing beat of a soaring night hawk.

I saw the bird high above me — a floating speck part way up to my newly located moon. The bird slid suddenly to one side and then finally an ululating trickle of melody came down to me. It was a soft woodwind salute — a lovely resonant muted air whistle.

All farm creatures and wild residents were more or less familiar to me, but this was new and exciting. The moon by day with an obligato from a night hawk! Nature's responses to my youthful questionings seemed normal and natural.

Each summer Mother reared a flock of several hundred White Holland turkeys. She purchased day-old poults and pen-reared them until mid-August, when they could be joined in one great stately band of awkward, pinfeathered clumsy creatures. Mother herded them daily for three or four hours as they gleaned the grain stubble and the hay fields.

Mother pointed out to me one morning that the turkey flock had inexplicably veered sharply in their slow walking and were drifting toward a grove of cottonwood trees and a hedge of tall, sweet clover. Mother turned from the flock and alerted her companion collie dog. "Hunt, Laddie!" she motioned to him, and he set his ears, made a short cast back around us and the birds, and exploded in noisy pursuit of a single coyote which had sneaked in behind us. By quiet and carefully-timed exposure to the flock, he had established a controlled turkey drift into coyote country. It was a primitive life for turkey survival!

Actually, the turkeys were put into this nomadic feeding pattern only after they were fledged sufficiently to use our great backyard cottonwood trees for a safe nesting place. It might require two or three days for them to grasp this concept. But after one coyote trotted by, the response was immediate and complete. They never forgot. One summer, Mother reared two thousand of them and paid off the mortgage.

A turkey patrol with Mother was a happy, learning experience. A great naturalist, she directed my attention to little signature behavior patterns that told us about our feathered neighbors. For instance, there were many meadowlarks, but they would not be nesting at this time of year. The young ones were always plentiful with their familiar soar-and-zip flight patterns; the white-edged tail feathers also identified them. There were many small ground birds — lark sparrows, horned larks, finches, and juncos. A bird singing sweetly in the tree top could not be one of these; it was in another habitat. And I remember the great day when between Mother's botany and Florence Merriam Bailey's *Handbook of Western Birds* we identified a pine siskin!

Mother developed bird lectures for schools and wrote about birds for local papers. She wrote and published a small booklet on *Some Birds of the Boise Valley As Seen From My Kitchen Window* for use in local schools.

As my eyesight for identifying such patterns improved, I learned that there were many bird watchers — amateur ornithologists — with impressive lifetime observation lists. There were similar amateurs with great knowledge of trees and wildflowers. Many of them would return each year to favorite nooks, where rare columbine or violets bloomed.

There were also enthusiasts in the field of biology, in geology, and in photography. They all loved to talk about their specialities. I liked to listen. I did not realize that this was valuable career preparation. But it was.

This was in 1917, when I was fourteen years old. I was a pheasant hunter, but not a very good one. My aim was terrible and I spent too much time looking at everything else.

In 1916 Dad traded the increasingly unreliable Studebaker for a 1916 four-cylinder Dodge touring car. The actual exchange value was a team of work horses, our reliable Sam and Star power combination, $35.00 cash, and a pig to boot. One final adventure had closed our friendship with the Studebaker. Our farm was under the Arrowrock Dam Water Program and The Pioneer Irrigation District. With headquarters in Caldwell, Dad had been intrigued by the finances of the project before he bought into it. Optimistically he scheduled a family weekend trip to go look at the dam. It was an awesome wall of concrete between great vertical walls of rock towering to the narrow crossways strip of sky at the apex.

It was a fun journey, and we were heartened by our guests Mr. and Mrs. John Lannighan. John was a neighbor who ran a blacksmith shop nearby and provided both the space for repair work and the expertise Dad needed to keep the car going. It was a lovely day on the crooked dirt road as we whizzed up to Boise and on to Arrowrock dam. The powerhouse was humming quietly as the generators turned water power into electricity. We headed home comfortably in the early twilight, but suddenly the car lights went out. Mr. Lannighan took over but, typically, had no success with the primitive equipment.

Dad had an old kerosene lantern, and as we had done earlier in Wyoming I finished the journey lying on the car hood holding the lantern. Dad followed the illuminated left front tire tracks while he steered us homeward in low gear.

Then, when I was seventeen Dad returned to the ministry as pastor of the First Baptist Church in Ogden, Utah. The family moved normally, but my brother Firth and I rode our bicycles from Caldwell to Ogden. It was about 450 miles, mostly over unpaved and rocky roads. It took nine days plus two days that we stopped in Mountain Home, Idaho, and worked in the hayfields.

Between several years of home ranch work in Ogden and part-time attendance at Stanford University, my naturalist interests went into eclipse. I became a Stanford senior, lacking only two quarters in residence and some residually required classes for a B.S. degree. But this never worried me — I had no problems with scholastics, having a solid B-plus average. The degree could wait! In 1929, I was twenty-six, still an amateur wildlifer. Girls and biology had a different context. I was admiring Maxfield Parrish's blues and reading Richard Halliburton's fantasies. His *Royal Road to Romance* (1927), a book about the excitement of travel, put me out of touch with the world for awhile. What a dream world he lived in! What a challenging way to travel! How could I get in on it?

While staying with my sister Margaret and her husband Willard in Council, Idaho, I had started working as a part-time apprentice on the weekly newspaper. I remember the able and kindly gentleman who was the publisher — Mr. William Lemon. His son Orange had been in high school with me. He was most helpful as he taught me about typecases and how to set a stick of type. Makeup of a page was nowhere near as simple as it looked, nor was the process of "justifying" columns, sentences, single letters, borders, and headings. The old flatbed press was a monster. But with the special "patent insides" newsprint we only set up pages 1, 4, 5 and 8 of an eight-page newspaper, and it looked great! Our linotype was a historic but dependable relic, so the handset portions of the four pages were mainly in the composition of advertising. It was satisfying to solicit an advertisement, set it up, check the proof, correct it, lock it into the page, run it, and then collect for the final product.

Willard was a ranger with the U.S. Forest Service and a very practical fellow. As I fretted over my prosaics of living, I realized that I was right at a crisis point in my decision-making. Should I continue only to dream of exotic adventure? If I were going anywhere I had better be about it. Willard, familiar with his agency boundaries, commented that I could start by investigating a job in Alaska. There were two National Forests, the Tongass and the Chugach; he knew the addresses, and, in February I sent a specific application for a 1929 summer job as a forest guard to the Supervisor of the Chugach at Anchorage, Alaska. Just writing the names gave me shivers of anticipation.

I received a very prompt reply offering me a job! I was to report in Seward on May 1. More shivers! This was a miracle! My ranger career was on the way! I would be a participant in a most exciting field — the U.S. Forest Service.

I learned during these summer months in Alaska that the Chugach was reorganizing. The year 1928 had been a disastrous fire year. The New Mexico District Ranger, Bill Sherman, was selected to take over the Anchorage District. Bill had vast fire-fighting experience; he had taken over problem fire districts before. One of his first decisions was to fire all the previous forest guards, recruit a whole new crew, and establish a fire training school. My application reached Bill while he was recruiting. I was a college student, had a western farm and work background, was mature and husky — new material for fire training. Bill would not have to "unteach" me anything. He could start on my fresh and unbiased mind. I fit his pattern. He fit mine! This experience started me on my generally optimistic approach to jobs and decision-making: Don't assume you can't get a job or that you will be rejected on a suggestion. Give it a try. Maybe your job application or your suggestion is just what the other guy is looking for. You may solve his problem. Quite often it works just this way.

I was instructed to report to the Lawing Ranger Station on Kenai Lake near Seward, Alaska. Transportation out of Seward would be arranged. I was told about the fire problem. Fire season started as soon as the snow melted at the edges of the meadows and forests, exposing the residual of dead grass and brush from last year. Alaska was a "new" land and had a very thin layer of topsoil. A flash fire in the ground cover often burned down into the layer of humus and roots and peat so that even the soil burned up. These fires were not roaring blazes. They were smoldering and stubborn smudges which literally had to be dunked in water to extinguish them. I read that in such a smoldering bit of wet moss a light breeze could stir up another puff of smoke and it would take off again.

I knew I must leave Seattle in late April. The only possible travel would be on the *S.S. Admiral Evans* sailing from Seattle on April 27. First class fare was $80.00; steerage $40.00.

But I could not forget Halliburton's strict admonition that a true vagabond, a follower of the Royal and Golden Path of romantic travel,

never paid for food, transportation, or love. At least, not full price!
Could I combine my exciting job prospects with the happy adventures
of a Halliburton? Hitchhike, bum a ride, work my way, stow away,
anything except buy a ticket! I went to Seattle a day early to give it
a try.

Hitching a ride to Seattle was no problem. I had hitchhiked for
many vacations. If you had luggage, you could ship your bed roll or
warbag ahead by Railway Express — collect. Prepaid express shipments accrued storage charges after 24 hours. Collect shipments had
30 days grace. My ride to Portland from Caldwell, Idaho, by chance
was with a salesman for Roebling wire rope who visited a string of
lumber towns on the Washington side of the Columbia River.

Portland to Seattle was easy. There was a war on bus fares. $1.50
took me to Seattle. My bed roll and warbag were waiting for me at
the express depot.

I had a friend who had a friend who was an engineer on a ship
operated by the Lomen Reindeer Company. He was willing to give
me a ride to Alaska, but he was not leaving Seattle until July, and then
he was going to Nome, not Seward. However, he would take the time
to take me to the *Admiral Evans*. I must sail on her the next day.
He whisked me past the dock police. A handful of waste in his right
hip pocket was enough identification, and we went on down into the
heat and clatter of the engine room of the *Evans*. Their chief engineer
was not interested in providing a work/transportation plan for a passenger who would jump ship in Seward, so my Lomen Reindeer friend
left. He had gotten me on the *Admiral Evans* and had demonstrated
the ease with which the imposing dock guard organization might be
bypassed.

I stopped at the beautiful main dining salon with its white linen,
crystal, gleaming silver and ornate candelabra. The chief steward's
response about passage was also negative. His entire crew of janitors,
waiters, dishwashers and helpers were "Niggers." No room for me.
I left with an admiring glance at the imposing phalanx of cooks and
stewards, a romantic vision in their gleaming white coats, braid, and
neckties. As I started up the long dock, one of these handsome fellows
followed me — the second steward, according to the pin he wore. His
name was Jensen. Beyond view of the ship's deck he whistled at me

and then ducked into a cargo embayment with a beckoning wave of his hand. He was a tall, lanky fellow with a droopy mustache.

"Do you need to go to Seward?" he asked furtively.

"Yes, I have a job beginning on May 1."

"Do you have twenty bucks?" he asked.

"Yes, I have twenty bucks."

"Go see the steerage steward," he said, and hustled back to the ship. So I returned to the *Admiral Evans* and found the steerage cabin on the third deck.

Bob Donahue, the steerage steward, had his name tag on, too. He was happily drunk even though it was only about 11 a.m.

But he talked to me. "Seward? You wanna go t' Seward?" He was astonished.

"Yes, I need to go tomorrow."

"Who sen' you down here?" he mumbled.

"Jensen the second steward," I replied. The second steward had suddenly become a character reference. Obviously I shared his larcenous traits.

Bob asked the second big question. "Do you have twenty bucks?"

Assured that I did, Bob waved his hand grandly. "Dozens of beds down here. We sail t'morrow nine 'clock. Bring your gear down here t'night," and he hicupped, tripped over the doorstep and staggered away.

I walked back to the Marion Hotel and packed my bed and the big canvas sack I called a warbag. I ate lunch and loaded up with reading material. A midafternoon taxi driver wheeled me down the dock to the foot of the *Admiral Evans* gangplank in a cloud of my own nonchalant cigarette smoke. I threw my bags over the rail and dragged them down to steerage. I had suddenly become furtive, too! Three-decker pipe and canvas cots were set up for two hundred cannery workers whose sailing had been cancelled that morning because of a spinal meningitis quarantine. Lots of vacant beds were visible. I settled in the second layer down and behind Bob Donahue's cabin and the toilet — the most inconspicuous spot I could find.

I couldn't imagine being so isolated on board a big ocean liner tied to the dock on the Seattle waterfront. But I was out of the line of lower deck traffic. I seemed to know what I was doing and nobody even looked at me.

The only entertainment was my cavesdropping through the airvent on the conversations between Bob Donahue and Sally, a hooker who came in to see him, and who stayed in his cabin to set up a temporary two-dollar cat house for the crew. There was a lot of noisy traffic in and out of Bob's cabin for a time. Bob also turned out to be the ship's bootlegger. Sally's cover story was that she was Bob's wife's sister and was going to go home with him in a few minutes — she left about 5 A.M.

My first ship's voyage — how exotic! I was a stowaway at half-fare, next door to a busy, cheerful, noisy, two-dollar whore who was shacked up with the ship's bootlegger, using the steward's cabin for a pad.

Halliburton? You only told half of it!

Things quieted down at daylight, but began to pick up again about 8 o'clock. More clanging on the steel decks, more foot traffic, but no questions for the stowaway. By 9 A.M. the vibration of the hull increased slightly and the pilings outside the portholes began to slip silently away behind us.

I waited until nearly ten o'clock, then rerolled my bed and dropped in to see Bob. His full flock of eight steerage passengers were all aboard and drinking coffee. Bob was badly hungover and bedraggled. But he had gotten all the required ship's clearances, and we were on the way. He had forgotten all about me. So we started over.

"Who sent you down here?" he demanded.

"The second steward." It was amazing the way I needed Jensen for a character reference! We must really be two of a kind!

Then came the big qualification question again — "Do you have twenty dollars?"

This test being passed, I was welcomed aboard. The list of eight farepaying steerage passengers was expanded to twelve by four of us with a reduced fare plan.

The stowaway organization planning was simple and tidy. I had a ticket stub to show at the gang plank on leaving or reboarding the ship. Actually, the ticket was out of date but the gate keepers were Bob Donahue, Jensen, the second steward, and the night watchman, who got five dollars out of the division of my twenty. Most of the full-fare steerage passengers knew of this system but no one seemed to be disturbed.

Two days later we were easing quietly up the channel into Juneau when the mate came to our dinner table. "We will load two thousand sawed hemlock railroad ties in Juneau. Do any of you want to work? We pay seventy-five cents an hour and it will take about eight hours."

Five of us put up our hands. But Bob Donahue objected after the mate left.

"Garrison, you can't work in Juneau!" stated Bob.

"Why not? I need the money," I replied.

"You ain't on the damned passenger list," a sober Bob explained to me. "The payroll will show that Garrison was paid off on the ship and some white collar jerk in Seattle will check it up and there ain't no damned Garrison on the damned passenger list. No sir — you can't do it."

Ralph Maxwell, one of the legitimate ticket holders, got into the conversation. "I know an old girl down here on the line who kind of expects me to come by and leave some money every time I'm in town. She'll know about it if I don't. I'm going on over and get my ashes hauled. Why don't you use my name, Lon?"

So Ralph Maxwell paid his compliments and his money to Becky while another Ralph Maxwell loaded railroad ties. When I was done I collected my six dollars. Then, since my Ralph was on the passenger list and "legitimate," I hunted up the crew's dining room and had a breakfast of four eggs, a slab of ham, sour dough hotcakes, and coffee as the *Evans* swung out and traveled towards Seward. A sleepy and contented Ralph Maxwell and another six-dollar-richer Ralph Maxwell quickly exchanged greetings and we both slept well.

I never got much of a look at the Alaskan scenery along the Inside Passage on that trip. I could see that it was blue water of inlets, channels and bays, towering barren mountains, a low timber line, dense shoreline forest with a lot of summer sunshine. But Bob encouraged us to keep out of sight. With only eight fares paid, our twelve bunks and twelve dinner plates and the like might easily suggest a head count to the purser and some of us might have to walk home — or dig up more money.

But that last afternoon, as we slid quietly up Resurrection Bay toward the Seward dock along the vertical shores, I felt more secure and joined the tourists at the rail.

Resurrection Bay! I was there! A great sight — great adventure! Halliburton spoke of using your youth while you had it. I felt content, but at the same time I realized ruefully that I really did not have that kind of irresponsible youth anymore. My vagabonding ended that afternoon.

And to provide some kind of climax, after all my stowaway cadging of meals, I got seasick as we entered this last channel. I was quietly and solidly really upty-chuck seasick over the rail. I guess I had been trying to eat everything in sight, particularly my last free lunch. But I arrived in Seward just like I left Seattle — hungry.

At the Chugach National Forest warehouse in Seward I checked in briefly to sign the necessary papers. Another forest guard met me and we took the Fairbanks train ten miles to the Lawing Siding along Kenai Lake. The Lawing residence and museum was the picturesque and lovely log cabin home of Bill Lawing, an old timer, and his famous wife, Alaska Nellie Neal. This tiny lady was a historically famous dog-sled driver and mail freight handler. Her museum exhibit of furs, mounted animals, geological specimens, sleds, dog harnesses, skis, snow-shoes, and the like was an excellent introduction to the realities of early Alaskan days and hardships.

Unfortunately, the local emphasis of the museum as an Alaskan relic was spoiled by a full-size, mounted African lion right in the mid-dle of the room. The lion had been a resident of a Seattle zoo. It was dying when Nellie offered them fifty dollars for permission to shoot it with her 30.06 and have it mounted. I suspect Nellie was mighty proud of this exotic exhibit but its mangy and partially hairless pelt was a sad contrast to the richness of the true Alaskan specimens.

The train paused only briefly at Lawing for the tourists to look around, and then "All aboard for Anchorage!" I stayed behind. I was no longer a tourist. It was the beginning of my new job as a forest guard! I shouldered my bedroll and warbag and made the ten-minute hike over to the ranger station where I met District Ranger Bill Sher-man and the rest of the forest guards who were to be in the school with me. At the last minute Bill's resolve had weakened and he had re-hired Si, who had been on the crew in 1928. The rest of us were new-comers. It took several days to work off some of our excess zeal and become a team.

I didn't help it much that first afternoon. We cranked up our out-board motor and took a skiff down the lake three miles, where we felled eight tall spruce trees. We limbed them out and rafted them home by a little towing bridle we hitched around the small ends. This was our summer wood supply, and our first chore was to buck the logs into fourteen-inch bolts and then split them. In getting the logs into position to snake ashore one-at-a-time, I needed to turn a crooked one over. Someway I found myself standing out in the lake on one log with a peavy to roll the crooked one. My hobnail shoes gave me good footing, but the peavy slipped. I took another jab at the log, the peavy glanced off, and then slid out of my hands into the lake. I remembered a north woods logging slogan — "To Hell With The Man — Save The Peavy! It Belongs To The Company," and I reached for the peavy handle bobbing just under the surface beyond the crooked log. I ended with my feet solidly on one log and my hands solidly on the next one as the two logs just slowly swung apart. I hung on for a moment, swore, and jumped in.

The water was only waist deep but very recently off a glacier and it was shriveling and cold. I didn't stay in long. I was a sissy and flew into the ranger station and up the stairs to dry boots and pants. By the time I got this arranged, the crew had yanked the logs ashore and two were on saw horses being sawed into bolts and then split for firewood. Our eager fire crew was on the ball.

CHAPTER II

THE ALASKA FOREST GUARD

BILL SHERMAN BEGAN CLASSROOM DISCUSSIONS THAT FIRST EVENING but he didn't really talk about forest fires. He talked about a new program called conservation. And he talked about professional forestry as if conservation and forestry were the same thing.

My reading had suggested that colonial British land managers, possibly a century earlier, were given the title of "Conservator" rather than manager. They were "Conservors" — conservators of forests, of game, of land, of agriculture. The title implied responsibility to preserve resources for tomorrow's generations. Someway, this concept keeps fading out of later definitions, but I liked it in 1929 and I like it today. And I use it in the connotation of preservation as simply a superior kind of conservation. I began as a conservator–conservationist on May 1, 1929. It seemed a good balance between the rigid practice of German, or "Scientific," forestry and the idea of managing forest resources for people to use.

Our fire school was a surprising review of history — particularly American history, and the King's Forests, such as the Ship's Stores Reserve at Santa Rosa Island in Florida, and later the President's Forest on the North Kaibab Plateau, in Arizona. There were stories of fire fighters and scientists such as Gifford Pinchot, whose professional approach to management and forestry in the early 1900s was a landmark of conservation history. Pinchot was the first Chief of the Division of Forestry in the Department of Agriculture. He had taught forestry at Yale University, and later became Governor of Pennsylvania. I first heard his name at Lawing in 1929. I met him in Yosemite in 1937. His philosophies of the greatest good for the greatest number for the longest time were tremendously inspiring and appealing. For their time they were true inspiration and idealism.

[27]

My own supplement was simply an overriding concern for the precious mystique of life. Forests, prairies, marshes, man — all nature and all natural processes — have survived for millennia by themselves. They do not need me or Pinchot to make "good" or "bad" value judgments for them. Nature in her own constant élan and drive has assured this. I was happily, but accidentally, a part of this special fire training and conservation scene of May 1, 1929. And I judged it by the mores of my awareness at the time. Bill Sherman helped me sort it out. He was ahead of his time, too, but he didn't know it.

I was a very inquisitive and dedicated forest guard. I felt I must learn the techniques, the standards, the goals, and the equipment. I was on the verge of great new horizons. I suspected that forest management changes were in the air; I first heard the idea of "multiple use" here, as Bill Sherman expressed it.

I was always one of the most fortunate of men. I had the outdoor life I loved and great people to work with. We would not have dared, even if we had thought of it, to refer to our work places as "environments." In effect, with the Forest Service we were in the lumber business. We had a great monoculture — we grew trees. The woods were storehouses full of trees. The economic steps beyond the forest were the sawmill, the lumber yard, or the paper mill.

This was a great mission. The Chugach and the Lawing Ranger Station with District Ranger Bill Sherman was a great place to be, and 1929 was a great time to celebrate just by living.

Bill Sherman asked me to take his field notebooks, and using DMD's (Double Meridian Distances) and a logarithm scale, to balance and close a survey he had made of twenty summer cabin sites to be sold or leased up near Moose Pass. I could not imagine where the people might come from to buy them, but it fit a good pattern — public use of public lands. Lakeshore lands and summer cabins all were compatible.

But even as this orderly economic plan unfolded there were some rumbles of discontent. Industrialists correctly foresaw curbs on their free and uncontrolled use of public natural resources. The John Muir-Sierra Club-Steve Mather faction thought the foresters were ignoring the most valuable resource of all in the natural beauty, inspiration, relaxation, and simple sense of wonder which these resources carried for burgeoning urban populations. This is my philosophy today. In 1929, to Pinchot and the practical foresters, parks and preservation were a lot of foolishness. They seemed to have said so often enough. But whether you counted board feet of lumber, sentimentalized over Peter Rabbit, or romanticized with Peter Pan, the message was the same. *Conservation was in.*

At the fire school at Lawing Ranger Station we spent a week in intensive training — fire line construction, fire behavior, tools, equipment, reports, and communication. This was part of the program of national standards for all forest protection such as forest fire control and resource management. Bill Sherman had developed his successful training pattern in New Mexico. Would it work in Alaska? He thought so. He was a hard taskmaster. He admitted he was a zealot. And he was on trial, too, with his new standards and new techniques for fire fighting. Before the first day was out we were all devoted to his cause. We would not let him down!

He was very blunt about one of the very human dilemmas he faced in his program — the change in attitude required for us to recognize fire as our Big Enemy. We must not accept the inevitability of big fires or be complacent in excusing poor forest fire control results. Sloppy work and poor fire management and reports were human situations we must overcome. Bill's first attack was on the attitudes that had been illustrated in previous fire records on the Chugach — good fire attack but poor follow-through. Thousands of dollars had been spent extinguishing fires and reporting them as extinguished. Only they broke out again and again.

This was anathematic to Bill, and it explained why he had been ruthless in firing the 1928 crew and selecting a new one. Bill laid it on the line, "If one of you reports a fire *out*, and we have to go back and fight it over again, just start walking or catch the first train to ship out. I'll send you your bedroll. I don't want to see you again. And don't ask me for recommendations for I will blast hell out of you." (This was mainly aimed at Si, of course. It was the kind of action that had created the bad fire record in 1928 when Si was part of the crew.) "Any questions?" Bill snapped. There were none. The point was well made. Back to our training programs.

On the Chugach, lightning was not a probable fire cause. Mainly, we must watch the coal-burning railroad locomotives. They burned Alaskan coal, a fair grade of lignite. It burned best if the engineers kept their blowers on. And often these blowers would boost tiny burning fragments of coal through the boiler tubes and out the smokestack. These fire starters would then ignite dead grass or brush and, in turn, set the tundra on fire.

In review of fire fighting techniques, extinguishing such a fire is a dull recital. You may douse one of these tundra fires liberally with water, wring it out, but it will often begin smoking again in the first breeze. Since absolute certainty that the last spark of live coal is extinguished was required, and I had lots of patrol time, I developed my own technique, which I called the "Ouch! test" for Class "A" small fires. My fire patrol times were long but my record of positive control was excellent. The two years I was a forest guard I never had a forest fire that was a blazing conflagration or that reignited.

The major piece of fire equipment at Girdwood was my Casey Jones speeder. The name was in remembrance of the legendary locomotive engineer, who "mounted to the cabin with his orders in his hand and opened 'er up for the Promised Land!" Actually, my speeder was about a four-foot-square box railroad car with a gasoline engine, loaded like an Arkie dust bowl refugee truck. The motor was a one-cylinder, two-cycle affair that would run in either direction. I was a mobile forest fire lookout, and I carried a full compliment of railroad equipment — a set of track torpedoes, a set of signal flags and flares, a collapsible telephone pole, a hand-crank telephone, and a five-gallon can of motor fuel. As a fire truck, I carried a shovel, a double-bitted axe, a mattock, a canteen, two days' rations, a backpack fire pump, a set of blank report forms, binoculars, and a first-aid kit.

There were only a few speeder operators such as the railroad section foremen, some field inspectors on specialty crews, and four or five independent operators like the Forest Guards. We were, of course, rigidly bound by railroad regulations: Before hitting the track I had to know about competing railroad traffic in my district, and I must keep the train dispatcher in Anchorage aware of my own location. Every morning at 7 A.M. the dispatcher summoned us all by our round-up phone call which gave us the line-up for the day. Work trains were listed along with the sidings where they would be based. One by one, we acknowledged the message. I completed my list on a form with a carbon copy. I left the original on the telephone shelf and took the carbon with me.

This was a ghoulish arrangement, with the expressed purpose of providing the routine to clear the air if I should get run over by a train. The record in my pocket would inform the coroner of my instructions. The copy on the telephone was to serve the same purpose if I was drowned or burned up or otherwise mutilated. The intent was to scare hell out of me so that I carefully followed instructions. It worked.

The only unanticipated operational factor was the occasional delay when I met porcupines. These free-roaming, bushel-basket-size critters waddled slowly, timidly, deliberately through the forest, and someway they found the railroad tracks fascinating. The tracks, of course, were twin streaks of rusty iron rails through the little green alleyway of clipped . vegetation where the trains mowed it open. A traveling "Porky" would usually be found between the rails, inching his way along suspiciously, parallel with my own line of travel. If I overtook him from behind he would hasten his two-miles-an-hour gait to his maximum of three. He would hurry, then tire quickly and relapse to his normal speed.

If he turned to cross the track, he would encounter the railroad rail and be afraid to cross it. The vibration in the rails transmitted from the speeder wheels would be just enough to turn Porky around to try to cross the other way. If I stopped, he might make it out of the way. But if I were still moving and the rails were noisy, indecision reigned!

Fortunately, the speeder wheels were high enough that I could let the speeder coast up to the critter and straddle him, and "Casey Jones" could just keep going. But we always had a moment of interruption. My feet had better be out of the way while Porky's tail slapped up at the three-inch drive belt as it brushed over him. He would be partially plucked and greatly indignant, but still in good health. I would spend the next hour pulling quills out of the belts as I resumed my trip.

Porcupine mortality from main-line trains was tremendous. This was particularly true in the winter months when snowbanks locked the animals in between the rails. Fortunately for Porky, he was frequently up a tree at that time. But it became a real disaster for a migrant moose as well as a Porky that found the open runway between the rails an inviting corridor through the snow. There was no escape when a train roared through.

We always had a warm respect for Porky, the only creature a man without a gun could kill if he was starving. So we tried to wait him out so he could complete his own journey. A footnote on a trip report or a daily log which listed "Porky" was explanation enough for late arrival.

On the north side of the Chugach Forest, toward Anchorage, the National Forest adjoined land of the General Land Office, or the Public Domain (now the Bureau of Land Management). Our two agencies had similar fire programs. One morning in the 7 A.M. line-up, the dispatcher reported an accident to the General Land Office patrolman north of Anchorage. He had been running north against the weekly Fairbanks-Mount McKinley-Anchorage-Seward train the day before. He had been delayed by porcupines, so he hurried to reach a siding ahead of an oncoming train. (Driving a speeder, you sat almost flat on the tracks looking ahead at these twin rusty ribbons of rails. They were unevenly full of bumps and vertical undulations. The horizontal dimension did not vary — it was always the same. I squinted along them often enough to be reassured about that hazard. But the wavelike, vertical variance was often exhilarating as I developed confidence that the wheel flanges on the speeder would always bring it back down in place on the rails. If I were in a hurrry, I must use one hand to control the motor speed and the other hand to hang on. It was not enough that the car stayed on the rails — I wanted to stay with the car!) But the Land Office fire guard went too fast and the speeder jumped the track. The fire guard was thrown free, knocked out temporarily, and the speeder crashed beside him. The locomotive engineer reported the scene just as the fire guard crawled away from the disaster.

This sent a chill throughout the system, and to all of us who used speeders including Bill Sherman and me. I checked my time-rate formulas often using the railroad mileposts and my watch; a four minute mile looked better and better!

I was delighted when Bill made his District Forest Guard assignments and I was sent to Girdwood, an abandoned mining town on the Anchorage end of the district. Miners had moved to Girdwood about 1910, obviously intending to stay; their household furniture stood derelict in the cluster of empty, staring cabins. There were books on the shelves and in the desks of the village school, and chalk lay silently on the blackboard rail. A railroad dormitory and tool house were lonely, but partially used. The railroad station telegraph office was the communications center. The Glacier Bar was open, still the social center. There was altogether a total of eight resident men among all of these otherwise silent dream houses, mostly at the railroad section house.

Exploring the empty houses or high-grading the contents was strictly forbidden. Interestingly, the eight residents — and many non-residents—were completely optimistic about the Girdwood Gold Field. This optimism is common to all miners, particularly gold miners. They are convinced the field will reopen one day and that all the former residents will return and get rich!

Near Girdwood, Crow Creek entered aptly-named Turnagain Arm, which became Cook's Inlet. At Girdwood it was a narrow, crooked, and rocky channel within a two-mile-wide tidal flood plain. The shores teemed with wildlife, and were lonely except for the Girdwood Store and the railroad maintenance sidings with their crews. One morning I was lucky enough to see a sea otter, an animal thought to be extinct at the time. Bald Eagles were common, and marmots (whistlers) were abundant. In the fall a fat marmot was a prized source of boot grease. One day I followed an incoming tidal bore which I timed at fifteen miles-per-hour. It was a relentless and steady four-foot wall of water rushing up the tidal channel. This was reported to be the second highest tide in America.

Around the time I moved into Girdwood and began regular patrols, Bill Sherman called one evening to report that Si, the Lawing forest guard, was out on his first fire assignment. He discovered a fire while on a patrol, doused it well with water, reported it out, and returned to Lawing. A follow-up phone call gave a disturbing report, however. The railroad section crew foreman had passed by the site and the fire was busily smoking again. Bill turned out the whole Lawing crew and kept them up all night. When they returned to camp, the fire was out completely. The following day, I waved goodby to the Anchorage train as it went through Girdwood. Si was on the train enroute home, now an ex-fire fighter. Bill meant business!

I used my portable telephone only once during my stay in Girdwood. I had stopped in a clearing on the main line to work on a small smoke I had discovered. By the time I was ready to leave it for my other patrols I had run out of safe time on the track. So I unfolded the collapsible telephone pole with its twin connectors and clamped in on the railroad phone line. I wired in the head set and gave the generator a fast turn. To my great delight, the Anchorage dispatcher responded promptly. It took him a while to understand who I was, where I was, how I ever got on his phone line, and then what I wanted. But he was a patient man. He sorted it all out and then advised me that I had time to run to Indian Siding ahead of an oncoming work train, but that I should slide in there and wait for traffic to clear. This may seem like a complicated procedure and a lot of red tape, but every day my life was dependent on this man's timetables, and I blessed him for the protection he provided.

I had an unusual experience with the railroad one evening in July — there was no real darkness in the summer — when Bill Sherman called to inquire if I was willing to run the speeder the thirty miles into Anchorage. There was an injury which required prompt transportation of a miner to the Anchorage hospital. I had the only available piece of equipment — the other district work speeders were out of service or away from their stations. The injured man could be moved sitting up; there was an aide with him. Time was a crucial element.

Another great adventure! What would Halliburton do with this one? The railroad officials developed a procedure to keep it legitimate. All district stations were informed by a telephone round-up alert from the dispatcher that Extra #666 — me — would be on the main line — Girdwood to Anchorage — from 7 to 12 P.M. "Keep the line clear!" The Girdwood ticket agent issued two tickets for my passengers. (I did not need one, since I was the engineer.) I was to collect the tickets and deliver them to the dispatcher in Anchorage. I had Bill Sherman's blessings. Extra #666 had a leisurely journey into Anchorage — we met no porcupines. The ambulance met us; I said hello to Bill Sherman and his wife, whom I knew well by phone but seldom saw, and by midnight dusk I was back in Girdwood.

A lot of Alaska fire fighting time was spent waiting. I developed my "Ouch" test for every inch of fire line before I reported that it was out. It took a long time to Ouch test a half-mile of fire line, but in my own few fires I always found enough live residuals to realize that it was time well spent. I was not just sitting there watching, but was actively on my knees feeling, squeezing, shaking out the burned moss, waiting and starting over. I never had any repeaters.

I saw an occasional fool hen or grouse; a persistent junco found that my tent window gave just the right reflection to encourage him to attack his image at six each morning. Goat or sheep tracks were there if I hiked up into the Crow Creek wilderness along the road to the mines. Another Cheechako and I made one such excursion, striking off above the six-thousand-foot timberline elevation to cross a lateral moraine and climb a nearby peak. But we found a brown bear track ahead of us. In fact, it was just ahead of us, and while the bear was not visible the tracks were fresh with crumbling sides as the sand began drying out.

We had no firearms and were glad we didn't, of course, because the plantigrade rear footprints of the bear slid down in the lateral moraine gravel fifteen inches long and ten inches wide, and those big claw marks were mighty impressive! We headed back to Girdwood.

One day from Moose Pass I spotted a smoke smudge on the horizon to the south. A Bureau of Public Roads (BPR) crew was in there surveying what is now Alaska Highway #1. So, after checking with Bill Sherman, I went in to take a look at it. I had a forest service replacement trainee with me, and just in case we had some business to attend to we went back to Girdwood and got a Pacific Marine Pumper, a gallon of gasoline, one length of hose, and lugged it all in about five minutes. Sure enough, it was a fire of about fifteen acres, obviously an abandoned lunch fire from the survey crew. It had been burning for several days. We were able to knock down all of the active arms of the fire, but we ran out of gasoline. I sent the other fellow back to Moose Pass to telephone Girdwood and get us some help. About all I could do was fill and refill our Indian Back Pump and work on my Ouch testing technique along the fireline. A relief crew came in about eleven the next morning and we soon rooted out all the fire line, finishing giving it an Ouch test, and headed back to Moose Pass. I still remember with some respect that after I had lugged a ninety-five-pound pumper back the five miles, an eager replacement who was also toting one of them challenged me to a race for the last quarter mile. It was a tie.

Small personal adventures at Girdwood were daily affairs. One concerned the BPR Moose Pass road into the old mining district at Hope and Sunrise — some thirty miles from Moose Pass and on the other side of the Turnagain Arm from the railroad and my patrol territory. The only piece of rolling stock on this road other than a wheelbarrow was a 1921 Model T. Ford carryall for road maintenance at Moose Pass. The caretaker was no mechanic. He and his wife used Old Asthma, as we all called their truck, for road patrols and incidental porcupine hunting to suply their mink farm.

One day in July, a combination highway-forest inspection crew of four men from Juneau and Washington came into Moose Pass and cranked up Asthma to go to Hope, thirty miles back in the wilderness. The inspectors were an overload; Asthma conked out in Hope. It was obvious that the clutch bands had burned out, but there seemed to be no way to do anything about it, and the weekly train would be at Moose Pass the next morning. Meanwhile, a miner from one of the back country gold prospects who had never seen an automobile had hiked into town that day so he could see one. When he found it, it was out of order. "What's wrong with it?" he asked.

"The bands are burned out," was the reply.

"What are the bands?" he asked.

The maintenance man could explain that much to him. The miner opened the gear box and looked at the bands. He took them out. He opined that if he had some leather he could reline them. So he punched out the old rivets in a nearby blacksmith shop, found some new rivets that would work and then started looking for leather. A box of dog harness provided some but not enough. The visiting engineers were cooperative — it was either get the automobile fixed or walk thirty miles to catch tomorrow's train. As they drove away, two of them were clutching their pants with both hands, for their belts were the new Ford clutch bands. And as Asthma triumphantly headed back to

Moose Pass, the Chief Engineer sounded the keynote message for the entire party.

"The trouble with you guys up here is that you don't know when you're broke down!"

Adventure stories of the Girdwood era abounded. Joe Burton was a self-reliant resident making a visit to the next railroad siding at Kern one April day when the humming of the railroad rails and an oncoming roar clearly indicated an avalanche was about to slam into the track. Fortunately, since he was hiking along the railroad track and the Kern snow shed was right there, Joe ducked into the North entrance just before a snowslide overran it.

Unfortunately, Joe's fur cap fell off as he wheeled to run and drifted away with the slide updraft.

Joe simply went back through the snowshed planning to return over the top and continue his walk to Girdwood, but another slide whistled in on the south end and he was nicely boxed in. This was no real cause for Joe to worry. However, the crew which brought the mogul snowplow down from Girdwood discovered his cap on the snow right there at the start of the snowshed. This made it appear that Joe had probably been trapped in the first few feet of the slide, so the snowplow crew and the railroad section crew and the visitors from Girdwood, who hiked down when they heard about it, got poles and long-handled shovels and began to try to locate Joe's body before they might hit it with the big auger. It wasn't there, of course, but it took a lot of long hours of trampling, whistling, and probing, while Joe jumped up and down under the shed and beat "S-O-S" on the rail with a rock for twenty-four hours before they found him.

Twenty years later Joe was still furious. With lots of profanity, this was one of his favorite stories. It was bitter cold, of course, and he had lost his fur cap. More profanity. There was no drinking water. Walk and pound some more. Try Morse Code. "S-O-S." More profanity. It didn't work. The greatest indignity was that the crew just didn't take time to listen! Also, they had established a supply of revival whiskey in case they found Joe alive and then drank it all up as hope waned. When they finally fished him out they had to make an emergency run back to Girdwood with a locomotive to get him a drink!

Joe was a brawny, tan-faced woodsman but with snow-white

hair — caused by this emergency exposure, he maintained, with particular emphasis on those loudmouths who had almost let him die of
thirst. Not exposure — curse, curse — but thirst!

This was the "windy" kind of conversation I enjoyed. Other bits
were on the more serious side. One night in the Girdwood Railroad
Station as I listened to the continuous clatter of the railroad telephone,
something sounded familiar. It was my telephone number — a long,
a short, and then two longs. And since there was time, I scooted across
the road to my tent and answered the phone at home! "Girdwood
Forest Guard Station, Garrison speaking." It was my boss, Bill Sherman, and he had urgent news for me. The railroad message lines had
just advised Bill that the maintenance crews had moved maintenance
repair shovel "Old 100" into my district. It would be at Indian Siding
for the next three weeks.

This was no great catastrophe. It was a historic piece of construction equipment which had been brought to Alaska from the Panama
Canal, and it was a magnificent kind of outfit used only for real
big jobs.

It was usually used when their major shovel-runner, Clancy, was
out of the hospital and jail at the same time. Clancy had come with
the shovel when it moved north about 1920, and legendry was filled
with tales of his great pugnacious characteristics. There had been a
controversy the previous year about Clancy and his "reluctance" to
use his spark arrestor in spite of a disastrous fire year. Bill thought
Clancy was part of the cause. But then Clancy got embroiled and
knocked somebody around "defending" a girl down in the Red Light
District and was out of circulation for a while. He had then gotten a
load on one night and confided to an Anchorage barroom audience
his great aversion to forest rangers and the spark arrestor.

Bill had been very specific in his instructions. "Go see that Clancy
has the spark arrestor on and if he doesn't you see to it that he puts
it on."

Clancy had been equally specific about the spark arrestor and
where he would shove it if any bling-blang ranger told him to put it
on. This sounded like the mouse putting the bell on the cat! I was no
barroom brawler. I was just a Chugach Forest guard. But my orders
were positive.

So I went back to the Girdwood ticket office and got the agent Bill Elliott to help me locate the railroad telephone directories — just mimeographed sheets — until I found the one that listed work trains. The code ring went with the train and not the location so I gave the phone generator a few whirls and soon had Clancy on the phone.

He might have been a nice guy but I thought he snarled. "Mr. Clancy, I am Garrison the forest ranger and I have orders to come up to Indian tomorrow morning and be sure you have your spark arrestor on Number 100. See you tomorrow morning." I hung up, although I don't think Clancy was through.

Then I began to figure this out. I would be coming in from the south on Casey Jones and would slide alongside the shovel wall for nearly one hundred feet before there was any break in the side or a way to get on. At that point there was a vertical ladder up to the cab where Clancy sat. There was no other entrance.

So I concluded that I had to be quick. If I could just stand there on my speeder with my left hand ready to cut the switch so that I did not leave the speeder drifting down the main line, then I could catch the ladder rung with my right hand and be up the ladder and into the cab with Clancy before he got unwound. Why? I wasn't entirely sure, but the stage was set. I was certain that once I got in the cab I had as good a chance of staying there as Clancy did.

The big diesel was noisy, so we were inconspicuous as we coasted into place. I stood on my floorboard, left hand on the switch to cut it, if needed, as I was sure I would. Then I looked up. Clancy was seated inside the cab glaring down at me from his cab window. I looked again and the spark arrestor cone was visible and bolted tightly into place on the smokestack. I did not cut the switch. In fact, I opened the gas a bit. "Don't stall it! Let's get out of this hostile territory!"

I waved a cheerful salute to Clancy and then gave the throttle another twitch. I was on my way. "Hi there Clancy! See you later."

I called Bill Sherman. "I got the job done. No resistance."

I wrote to my mother. "Hey, Mom, do you remember telling me that the worst worries in life are the things that don't happen? Well, today . . . ."

I remember one delightful last incident with the Forest Service, the

Bureau of Public Roads, and one of the highway engineers who had been involved in the Model "T" clutch job at Hope.

Bill Sherman called as I was ready to leave. "Can you drive a gear shift truck?"

I reckoned that I could.

"Well, the BPR has a brand new one-and-a-half ton Model A Ford truck on a flat car at Moose Pass and they need help in unloading it to avoid demurrage. Can you go over and drive it off for them?"

I could and I did and the last time I saw it, it was safely parked by the BPR horse barn at Moose Pass until they could get technical help to train a driver and put it to work.

Meanwhile, "Asthma" was comfortably back on duty. The clutch bands were still working.

It was mid-August. The predictions of my adventures in Alaska had been met and oversubscribed. Being a forest guard was very rewarding, and I got paid $140 a month for it, too! But I wanted to make it "full circle," and winter in Alaska if I could find a way to finance it. Bill Sherman's promise of a summer 1931 forest guard job was enticing. But I knew of too many cheechakos who didn't make the winter. I needed a job commitment of some kind.

Fortunately, I met an engineer whose wife worked in the Juneau office of the Alaska Commissioner of Education. He knew about a high school teacher bound for Haines, Alaska, who had resigned before he got there. So there was a sudden vacancy. A telegraphic inquiry to Juneau with a quick mail response indicated that the job was open; a temporary teaching certificate was available. Another wire to the Haines School Board announced my availability, and a response offered me the job. In less than a week I was on the *SS Yukon* enroute to Juneau and then on to Haines, this time as a first-class, $80 fare-paying passenger.

CHAPTER III

HAPPY GO LUCKY

I ARRIVED IN HAINES ANTICIPATING STIMULATING FRIENDSHIPS with the young people and the local residents. It was this and more: The towering mountain background, the changeable fjord of Lynn Canal before my door, the moaning midnight howl of husky dogs, the flaming northern lights, the friendly and supportive people, the mixture of whites, natives and "Squaw Men," the eulachon fishing, the Indian fishermen (trolling the bay for halibut and then the next morning selling their catch from wheelbarrows, announced by a vigorous school bell), the small fishing fleet, the tie of all activity to the boat docks (both the Alaska Steamship Company in Haines and the military post dock at Chilkoot barracks), the Chilkat and the Chilkoot Rivers, the Alaskan Native Brotherhood and their meeting hall as well as the Alaskan Brotherhood's similar structure, problems of the Alaskan Bone Dry Law and booze, and the nearby historic community of Kluckwon. It was a different world. The police force was a United States Marshall. Small, round, brown children played solemnly in the rain and the mud puddles. I hired an Indian woman to clean the house I rented.

One wayward Indian wife and her teenage daughter partied with a group of soldiers to the point that the husband beat them severely with a stove poker. They ended in the Chilkoot Barracks Hospital and the U.S. Marshall came to call on the husband to learn more about it at the hour of midafternoon school dismissal. The Indian home was next door to the schoolhouse. The Indian sent word to the Marshall to stay away, but he went over anyway and stood behind a tree and tried to converse with the Indian through the door. As he stepped away from his tree shelter, the Indian, an old pelagic seal hunter, killed him with one rifle shot through a window.

[41]

The street was full of school kids, the armed Indian was still in the house, and the Marshall was dead under the tree in front. Suddenly, everyone vanished. There was nobody in the street except a row of faces peeking around house corners. The school kids had raced for home. Two of the local white residents tried to talk with the Indian by calling to him from behind trees, but he simply told them to stay away. Somebody got a tear gas bomb from the military post and threw it through the back window of the house. The gas was obnoxious but the bomb set the curtains on fire and the house began to burn. Suddenly, there was one last sharp rifle shot and the knowledgeable residents moved in without hesitation. The hunter had been shamed by his wife and daughter, and he had killed a United States Marshall. There was only one possible ending, so he had killed himself. The furor and the tragedy and the reports so disturbed our United States Commissioner, a kindly retired Presbyterian missionary, that he had a stroke and died. Death was heavy on every heart in the community for a few days.

Ralph Wright, the school principal, and I divided the high school curriculum as best we could. His major subjects were English, history and civics. I fell heir to classes in algebra and geometry; typing was not a demanding subject and we elected to try an introductory class in physics, mainly because I had studied this most recently. I spent hours checking lists of laboratory equipment only to learn that just $400 was available for supplies to meet my optimistic $1,000 budget.

However, by this time I knew the students well, and the effective ingenuity of these big fishermen's kids plus their skill as motorboat operators and repairmen was another victory. We would read the text and the lab manual on various kinds of thermo-couples and electric hookups and then we would build them ourselves. Usually they worked. These were great adventures for me and the kids. I loved them!

One of the prerequisites for my selection by the Haines School Board was an ability to teach Latin. The board believed that any quality education must include the basic of the Latin language. I professed no great competence, but had an acquaintance with the usual high school level Latin courses up through the adventures of Gaius Julius Caesar and even a bit of Virgil. I recall the pleasure my mother and father had in Latin grammatical structure and its precision; I should have done better by those ablative absolutes, but I did learn about gas boats.

I really wasn't a skilled basketball coach, either, but we started practice faithfully in mid-October and played our last game five months later in mid-March. The snow was so persistent that we ended the school year about June without even having open ground to play catch. Baseball was not a pressing interest.

A lot of things crashed in on me all at once. Teaching was a full-time job, considering the daily preparation I must make. Learning to live in the northland was another problem. Montgomery Ward and Sears Roebuck were old family friends. I met them again — and again — and again!

The greatest adventure of all caught me unaware one evening when Ralph Wright asked me to join him and his charming wife, May, on a stroll of about half-a-mile from Haines over to the Chilkoot Barracks' boat dock to meet a new school teacher. The Commissioner's office had established a new school district called Chilkat River two miles out of Haines where there were two fur farms on the Chilkat River.

There were only two or three automobiles in town so we walked to the dock with our flashlights. It was a misty, foggy, kind of wet-foot expedition. I remember the tendrils and wisps of fog at the dock in the ship's floodlights and the echoing voices through the timbers of the deck structures and the ramps of the ship. The companionway lights were feeble and uncertain and we were all creeping through the mist when suddenly someone turned another light switch on the ship and in the brilliant new illumination the most beautiful blond girl I had ever seen came drifting down the stairway, struggling with a suitcase. It was the charming and beautiful Inger Wilhelmine Larsen, the new Chilkat school teacher. She was just five feet tall, compared to my own six feet-three inches. She was nineteen years old, weighed one hundred pounds, wore a size four shoe, and was a native of Norway with her home in Juneau. My winter courtship started immediately! Six months later we were married. Three children and forty-eight years later she is still beautiful and a delight to be with — a happy part of a Halliburton-sponsored experience! "Let events take you where they will." It was often more interesting than what I had planned!

But this changed my plans a bit. In fact, quite a bit!

I lacked only two quarters of credits for graduation from Stanford University. I had my mind set on a degree in psychology, probably because my dad had taken a graduate degree at Harvard University in 1909 in behavioral psychology. It had become a goal which I accepted without question, even while I was gathering naturalist experiences. It was mixed up but I decided that I must get the degree. I still planned a psychology major. I would look at ranger dreams later.

At Stanford my friends generally had classed me as a "happy-go-lucky" type, but those casual days soon ended. Mr. William Keller, the Territorial Commissioner of Education, convinced me that a Master's degree was needed if I was interested in school administration.

But there might be other ways to go than teaching, and I must explore them, too. This was no longer a "someday" approach, however. This time it was for keeps. And what about my ranger interests?

I had committed us for another Alaskan year as a forest guard and a Haines high school teacher. In this second year of basketball coaching I not only played on the town basketball team, I refereed many community games and, of course, enthusiastically coached the high school team. Fortunately, fate delivered five eager and active boys, plus John Heintges, a lanky young fellow, stepson of an officer at Chilkoot Barracks. His six-foot-two height and great enthusiasm and coordination promised us a much brighter basketball year!

That second year, in cooperation with the Chilkoot Barracks recreation officer, we sponsored a Lynn Canal Invitational Basketball Tournament. Both Skagway and Juneau High Schools responded. The Army recreation program provided housing and meals — we ransacked all manpower to provide referees, and we had a very successful tournament. It was continued for several years after my departure.

In August of 1931 we visited my family in Idaho. We bought a 1926 Buick Roadster and were ready for another kind of move. Inger was eager to continue her own education and we agreed on San Jose State University for her courses in homemaking, education, and art. My own plans were for one quarter at San Jose State to save tuition money, and then to transfer back to Stanford for a March graduation.

That is the way it worked out. Our savings of $1,200 lasted just long enough to get the Bachelor of Science in Psychology, and I was again seeking employment, preferably in the natural history field. Something like the forest guard would be great. We heard about the National Park Service that winter. Were there openings?

My job experiences and advancements seem almost capricious. I was enrolled at San Jose State University the fall quarter of 1931–1932 and met a young geologist who was a summertime park naturalist in Grand Canyon National Park. My own experience in outdoor work was not professional enough at that time to qualify me for such a job, but there were other seasonal jobs in parks. I was given the name of Mr. Jack Diehl, the park engineer in Sequoia National Park. He lived in Redwood City in the winter months. A Sunday afternoon visit to Mr. Diehl had the strange side effect that Mr. Diehl recognized Lemuel A. Garrison as the name of the one-time pastor of the First Baptist Church in Ogden, Utah, and Mr. Diehl had been a member of my father's congregation. In fact, Dad had performed Jack's marriage ceremony! So Jack Diehl not only referred me to Larry Cook, the great Sequoia Chief Ranger, Jack actually spoke to Mr. Cook personally at a strategic moment, and four months later I was offered a seasonal park ranger job.

This was following the 1932 election. Franklin Roosevelt promised to cut down federal employee numbers by the simple device of closing off the hiring machines. Strangely, this reduction in hiring led to a job offer for me!

The National Park Service had been vigorously working to establish a new ranger at the North Rim of Grand Canyon National Park. The U.S. Civil Service Commission in early June agreed to issue a register, but the job had to be filled before June 30. The ranger candidate certified for the new job was Warren Hamilton, a long-term, backcountry, seasonal ranger in Sequoia. In fact, he was out in the remote Kern District and it was necessary to get word to him, get him moved in, which involved a sale of his horses and a few problems of this type, and then get him on the road by June 20.

Someway it all fit together and Warren Hamilton got to Grand Canyon. (Twenty-five years later, in 1956, Warren was Assistant Superintendent with me in Yellowstone National Park.) His move left Larry Cook, the Sequoia Chief Ranger, with a seasonal ranger vacancy almost in mid-summer. Even in the bottom of the depression it would take at least two weeks of procedure to recruit a new ranger fire-fighter, which had been Hamilton's specialty.

But Jack Diehl remembered our Sunday afternoon visit. I was a recent Stanford graduate, a trained fire-fighter, and immediately available. I was interviewed by Chief Ranger Cook and Park Superintendent John R. White at Ash Mountain, park headquarters in Sequoia. I was hired late that afternoon, July 3, and reported to the Lodge Pole Campground. Larry Cook had just completed his fire training school; it was remarkably similar to my Alaskan training. I felt right at home with this part of the job, and Larry Cook was content with my own readiness.

CHAPTER IV

RANGER GARRISON

I HAD ONLY HEARD GENERALLY ABOUT THE NATIONAL PARKS and the National Park Service, and suddenly I was a park ranger on the job. I drove overnight back to San Jose in my old Buick Roadster to arrange for this new career.

My first concern was for Inger. In just seven days, on July 10, she would enter the hospital in San Jose for the birth of our son Lars. Meanwhile, I had reported to the new ranger job with our few belongings. My salary was to have been the same $140 a month as with the Forest Service. But on July 1, F.D.R. had not only cancelled all new permanent jobs, he had also cut all salaries by 15 percent. My salary was now $117.50 a month.

On the afternoon of July 4th I put up my 12×14 tent with a protective fly on a platform by the Marble Fork of the Kaweah River in Sequoia's Lodgepole Campground. I unloaded my gear, got a bucket of water from the river, split some firewood, fired up the Lang Alaska stove to heat coffee water, and unrolled my Alaskan blanket roll. Later, I would have a sleeping bag, but this was my new address for three months. *Ranger Garrison was at home!*

This same tent with the U.S. flag flying was a ranger station. A crank telephone on a tree near the door was the communications system. My ring was three shorts. The quick signals such as two or three shorts were reserved for emergency points such as ranger stations. One long ring signaled the "central" switchboard in Giant Forest. My first tool kit included telephone lineman tools — just as in Alaska. But here I was surrounded by campers in tents of various sizes and colors. There were also a few luggage trailers. Wood smoke tinged the air. A family walked by to ask directions to Giant Forest. Fortunately, I had seen the trail sign.

Ranger Garrison was at work!

[47]

The privy was behind the tent away from the river, smelling of chloride of lime. A rock-to-rock stepping stone path led across the shallow river to the big pole corral for my horse Pico and a red pack mule. Tack was on a pole between two trees. Bales of hay and a tightly covered garbage can full of rolled barley were tarp-covered on the ground.

On my first full day on duty, District Ranger Irv Kerr assigned me to campground foot patrol. Since my new uniform had not arrived, Irv loaned me a ranger badge in case I needed it. I didn't.

The first camper I interviewed had a few questions I could not answer about specific trail distances. A second camper answered them for me, so I returned with help for number one. I carried a short crow bar or nail puller — a quiet conservation reminder as I pulled pitch-encrusted nails out of trees. I needed only occasional visits to Irv Kerr's ranger station for help with questions. Courtesy, accuracy, helpfulness to park visitors, and concern with nature preservation were the names of the tasks. I liked it!

Short horseback trips taught me the local trail system up the Toko-pah Valley to the Falls, to Heather Lake, and to Clover Creek and Twin Lakes. This was the full moon, and campers were having problems with marauding bears. A full moon facilitated travel for bears through the congestion of forest and campground.

Visitor conversations, campfire programs, and late exchanges with Irv and other rangers and naturalists filled the days and nights.

On July 10 I was assigned to lead a rescue expedition for a heart attack victim at Scaffold Meadow on the Roaring Fork of the Kings River, north and west of the Park.

I am certain the Sierra Club High Trip leadership did not realize the extent to which this Los Angeles school teacher, Miss Jane Spalding, was on medication for an ailing heart. She had been on other High Trips and she was determined to take this one even if it killed her — which it did. She somehow made it out of Giant Forest and over Elizabeth Pass, but by the second day she was unable to walk even with her reinforcing pills, and she rented a saddle horse. On the third day, on the Sphinx Crest, she collapsed and the hiking party constructed a bumpy stretcher of lodgepoles pushed through sweater sleeves to carry her down to the summer camp of Ralph Merritt at

Scaffold Meadow. Kate Smith of Los Angeles, a companion from the Sierra Club, stayed with her. Their hope was that somehow Miss Spauling would recover strength enough to ride out if someone could provide horses for them.

Colonel White, the Sequoia National Park Superintendent, heard of the situation and asked Dr. Morton Fraser of Woodlake, the Sequoia National Park Physician, to see what he might do. Even though I was a brand new Sequoia ranger, I was a good mountaineer and rider, and was appointed escort for Doc Fraser. Early in the morning of July 11, we left the Lodgepole campground for the twenty-eight-mile journey. There were three of us with five horses — Doc, myself, and a packer with two extra horses just in case the patient and her companion would be able to ride.

Doc Fraser was a great mountain man but fifty pounds overweight. At 5:00 P.M. we dragged into Sugar Loaf Meadow with six miles to go. Doc was beat and gray with exhaustion, but we lined up on a log while he fumbled with his saddlebags and produced a bottle of a rare 1932 elixir known during prohibition as Medicinal Whiskey! After two short libations mixed with spring water, we trotted back into the main trail, and about 7 P.M. came to Scaffold Meadow and Miss Spalding.

The best Doc could do was leave medicine. He called her problem Tachycardia, which meant a racing heart at this 8,000 foot elevation. There was no way down except to go up. Helicopters were still a visionary concept. We must depend on the horses.

The next morning Doc and the packer and I with our five horses were on the way by daylight, and at midafternoon were back at the Lodgepole Campground.

The third day the packer and I were again enroute to Scaffold Meadow. Again we took the extra horses just in case of a miracle. But we were escorting a nurse this time with a satchel of pills and lots of instructions. She was a novice horsewoman, a city girl, but game throughout. We broke the trip by camping at Rowell Meadow just outside the Sequoia northern boundary, and came to Scaffold Meadow early the next afternoon. The nurse created a great optimism; the new drugs would hopefully improve the pulse count.

The packer and I left Scaffold early the next morning. He went directly home, but I crossed over to Ranger Lakes and Silliman Pass above Twin Lakes. Here I picked up the trail register sheets and then slid down the dusty switchbacks to Clover Creek and on home.

Three days later I was on Lodgepole campground patrol when Doc Fraser called.

"Garrison, we had better ride back in there tomorrow."

Another twenty-eight miles to Scaffold Meadows followed by another twenty-eight miles back to Lodgepole. By that time, I was using my second saddle horse. The patient was not improving. We would take in a stretcher and carry her out. Irv recruited eight stretcher carriers who walked the twenty-eight miles. We had a packer and a cook; we were back at Scaffold Meadow one more time. (This was trip number four.) The nurse was eager to get started but we were delayed the next morning because some of the mules had slipped their hobbles. We searched half a day for them.

Then one of the stretcher bearers developed a heel blister — he had been idiotic to try this trip in oxfords. I was idiotic to let him do it. Now he rode the horse and I took his turn with the stretcher.

We came into Sugar Loaf Meadow in good time that afternoon and the nurse got Miss Spalding settled in for the night. Then she took me to one side.

"The patient is not doing well. Please send word to the doctor at once."

It was my responsibility, so without supper I saddled up and rode seven more miles to the cow camp at Rowell Meadow. There was a grounded return Forest Service phone line at Rowell, but it was not working. "Trees across it someplace," Walt Goins, the resident cowman, told me. "But at 9:00 P.M. the Buck Rock fire lookout comes on to give the fire reports and if you are on the line, you can get him to relay a telephone call for you."

Buck Rock was not early! From 7:30 until 9:00 P.M., I stood in the cow camp cabin kitchen listening to the silent phone line. Scratching mosquito bites, burping with the rumblings of my empty stomach, fretting over the snail's pace of my watch, observing the beginnings of a moonless night, knowing that I must ride through two or three hours of darkness back to Sugar Loaf.

I immediately butted in on the Buck Rock schedule and the dispatcher arranged for an end-of-report time to handle my emergency. The phone receiver filled my ear with scratchy noise, occasional howls, a fading rock compressor, and suddenly it cleared completely and I heard Doc Fraser tell Buck Rock to inform Garrison that he would start that night.

And he did, with a good guide, Ord Loverin. But losing the trail down in the lower end of Cahoon Meadow, they unrolled sleeping bags and resumed travel at daylight.

Meanwhile, Walt Goins helped me make a candle light flare out of an empty two-pound coffee can, and I started back to Sugar Loaf. Unfortunately, my regular reliable mount, Pico, was being rested for that trip. My strange horse was steady enough, but he wanted to go north up to Ranger Lakes. I soon ran out of candles for my flare, so I just waited until it got fully dark and then led the horse through the dark tree spires overhead, feeling the impacted soil of the trail with my feet and stumbling on into open meadows where starlight would let me ride. About 1:00 A.M. I found our camp. I unsaddled in the dark, fixed a nosebag of grain for the horse, found the supper the cook had left for me in a Dutch Oven, awakened the nurse to reassure her that Doc Fraser had the message, and settled down with my own sour and bitter stomach to await morning. Soon the packer rolled out to begin getting the stock ready for another day of travel. Seven miles to Rowell Meadow.

We tacked some willow withes over the stretcher to create a sunshade out of dishtowels; we hewed out extra-thin and -long lodgepole sticks and lashed them to the side of the stretcher so the carriers could go in tandem rather than abreast; we teased the nurse who was a cheerful greenhorn. The procession became a parade. I was one of the stretcher bearers, and the fortunate guy with the sore foot was both blessed and blasted for his ill fortune. About 4:00 P.M. we met Doc Fraser and Ord. We chatted briefly and then hastened on to Rowell Meadow so that Doc could have ample time with the patient. She relaxed in an extra bed which Mrs. Walter Goins found for her.

It was a happy evening. We even had an impromptu campfire program with some singing and amateur star-gazing.

The eastern sky was lifting its lower edge when I awakened. Doc hovered over our campfire in his underwear and huffed and puffed

on the coals to get a beginning blaze. As I sat up, he came to me bare-
foot over the rocky ground.

"Garrison," Doc whispered, "she just died." The nurse had called
Doc; Miss Spalding had had a sinking spell and Doc, with his stimu-
lants, someway had brought her out of it. She almost immediately
went into another lapse and this was fatal.

Sensibly, we should have folded the body over a pack mule and
gone on to Lodgepole, now about fourteen miles farther, but I had
seen one or two corpses that had been packed on a mule and the pooling of coagulated blood in the face was beastly and irreversible. I
called Irv Kerr, since we were now back in phone contact through
Buck Rock. I asked for two more men so that we could carry the body
on in. We had all become very fond of Miss Spalding — the thought
of delivering her to her family disfigured was distasteful. Doc and Irv
agreed, and so about 4:00 P.M. we came down the long, dusty dugway
trail into Lodgepole to an audience of several dozen visitors, newsmen,
curiosity seekers, and the ambulance which had now become a hearse.

I shook hands all around with the willing and dependable crew,
took care of my horse, and got word from Irv that I was now the father
of a son born in San Jose. The Chief Ranger wanted me to take two
days off and drive up to say hello to the young man! The old Buick
was equal to the task, although I had to borrow money from Doc
Fraser. He had become a firm friend by this time.

Soon after I returned, Superintendent White asked me to come
to Ash Mountain. There I met Mr. Spalding, the father of the recently
deceased Sierra Club hiker.

"What did all this travel and manpower cost?" asked Mr. Spalding, who was a banker.

"About $800," replied Colonel White.

"Who is paying for it all?" asked Mr. Spalding.

Colonel White's response was simple. "Why, you may if you wish,
Mr. Spalding. But if you cannot we shall just consider it a public
service. Our job is to be helpful to park visitors. Not many of them
get into the difficulties your daughter did, but she needed help, and
communications and time made it impossible to ask her advice and we
didn't even know about you."

Mr. Spalding responded graciously. Of course he would pay. His daughter had been foolish to try the trip. He was delighted to find in American government an outfit that put public service on the front line even if it were expensive.

And this is partly why I made a career as a ranger in people service as part of natural resource management. I never got over that one, either!

Lars was a long, skinny, blonde fellow with big feet and a red face. I suspected his eyes would be blue! Inger was very lovely. She and Lars stayed in Oakland with Helen until mid-September. When they arrived in Lodgepole campground I moved another cot into the tent. A dresser drawer with a pillow made an elegant crib.

But in late July, I had gotten back to regular duty.

I was enjoying this ranger "work" in a disrespectfully happy fashion. One morning we planted rainbow trout in Pattee Meadow Creek. There were three extra mules and one horse in the Lodgepole ranger corral. Their tack was astraddle the pole saddlerack. It had been a mighty short night. By two o'clock I was up feeding the horses and mules; my coffee and eggs in my ranger tent were by the light of a Coleman lantern, and I had stuffed lunch into my saddle bags. By three o'clock I was fumbling in the dark with curry combs, brushes, saddle blankets and the complicated rigging which girdles a pack mule properly dressed for work. By three-thirty I had swung into the saddle on Pico, strung out the four mules in a head-to-tail hitch, forded the Marble Fork of the Kaweah River, and rode into the parking area at the Lodgepole Ranger Station.

District Ranger Irv Kerr was the planner and leader of this expedition. He was already deep in conversation with Chief Ranger Larry Cook, who had come up from Ash Mountain with the fish truck. The air pump was running quietly and little air hoses with carborundum tips bubbled compressed air up through the eight pack cans, each loaded with ten gallons of hatchery water (more-or-less, according to the splashing endured) and one thousand rainbow fry or fingerlings from the Kaweah Fish Hatchery at Three Rivers. I was told that a quart of fingerlings this age and size weighed about two pounds, which was the capacity for ten gallons of water. It all sounded very scientific and precise to me.

Irv and Larry were dropping chunks of ice into the fish cans to keep the water temperatures low for the four-hour trip. Screen tops were added to the cans, and one-by-one we led the mules to the truck, checked the cinches, and then slung the cans to the cross-buck pack saddles we were using. A simple box hitch with a lash rope screwed each one down snugly, and by 4:30 A.M. we were strung out ready to head for Pattee Meadow.

As the icy water splashed through the screens of the open can tops onto mule hide there was some twitching and complaining from the mules, but they have an endless capacity for contrariness, submission and routine, and soon settled down. Against the rosy glow of approaching sunrise, through the early morning dusk, we rode across the still-silent campground, splashed across the Marble Fork ford again, and went single-file up the narrow side-hill dugway trail as it climbed out of the Marble Fork Canyon towards Willow Flats. I would have other adventures on this steep and precipitous trail, but this was my first fish-planting trip, and the mules and horses held my full attention. As the sun rose, I checked the saddles — were they riding straight, the straps all in place? Were there any slipped saddle blankets? After all, I had put them on in the dark by feel! The fish cans were rocking along steadily as the mules began the journey one rough step at a time across slick rocks, through the dust, stumbling on loose stones. I was leading the pack string, Irv was the caboose observer.

But leading a pack string while riding Pico was another kind of an experience! A younger Pico had been one of the prized performers in a rodeo string of bucking horses. Why a government horse buyer bought him in 1925 as a ranger patrol horse for Sequoia National Park remained a mystery. There must have been some ironic humor behind it. His smooth-mouthed age of twenty-five years in 1932 was only four less than mine. I envied his sure-footedness, his stamina, his competence, his even disposition, and his pride in leading a pack string.

As a rodeo performer and a vigorous bucker, he responded wildly to the use of a bucking-strap cinched around his loins. He had also developed an absolute passion against a lead rope under his tail. So when I was riding Pico and leading mules I dared not doze in the saddle nor let the lead rope go slack.

Pico had been a faithful ranger patrolman's mount for several years — sleek, black, glossy, with white feet, head high, ears alert, proud — just the show horse for Chief Ranger Guy Hopping, who had ridden him leading a mule string as part of a 1931 Fourth of July parade in Giant Forest. Only Guy's attention had faltered, a wasp stung a mule's nose and it bolted, and Pico got the lead rope under his tail! Guy was no buckaroo, and no ranger ever quite finished relating the tale without real Freudian laughter. Between the rambunctious mule and the bucking horse, the Chief Ranger ended on his ass beside the parade, and Pico again became a back-country ranger patrol horse!

In 1932 I was the newest seasonal ranger. I was riding Pico, and I was very careful with lead ropes. I was no buckaroo, either! It would have tickled some of the Sequoia old-timers greatly to see the college boy get his ass busted by Pico!

As we rode up the trail the mule lead rope was looped loosely around my saddle horn. But I had a firm grip on the action end of it, holding it high and free.

We made a brief stop for a breather at a wide place in the trail. I made a quick walk around the mule string and slipped my fingers under each cinch. I checked each lash rope — were the strainer tops riding securely? The Number Two mule had stumbled but there was no rock stuck in a shoe. Back on board, we were on our way in the full early morning sunlight, brilliant on the granite boulders through the blooming and aromatic manzanita and chinquappin and deer brush heavy with dew.

We stopped at Silliman Creek to water the mules, but the fish were the control — so we were soon back in the saddle and on across the creek. Past Cahoon Meadow and Cahoon Gap, we reached upper Clover Creek and the cabin at the trail fork, but did not hesitate. The J O Pass trail led on through the scattered pine trees, and we plodded ahead.

Always uphill. We had two more miles to go and 2,500 feet of altitude to gain. We stopped to let the mules catch their breath. Each mule faithfully stopped with a half-turn across the trail and panted quickly and heavily. In a few seconds respiration caught up with circulation and the mule took one or two deep breaths, relaxed visibly, and was ready to start on again. The packers who trained me in this routine taught me well to watch for heavy sweating or distress in breathing. "Take a quick break," they advised, "let the panting subside, take a few more deep breaths — and the mules will reach your destination tired but still in good condition."

We came down on the west side of Pattee Meadow. It is about ten acres, the first in a descending string of small meadows down Pattee Creek. It lies in a small cirque under the rimrock of J O Pass at an elevation of just over 9,000 feet. (This gets the full pronunciation — Jay Oh Pass!) It was named for John Warren, an early cowboy who could spell his name and had a jack knife. John decided to carve his name on a big lodgepole pine tree in the pass. But his pride in his name and carving led him to adopt such an heroic scale that there was room for only the first two letters. They stand today as they stood in 1932, a mute memorial to his frustrations!

Pattee Meadows Creek gathers here from a million tiny dripping rivulets. The marshy soil is lush with sedge, shooting stars, and cone flowers. It is rimmed with tall fir and lodgepole spires.

Irv took the lead. We reined the mules alongside the meadow and one-by-one led them into the meadow and unloaded the fish cans. Each mule and each can was an individual project. These tiny wriggling slivers of rainbow trout represented life itself, plus much work by many people. It began with the gathering — stripping — of roe, possibly from Lake Eleanor in Yosemite (where I later did this myself). Careful rearing followed in the Yosemite fish hatchery, in a flow of clean and cool water. The bad eggs were sorted out, the survivors fed, and troughs cleaned daily. Months later the fry were turned over to a park ranger, ready to plant in a stream or lake. There was a lot of brain power, manpower, and technological achievement — as well as life — in those fish cans! We treated them with due respect.

Irv selected a short run of the stream where we could approach the water easily. We had no stream thermometer, so Irv hand-checked the comparative water temperatures in the stream and in the cans — there was ice remaining, so the water in the cans was colder. We tempered the water slowly and carefully. (Sudden temperature rises will kill fish very quickly, as I learned to my distress with some adult trout in later years.)

I had just learned about baby bottle temperatures. The same technique of wrist tests applied to fish planting. In about fifteen minutes Irv concluded that the temperatures matched. Only then did we carefully tip the cans and drain the little fellows out into their new home. They were almost invisible in the clear water, but immediately began feeding on some of the *minutae* in the stream. With no predator fish, they would do well!

We did not overload any pool — from the eight cans, we dumped little fish into at least twenty-five different places.

There were only a few dead fish in our cans — they could have been bumped by ice chunks. Generally, however, it was a very successful venture. Irv was a meticulous, thorough, patient, and knowledgeable tutor for my first fish planting expedition. I remained grateful to him, for I later repeated the thermometer procedure many times — at Glacier National Park and in Bright Angel Creek at Grand Canyon where I was in charge of the snow. His routine was always successful. Pattee Creek had been a "barren" stream as it gathered into a trickle, into a flow, and into a stream. It was now a dependable home for these youngsters.

According to modern philosophies, we might not plant Pattee Creek at all today. We would leave it to the water bugs and the striders and salamanders and stream bottom fauna which were considered to be only curiosities or fish food in 1932. We now accept a new principle — just because a stream will grow fish does not mean that we must put some there.

But this was the kind of informal planting plan that early cowboys and rangers had followed, and even most park administrators in my early career. And since I am a fisherman it made good sense to me! Why not? Subdue the earth — use it, plant it, harvest it, go fishing! This was the Forest Service philosophy of resource management as I learned it on the Chugach. I must wonder now why I concluded that there was any great difference between the consumptive use of lumbering or cattle grazing, which were park no-nos on principle, and the consumptive use of fishing. My questioning did not occur at Pattee Creek — this first fish planting was a constructive mission, scattering good across the world and around the park!

Some years later in the Omaha regional office, I checked fish planting plans for Isle Royale National Park. I came across an impassioned and beautifully reasoned letter from the great University of Michigan ichthyologist, Dr. Carl Hubbs. He urged that some waters in Isle Royale remain forever "barren," simply as a control for future reference when scientists would begin to try to understand how the state of Michigan had created the mixture of species that it has. His letter made sense to me and still does; yet I am still a purist dry fly fisherman. I do not suspect that I will change, although I now thoroughly enjoy fishing for fun, and even in good water seldom kill a trout.

But at Pattee Creek, mule-by-mule, fish can-by-fish can, we dropped the little fish into the clear and cool waters. The empty cans were piled at the base of a lodgepole pine tree.

We loosened the mule cinches, unsaddled the horses, and turned them all loose in the lush grass to graze, which they did with evident gusto and glee. Irv and I sat beneath a giant red fir to eat our 10 o'clock lunch. I questioned him about his ranger career and he related more of the story of the National Park Service and of Sequoia National Park.

It was like listening to Ranger Bill Sherman, only from a different pulpit than the Lawing Ranger Station in Alaska. Irv named Steve Mather, only recently deceased; Director Horace Albright; Harold Bryant, who was stirring things up in the field of park interpretation; Carl Russell, the interpreter at Yosemite; Larry Cook, the professional forester who was the capable Sequoia Chief Ranger; and Colonel John R. White, the romantic and dynamic Superintendent whom I had already met. Irv was a magnificent teacher and exemplar — dedicated, articulate, a great physical specimen, handsome and homespun, a ranger's ranger and a pipe smoker. He brought alive for me a whole new concept of natural resources and what they meant in the life of man and the world of men. I discovered anew the balance of nature— ecology.

The two summers with the United States Forest Service in the Chugach National Forest had developed my skill as a fire fighter and my knowledge as a forest timber manager. I was deeply impressed with an awareness of economic and social responsibilities for wise land use. National Forest conservation was geared to the harvesting of lumber. But in some way my short time in Sequoia had introduced me to the possible alternate use of this same forest resource just for public enjoyment and inspiration. In some way the "rightness" of park preservation, of the concern for identity with natural law, was impelling to me. Recreation was as legitimate a use as logging, and a lot less destructive. I liked it.

Of course, I was frankly job hunting — or rather career hunting. I was a ripe candidate for ranger recruitment. I was almost thirty years old, married, with a newborn son and an almost equally brand-new degree in Psychology. It had taken me ten years to capture this degree from Stanford University. But I was also interested in nature and in people. Parks were for people. Could I fit it all together?

From beneath the huge fir tree on a bright and clear morning, Irv and I were looking west to Kettle Peak and North to J O Pass across Pattee Meadow. The mules and horses were harvesting the grass and flowers with great and noisy munching. A halter chain would jingle, a mule would snort. It was all inspiring — serene, beautiful mountains around us, clear, blue sky overhead, the quiet of Pattee Meadow and the tiny Pattee Meadow Creek in the foreground.

We had just completed a successful manipulation of life in the fish world and given our proteges a complete habitat change. Suddenly I recognized the decision before me. I must quit dodging around. If there was a way to make a living out of what I was doing, this was for me! I still had to ask Inger — and I still had to harmonize a social science major with a life in natural history. I had to learn about qualifications, standards, examinations, titles, salaries — but these were details I could cope with.

As the Indian youth who goes out to seek his Medicine and his Spirit, I went forth to plant a fish and suddenly I met my Spirit that morning at Pattee Meadow.

I looked again—I had been in Alaska and I also knew the Western mountains. What would this look like in the wintertime? The gentle round meadow with the north fringe of pointed trees climbing to the park boundary just above it would be a quiet snow basin. There might be occasional deep-snow tracks of the large predators — fisher, wolverine, pine marten, or lynx. But generally these animals frequented the brushy hillsides or bottoms where rabbits or squirrels concentrated. So I might ski freely through Pattee Meadow on snow gauging trips, and the creek would be an invisible but gurgling stream beside me.

For four summers my duties would keep me busy along portions of this J O Pass trail from Lodgepole — and many of these adventures held the impact, the satisfaction, and the happy remembrance of the first one. But my search for a home was over — the out-of-doors, nature-saving, and people-sharing, would be my career.

It all turned out even better than we had expected. I had the interest, but my formal training was inadequate. To even take the Park Service examination in 1932 I needed a degree in a natural history field — forestry, geology, or entomology. I could substitute history or archaeology, and *pro forma* I could qualify to be a ranger by substituting my work experience for classroom work. Permanent jobs were frozen. My succession of seasonal tasks was a livelihood and an asset, and there were new hirings of park rangers in 1935.

CHAPTER V

THE NATIONAL PARK SERVICE EMERGES

ON AUGUST 25, 1916 THE NATIONAL PARK LEGISLATION had combined the various National Parks, which had been operating more or less independently within the Interior Department. But this consolidation could not be instantaneous. For example, Sequoia had been established in 1890 to preserve the Big Trees and to forestall a lumbering and homestead takeover. Between the Interior Department and the United States Army, the park had had some protection and a management organization. But in 1916 the new agency had the responsibility. What could Steve Mather and Horace Albright do in Washington to speed their new goals? How soon should they do it? And in the interim, Interior Department management must continue.

Mather and Albright were handicapped by Mather's physical breakdown. Albright, as Acting Director, moved carefully to protect Mather and to prepare for his return to duty. They had evolved specific goals. They had envisioned professional quality staffing — they convinced Secretary Lane to establish policy guidelines — and they developed cooperative relationships. The Park Service was taking shape rapidly over the next decade, when Mather died suddenly in 1929.

Thus, when I came on board as a seasonal ranger in 1932, and then as a permanent one in 1935, the last specifics of their policy and procedural changes were just emerging. These are the conditions I met and adjusted to, not knowing, of course, that so many of them were innovations. The agency was only sixteen years old.

For example, in my first summer I met Dr. Emilio P. Meineke, Principle Pathologist in the Division of Pathology of the Bureau of Plant Industry, United States Department of Agriculture. The park rangers had been concerned about a large number of dead trees in the Lodgepole Campground and had asked the Washington office for professional assistance. The rangers assumed that it must be a root blight or some kind of an obscure disease. However, both Mather and Albright had been determined not to hire specialized staff to meet Service problems, but to seek help from existing specialists in other agencies. Hence a referral to the Forest Service, then to the Department of Agriculture, and thence to Dr. Meineke.

In 1928 Meineke had written a Forest Service report on damages to forest campgrounds arising from campers and unrestricted automobile driving. The pattern of damage was obvious once he looked at the facts of increased trampling from campers, injury to tree roots from automobile tires chewing up the forest floor, and automobile oil drip from the 1927–1928 season adding to the damage. The same things were happening in Lodgepole Campground in Sequoia.

Helpfully, his report included a section on the remedy. Roads must be established and well-marked to keep automobiles upon them instead of wandering all over the forest floor; parking or garage spurs must be established for use by camper automobiles. Fixed locations were needed for camper tables, tent sites, and fireplaces. The major suggestion was construction of one-way roads.

It was decided to establish an example of such a protected campground as a part of the Lodgepole Campground in Sequoia. Our old friend Jack Diehl, the Park Engineer, and his staff would do the surveying and recording. Tom Carpenter was the landscape architect and planner. Irv Kerr was in charge of the work crews, which brought me into it as Irv's support. Dr. Meineke came into the park to provide professional oversight and control as we tested his philosophies and plans.

We did not have topographic or tree maps of the new campground site. We developed a sketch and then generally built things to fit the topography. Most of the major decisions had already been made. The one-way loop road had become a series of interconnected one-way loops. The barriers for traffic control were four hundred- to six hundred-pound big river stones placed among the trees. We moved them on a stone boat which was just a heavy wood or metal sled we towed around with a truck.

As we completed a section of the road and camping sites we would try it out with our pickup truck. Some of the first roads were too narrow and the curves too tight. In our zeal to keep them strictly one-way we were aggressively restrictive. Some of our parking spurs were too narrow, or the angle of approach too abrupt. We learned that most drivers, even good drivers, had difficulty reversing their cars to get out of a parking spur and into the loop road. Some of our barrier rocks were too easy to move out, or visitors could drive around or over them. Carefully placed, it only took a few rocks to supplement natural stones or trees to close a loop. We mapped them as they were completed.

When we opened the new roads and spurs to the public, there was very little public acclaim. We were surprised at the resentment of restrictions on driving. We were amazed in particular by the power and ingenuity of a little old lady in digging out and moving a six hundred-pound barrier rock! She wanted to come in from a different direction and park two automobiles. But our intent was to restrict use to the established driving lanes, and we built by trial and error until we got it done. We just put in bigger stones.

Irv was very busy with fires, new interpretive programs, and sanitation and maintenance jobs; I spent a lot of time on the campground job and with Meineke. He was as fascinated with my psychology degree and my belief that it was a proper background for a park ranger as I was, after I found out what it meant, by his forest pathology profession.

He was a rigid and precise scientist but also a lively and inquisitive fellow. He was very much interested in the philosophy which led to the creation of this new land management and park protection agency. He was also deeply interested in the interpretive programs. I was the greenest of all employees of the National Park Service, and a seasonal one at that. So when Meineke challenged me as to which direction we might be going in the apparent conflict between preservation and public use, I simply promised that I would watch it closely until I found out for myself. I could not see why we could not follow both directions.

With this brief and provocative contact I immediately became acquainted with the major question of policy the Service has asked for over sixty years. And when I reflect with wonder and inspiration on the ecology and beauty of my role, I am again content with the mixture. The Lodgepole Campground one-way road was an example of the newest standard for combining preservation and visitor enjoyment in camp layouts. I feel a distinct touch of pride every time I see such a plan. I helped build the first one! It was illustrative of the emerging thoughts, policies, and programs that were guiding the National Parks. I had to learn and develop with them.

Forestry was a new and active dimension of park management. It had evolved quickly through the leadership of John Coffman, a respected recruit from the Forest Service who was no stranger to nationwide forestry programs, and Sequoia Chief Ranger Larry Cook, a Syracuse University Forestry graduate. In the mid-twenties Steve Mather had recognized the need for professionalism in our vast National Park forests, and people like John and Larry had been eager to take on the problems of fire protection and forest insects, and issues of watershed protection, land carrying capacity, fire protection, tourist blight, and competitive use. The term "recreational forestry" emerged to describe our particular program. Larry's zeal and dedication for forest fire programs was as intense as ranger Bill Sherman's was in Alaska. (Larry later followed John as Chief Forester for the Service.)

Interpretive programs were just entering the mainstream of operations. Dr. Harold Bryant, Dr. Carl Russell, and Ansel Hall were key people I met as they came through Sequoia on field trips. Dr. Bryant was a graduate of the University of California in ornithology. For a time in the late teens he was the Customs Inspector for imported birds for the Port of San Francisco. Dr. Carl Russell had been another man in the right place at the right time; in this case Yosemite in the early twenties. The men and women who interpreted nature were called "naturalists" at that time. Dr. Bryant and Dr. Russell began the experiments, and Ansel Hall became the first permanent Naturalist, then Chief Naturalist at Yosemite, and later Chief Forester in the Educational Division of the Park Service. All three went on to illustrious careers as Superintendents and Regional Directors.

Leadership in land planning, design, and nature preservation have been hallmarks of the National Park Service. Steve Mather had attended planning sessions with the American Society of Landscape Architects and adopted many of their principles for planning development and management. His memory and ideas persisted. In every National Park a memorial plaque reminds visitors that "There Never Will Come An End To The Good That He Has Done."

Thomas C. Vint, Landscape Architect, was most influential in the way we *see* parks. He entered the Service in 1922 at Yosemite, and for the next forty years park entrances, roads, and buildings reflected his philosophy that nature is the best teacher. By 1937 his offices were moved to Washington and organized as the Branch of Plans and Design, with him as Branch Chief and Special Advisor to the Director.

Harry Homman was a specialist on water and sanitation systems in parks. For years he was involved in setting standards and then designing and building facilities. He was attached to the U.S. Public Health Service.

The Bureau of Public Roads (BPR) was invited to help on road layouts and standards. It was divided into regions, as was the Park Service. (At Glacier and Yellowstone we worked with the Portland regional office [Baird French was Regional Engineer, his wife a classmate of Inger's from Juneau High School.] During our stay at Yellowstone the BPR won a national award for the design of the bridge it had built on the Tower road near Mammoth Hot Springs.) The BPR was not as strict about aesthetics as the Park Service. For instance, when building roads in the parks we covered the trunks of trees near blasting areas to protect against scarring from flying rocks. Park roads were built narrower than public highways to deliberately slow down traffic. Turnouts were later added so that visitors could pull over to view wildlife or a particularly beautiful scene. Planning the design of a new road or the change of alignment of an existing one has always been a bone of contention. At Tualume Meadows in Yosemite there was an uproar from the Sierra Club and other friends when a large slope of glacial polish was to be blasted away. As a compromise only a small edge of the granite was taken. (Our old friend from Yosemite days, photographer Ansel Adams, was one of the leaders of this protest.)

Wildlife programs were borrowed from both the old Biological Survey (which later became the Bureau of Fish and Wildlife) and from university biologists. Records were kept of wildlife counts in the existing parks even before 1916. (In Yellowstone the records on elk and buffalo go back to 1914.) The Wildlife Division of each park usually had one man assigned as Wildlife Ranger, who was responsible for counting animals, for watching their food supply, for recognizing diseases and signs of over- and underpopulation, and for assessing the impact of man in the natural habitat. The Wildlife Ranger was not always university-trained, but was wise in the ways of the animals, particularly in the early days of the Service.

(At Yellowstone we later studied the carrying capacity for elk, conducted a five-year study on Grizzly bears with the Craighead brothers and a study of the black-footed ferret with Walter Kittams; and studied the fish in Yellowstone Lake, atmospherics at Old Faithful in the winter, and interrelationships between various animals, weather, and disease. At Big Bend the Service reintroduced desert bighorn sheep to their native habitat, and at Grand Canyon the burro herds were thinned so that the desert bighorn could exist there as well. The National Parks and Wilderness Areas are the only large, undisturbed acreages where scientists can watch the evolution of nature.)

State Parks. Mather had in mind an organization of state park managers to supplement National Park plans, and in 1921 had started the National Conference on State Parks. By 1971—fifty years later—parks were authorized in every state, although in some they had become political footballs. Colonel Leiber of Indiana was a nationally-known leader in the expansion of state park systems. New York, California, Colorado, Indiana, and Maine had particularly fine systems in 1921. After World War II the country had time to assess its resources and pride in states, so a natural outcome was an increase in state park systems. (Colonel Leiber's grandson was on my board when I was president of the National Conference on State Parks in 1973.)

Forest fire control was always a joint endeavor with our neighboring National Forests and state governments. The three political entities by invitation would be included in each other's training programs. During fires we helped each other when we could spare men and equipment. At the field level the relationships were cooperative and friendly.

The U.S. Geological Survey produced maps needed for park planning and for tourist guidance. Names for topographic features were historic or geologic, or taken from some person who had been important to the area, and were formalized by the National Board on Geographic Place Names.

Professional engineers took over park maintenance — electrical, mechanical, and hydraulic engineers were borrowed as needed for planning from other Federal agencies in the beginning and later from the National Park Service Design and Planning Center in Denver. There were some engineering "greats" in the Service. Hiram Martin Crittenden was an early engineer "borrowed" from the Army Corps of Engineers. His beautiful bridge over the Yellowstone River and the figure-eight road system in Yellowstone were monuments to his aesthetic values. (The bridge has been replaced in the same form, and the road system is still in use today.) Frank A. Kittredge became Chief Engineer in 1927. He was a road builder "par excellence." The White Spar between Prescott and Wickenburg in Arizona; the Knife Edge; the entrance to Mesa Verde; and the Going-to-the-Sun Highway in Glacier were his designs. (He also became the Superintendent of Zion, Yosemite, and Grand Canyon.)

All paperwork (payroll, budget, purchasing, property, personnel, accounting, etc.) was combined as Park Administration.

Ranger and park superintendents' employment standards were raised, and United States Civil Service Commission standards were set for the new agency. First, however, Mather and Albright surveyed their top crew and completed a weeding-out process.

These were the obvious kinds of common working dimensions I would see or could infer from the direction things were going in the administration of Sequoia. We never really had any published guidelines informing us of policies. It was mostly word-of-mouth from Irv. All park personnel were there to help the visitors (never called tourists) enjoy and learn about the park. All the while we never forgot our role as conservators. Law enforcement was required, but never emphasized unless needed. From the Superintendent to the maintenance and sanitation people we were idealists. The goal was to keep the parks unspoiled, even as we, the people of the world, used them. Use and conservation did not always go hand-in-hand, however. The burgeoning visitation after World War II strained the facilities (especially campgrounds, roads, water resources, park personnel, and concessions). In response to this pressure, many ideas emerged over the years, among them closing parks when they are "full," reservation systems, and the suggestion of enlarging the facilities. Several of the more popular parks have instituted reservation systems successfully.

I soon learned about the "Lane policy letter" of May 13, 1918, which had established program policies for the National Park Service, and this simply reinforced my conviction that I had joined the right outfit. This letter made our job more explicit: "Preserve the parks unimpaired for the use of future generations; they are for the use, observation, health, and pleasure of the people, and the national interest must dictate decisions about public or private enterprise in the parks." Even a beginning ranger could understand this kind of instruction, particularly when it was reinforced by the ongoing job and the direction in which programs were moving.

I never met Steve Mather — I just knew of his effective leadership. I did work for Horace Albright for over a year, however, and the great loyalty and idealism that pervaded the 1932–33 park crew made an indelible imprint on me that never faded. (Inger and I got to know Horace and his charming wife Grace as well, and their sharing of courageous and gracious counsel has always been rewarding.)

The year 1932 was highly exciting. There was a staff ferment of pride in the parks and in their new direction. Fortuitously, I arrived just as a new flood of excitement and procedure pervaded the Service. A great spirit was developing. I could grow with it. Historical parks were increasingly prominent: Colonial (Virginia, 1930); Cumberland Gap (Kentucky, Tennessee, and Virginia, 1930); George Washington's birthplace (1930); and Hot Springs (Arkansas, in 1932, as a public land withdrawal because of its importance as an Indian treaty ground). Archaeological sites were also being preserved, the best example being the ruins at Mesa Verde (Colorado, 1906).

The old ranger purist protection policies continued, but the "people" services began to grow: park interpretation, quality maintenance, sanitation, law enforcement, planning, community services, use of professional skills through research, demographic measurements, concessions (hotels, stores, and service stations), and the concept of park carrying capacities. I was a psychology major; I could help with this dimension.

All of the new people who were moving into park operational jobs and who worked with me thought I was an "old-timer" because I knew how to ride, care for a mule, run a pack string, and use dynamite on trail maintenance. But I was still a brand-new seasonal, searching for that elusive permanent status.

CHAPTER VI

THE GOLDEN TROUT

I FELT LUCKY TO BE PAID FOR THE WONDERFUL TASKS I PERFORMED.
Ranger work was never routine. There were always interesting things
to learn. After the Sierra Club rescue of Miss Spaulding, I went to
Park Headquarters at Ash Mountain for more supplies and equipment. Then I was back on a camp-by-camp foot patrol of my campground, getting acquainted with the people there, helping where I
could.

My last assignment that summer of 1932 was the Clover Creek
Ranger Station boundary patrol. This was during the last two weeks
of September, during the California deer hunting season. My responsibility covered park boundaries from the Dorst and Stony Creek junction on the Marble Fork of the Kaweah River, up to Jenny Lake and
J O Pass, and across to Kettle Peak and Silliman Pass.

The most obvious and effective way to survey the high country for
possible trespassing hunters was to make an occasional circle to observe
all possible campsites. A little visibility to indicate that a patrol ranger
was on the job was usually enough to deter hunters. It was not a
highly productive deer area anyway, but tradition persisted that there
were always a few mossy-horned big bucks around Silliman Pass and
outside Kettle Peak above the Ranger Lakes. However, all the out-
fitters who hunted up to the park boundary were just as visible as I
was, and we never had any conflicts.

Just as a precaution against sneaky poachers, I spent some hours
climbing over Kettle Peak looking at deer tracks. Were there any big
ones that might tempt a trophy hunter? I was a good walker, and
Pico could get almost anywhere. We were always questing along the
rimrock. None of the few deer tracks looked like big buck to me.
So I relaxed a bit.

[71]

On Kettle Peak one afternoon, I decided that instead of climbing back around to J O Pass and returning to the Clover Creek cabin, I would just ease off the side of the peak and work my way down to the dry fork of Clover Creek below us and then on down to the main stream and the cabin. It was a long detour, and just as we slid down into the valley and turned downstream, I realized that we were crossing a rock dike which surfaced on both sides of the valley. Unexpectedly, there were several pools and ponds of water and a short, living stream instead of the sandy dry streambed.

A trout surfaced in a pool as I watched. It flashed like a rainbow or a golden trout. These were mythical creatures of secret places, only rarely seen, except in places like Golden Trout Creek in the Kern.

Pico and I hurried on to the cabin and I made my daily reports. I had been looking for big buck tracks and that afternoon there were none. I got out my old collapsible steel fish rod. The guides were only bailing wire soldered on; my reel almost a junk pile donation, but it could hold the line which was little better than grocery twine. My flies were from a Woolworth closeout sale. After I returned to the pools, I turned Pico out to graze with a loosened cinch, and fumbled with knots until the fishing rod was threaded up. The stubby and stiff rod whistled through the air as I made my false casts. Somehow the fly shot out over the stream and dropped.

A trout hit it immediately. I overcompensated on my first jerk and a ten-inch golden trout flipped up out of the water and lit on a steamside bank of spongy green moss. I have a memory center behind my breast bone where only great events are stored — like the time I met Inger. And this was one of those special events. The trout turned and flipped and almost visibly began to fade — aye, it was beautiful! It turned again and I reached over and flipped it back into the pool as it fell from the hook.

It swirled briefly and vanished. I did not cast again. I ate spam for supper. A rainbow would have been someway unsettling!

In the spring of 1933 there was a new feeling of anticipation in the air in Sequoia National Park. The park was to have one of the early Civilian Conservation Corps (CCC) camps, probably at Lodgepole.

So suddenly I was assigned to take an initial enrollee crew of twenty up to Silliman Meadows. We were to build a horse pasture about three miles above Lodgepole on the Clover Creek trail. Actually, this job was a "make-work" project, until materials arrived for major programs.

Irv went up with me to look over the pasture fence. It was to be very primitive. We were not to cut any fence posts. We were to use barbless wire — in this case coils of #9 telephone wire. I was to lay it out starting at the Silliman Creek crossing, unrolling my coils of telephone wire to enclose about ten acres. I was then to suspend the wire from trees, pulling it sideways to tighten it.

This streamside grove of conifers included a beautiful open meadow with a rustic sign, "CAMP BETTY." The land had been admired by Steve Mather. It had been privately owned and for sale. Mather had purchased it and then donated it to the park, meanwhile using it for a camping site and naming it after his daughter, Elizabeth. Years later I asked her about Camp Betty, but she had no memory of being there.

[margin annotation: Camp Betty]

The work with the CCC crew was a surprising experience. As we carried the wire around the perimeter and sashayed over to the nailing points, I was often briefly concealed from our starting point and most of the crew. Yet I always seemed to be in the middle of a crowd. The enrollees clustered around me, whatever I was doing. By noon I had learned about their problem. I had ridden in on horseback with my pack mule, while they had walked in. They were scared to death that I might leave them, and they didn't know how to get back to the truck. So my ranger hat was their security blanket — they just kept it in sight!

Our first lunch was a dismal affair — a typical early CCC primitive with thick slices of bread, bologna and cheese, a #10 can of peaches, a jar of pickles, and a coffee pot.

The CCC mess sergeant apparently knew nothing about campfire lunches, and since I was to be with this crew for several days, I organized an early morning raid on the commissary the next day. I came up with all the same food plus better pickles, mustard, jam, condensed milk, sugar, cookies, an enormous onion, and plenty of Bull Durham tobacco. At noon I clipped out some pieces of fence wire and showed

the boys how to make a crude grill. Then we built a fire and they
learned how to face the grill, so that it toasted the bread, frizzled the
bologna, and melted the cheese. We used long twigs to spear the
canned peaches and divided the syrup into the mess cups. I made
coffee and they used lots of condensed milk and sugar. It all turned
out well although their ignorance of how to make do was unbelievable.
But they all were willing to learn.

As we sat around our campfire with a second cup of coffee, we
talked. I found that my ignorance of their backgrounds was equally
unbelievable. Their experiences were mainly home town events. They
were honest, tough, disturbed young men from the Southeastern
United States. Their away-from-home adventures had been as hoboes
or vagabonds. We had three University of Kentucky students who
were especially articulate. Around the campfire they all spoke their
hearts.

"Have you ever been in jail in Nashville?" asked one of them. He
had and it was tough. You might get a jail sentence or run out of
town, depending on whether or not the sheriff needed a work crew
that day. Others contributed to the discussion. Jails were tough in
Portland, The Dalles, Memphis, Pocatello — these kids had been in
jail literally across America. Often they just went on to roam America
seeking work or sustenance in any way possible. They rode freight
trains, hitchhiked, even walked. Mostly they disapproved of stealing but
they were not fanatic about it, and it was better than going hungry.

I soon respected them as I recognized the grinding poverty they
had at home and the hope that the CCC offered them. Twenty-five
dollars a month to be sent home and another five dollars for spending
money may seem pitiful wages by later standards, but not in 1933.
The families needed it. The young men worked cheerfully, and most
of them knew how to work — "just please Mister Ranger don't leave
us alone out here with the bears!"

The three University of Kentucky students stayed with us only
ten days. Now that they had had their fare paid to California and
had seen the big trees of Sequoia National Park, they went "over the
hill" and on the bum along California highways. There were hundreds
like them along the roadsides. We never heard from these particular
students again.

But over subsequent years in the National Parks, and I am certain in National Forests as well, a middle-aged man with teenage children might introduce himself. He had been here in CCC camp, and he wanted his sons or grandsons to see the place he had worked, and the buildings or roads which he had helped to construct. It was a great adventure in being an American! I wish we could do it again!

This was the end of the 1933 season. As a CCC Junior Foreman and a Sequoia National Park seasonal ranger, over the next two years I continued to add to the months of experience needed for permanent ranger eligibility. Chief Ranger Larry Cook was transferred in the summer of 1935 to a new National Park Service forestry office in Berkeley, California. The new Chief Ranger, Ford Spigelmeyer, obtained approval for my status as Special Patrol Ranger and CCC Foreman to rework the tourist trails in the northern end of Sequoia. I had recommended this in my two annual reports. Suddenly, I was told to go do it.

I had three seventeen- and eighteen-year-old enrollees for the work crew, and three burros as the transportation system. We would set up a roving camp work out of Lodgepole, with camps at Twin Lakes, Pattee Meadows, and Alta Meadow.

None of my three crew members were skilled. They had not learned to use tools, they could not manage the burros, and they even had to learn how to roll their beds. But they were eager, and it was the best of summers.

Up at six A.M., I fixed a sourdough breakfast, while the boys — dubbed Hungry, Weary, and Sleepy — did the chores. Four plate-sized pancakes with syrup, bacon, and two fried eggs were the quota for each youngster. This carried them until noon.

As I finished breakfast, I would heat the Dutch Oven. I used my residual pancake batter with the addition of flour, an egg, raisins, sugar, canned milk, soda, and vanilla to create a sourdough trail cake which baked as we finished the camp cleanup. Packed while warm and opened for lunch, it looked like a chunk of concrete block, but was wonderfully moist, sweet, fragrant, and substantial!

Lunch was crackers, cold biscuits, ham, cheese, dried fruit, peanut butter, jam, lettuce, and cake — the equivalent of about two thick sandwiches apiece. For supper we had trout or canned meat, or a roast if there was meat and time to cook it. For supper I always turned out biscuits. The kids loved them. A can of fruit, cookies, coffee, Sleepy with his guitar — we did well by ourselves under the open sky! Our tent was used mainly for bad weather.

As far as we knew, our three burros came to us nameless. The number one burro was a large jennet, perfectly tractable and well behaved, but the most noisy and outspoken burro I have ever known. At Pattee Meadow on our first day in camp she was speaking to some other burros that had just passed our way and were up to J O Pass. She continued companionably as long as they were in earshot in an unmelodious, grating voice. Our work crew was assembled for the first time. To my surprise, Weary's Mexican background included some rudiments of music, and he believed that she sounded just like a soprano his father liked on Red Seal phonograph records. So "Madame Honk" came into our family.

The male burro was the Madame's son, a six-year-old sneaky and rebellious fellow who had a great swagger and personality. He thought he was a horse and he refused to associate with burros if he could find a way around it. He did not like rangers either.

One day at Alta Meadows, we used him as our daily load bearer to the top of Alta Peak. As we moved down the rocky back trail into the basin where we were camped, the Madame welcomed him to camp. He responded in good voice, but out of tune and with less volume. He saluted his mother, and between them the mountain valley rang with the bellowing. Weary came through with a characterization. "Welcome home, Admiral Byrd," he announced, recalling the great and noisy welcome we had heard on our radios for the Admiral as he had entered New York Harbor on his return from the South Pole. Yes, indeed — "Welcome home Admiral!"

Our third burro was a well-behaved female, small, quiet, with no color identification. I used to wonder about her, keeping in mind Josh Billings' warnings about some of the ornery Erie Canal mules that would behave themselves for weeks just to get a chance to kick somebody. But this burro was modest. We called her Freckles, because she did not have any.

They were part of our family all summer long.

I must describe Sleepy a bit more — he was the kind of helper you always wished you had with you on camping trips. The water pail was always full, the woodpile was adequate, dishwater was always heating when you needed it, coffee water was always ready. Hungry, on the other hand, was a sleeper — he needed a constant prodding to be up for breakfast, to have his bed rolled in time to leave camp. His name was descriptive because he was a prodigious eater. He loved to fish and to eat fish, but "yukked" badly when I expected him to clean his catch. I asked him one day what his civilian jobs had been — as much as a seventeen-year-old had a job. He had a job — he was expecting to return to it. He was a mortician's helper! He "cleaned" people, he said, but fish — NO!

My ranger hat was all across the north end of old Sequoia. We built water bars, we adjusted grades, we went around big trees and trimmed growing shrubs. We pried out big rocks, and found that a little massage with a sledge hammer would smooth out rugged trails. I blasted out trees with dynamite (seventeen- and eighteen-year-old boys were too young to use explosives) and we repaired switchbacks. We were careful, and we had no bear raids.

Any single-blanket, jackass prospector will tell you that for every week of prospecting with burros you spend two days hunting them. We learned the truth of this from the Admiral. He had been raised with horses and always believed that he was a horse. He always wanted to follow pack strings we met on distant trails; he tried to run away searching for horses that had passed our camp during the day. Associating with other burros — or with rangers — was degrading. He would forsake camp and friends, everything except the barley sack, to look for unappreciative horses.

With front feet hobbled, and a small, clear Swiss bell around his neck, the Admiral could pick and shuffle his way through a sleeping camp, head and neck held immobile so the bell would not ring. He lifted both front feet together, to step quietly over me and other sleepers until he was beyond our immediate reach. Then he would soon be gone. Every morning we fed each burro a handful of barley using a burlap nose bag to keep them accustomed to being handled. In fact, using this nose bag was the only way to catch the Admiral if he were loose. Carelessly, I left the barley sack among our camp gear one day. The burros ate it. From then on the barley sack hung high in a tree.

The Admiral was a true loner. Camped at Pattee Meadows in late summer, I decided that probably he was sufficiently imprinted and I could leave him in camp for a day with the others without hobbles. I hated to keep him under continual restraint. When we returned in the evening, the Madame and Freckles were at the tent. A bit of grain was welcome, they said, and we tousled their long ears. The Admiral had disappeared. He stayed invisible for a week, although I made several long scouting hikes looking for his tracks or listening for his bell. He probably had followed a horse somewhere, but J O Pass trail parties had not seen him. He was not at Rowell Meadow, or Clover Creek, or Twin Lakes, or Ranger Lakes, or back in Lodgepole. Finally, a passing rider, seeking stray stock of his own, told me there was a little gray burro with hobbles and a small bell running with three stray horses several miles down Clover Creek. The burro was as wild as a jack rabbit, he said. This sounded like our friend the Admiral, so the next morning the three boys and I went down looking for him. By this time I would have been content to let the winter snows get him, but I had to get my bell and hobbles back. At least three miles down Clover Creek below the cabin we began to find burro tracks, and then we could hear his bell.

So we made a plan. We had run out of barley, but the Admiral didn't know that. The empty sack still smelled good. With the open noose of a lead rope around the open mouth of the empty sack I moved down to him, and after some endearing but unprintable conversation I got close. The fellows spread in behind him. He was very suspicious, wheeling and snorty, but greedy. He finally boldly pushed his nose into the empty sack. He wheeled to run when he discovered that he had been trapped, but my hand was quick and the rope loop flipped over his long ears and settled around his neck. He charged valiantly away. My two hundred pounds slowed him down.

The enrollees got ahead of him and charged in to turn him back, but he ignored them. With a downhill pull the little beast could drag me against my sliding dug-in heels. As I skidded down the hill I encountered cross logs, and I had to suddenly abandon my sliding and run for a few steps to leap them. The CCC enrollees were wildly running with us, trying to intercept the Admiral or hang on to the rope with me. They did not make it. Only the dead drag of gravity beat him as we got to the bottom of the hill. Although the strength in his neck was amazing, he simply could not haul me uphill. At the bottom of the hill I slid among a few small trees, and soon we had him snubbed down. The rope did not break, although he put a real strain on it before I got a halter over his contrary nose. We admired his determination as we cursed his unwillingness to comply with ordinary restraints.

After Admiral Byrd had his holiday along Clover Creek, he became increasingly difficult to handle. He worked willingly enough when saddled and on the job, but his sole goal at rest was to elude us or untie his rope or in some way break loose from our control and find horses. His final gimmick was simply to lunge backwards to break his lead rope or the hitch rail. His power in pulling back with his head and neck muscles was tremendous.

We tied him high to a young tree for a day so the spring of the branches would haul him back, but we had only a few yards of rope strong enough to withstand his assault. We left the hobbles on his forefeet and turned him loose with a forty-foot lash rope tied into the hobble.

Finally, the Admiral broke it up himself. Early one afternoon at Pattee Meadow, as I reached for his halter, he jumped backwards, broke the hitch rack and galloped away across the meadow in evident disdain for our constraints. He had just gotten into high gear in his flight when the loose end of the trailing hobble rope whipped around a small pine tree. As the Admiral reached comfortably for his next leap ahead he ran out of space and the rope pulled his front legs neatly out from under him. This was a very lush, very marshy and mushy meadow, so that the aerial flip he performed simply laid him out on his side in the marsh with a great splat.

It knocked the wind out of him and he lay flat, gasping and quivering, completely subdued for the moment. I wondered about artificial respiration, but could not see how to do it. (Years later we learned to manage this with overtranquilized bears simply by jumping on and off the rib cage. But we didn't know how to do that yet.) The Admiral stirred, gathered his front feet, and gently rose, and we walked back together to the broken hitch rail where he had started. When I took the hobble off and tied the Admiral with his normal lead rope he was uncommonly sensitive about it. He had learned a lesson.

He had related his catastrophe to the lead rope. From then on you could tie the Admiral to a tree with grocery string. As long as it was visible he would not pull it tight. He had good manners. But he still thought he was a horse.

CHAPTER VII

A RATION FOR A HORSE

IT WAS NOW SIX YEARS SINCE I HAD PUT HALLIBURTON ON THE SHELF. I remember one of my early psychology professors commenting that the difference between a nineteen-year-old buying flowers and a twenty-nine-year-old buying flour was ten years. My sequence only took six. My free-wheeling, scattered enthusiasms finally had been channeled. I wanted to be a ranger — my own kind of ranger.

I blessed Inger almost every day, as her loyalty and her own ruggedness supported our spirits through the rough beginnings. We lived in tents on platforms for four years; only the last one had electricity and running water. She was positive, creative, and cheerful. (At first I thought of sending a note of appreciation to her domestic science teacher, for Inger was a superb cook and a graceful homemaker. I never got it done. Besides, it should have been shared with Inger's mother, who exhibited Old Country graces so naturally.) Inger's skillful hands and natural talent for appreciation of color, textures, line, and harmony evolved gradually, and I just relaxed and enjoyed it with her. She knew many crafts, but particularly ceramics, sculpture, and basketry. Arts and crafts fit well with parks.

At this time I was still in the elementary phases of park management. Much of my enthusiasm came from my goals of preservation and public enjoyment for the parks, so the work at hand satisfied both my ethos and my ethics.

One of my keepsakes is a portion of a copy of a 1932 Sequoia National Park office order which established guidelines for "A Ration for a Horse." New procedures about 1930 for the National Park Service authorized the government purchase of horses for patrol rangers to ride, and it was now necessary to establish controls on how much the government expected to feed them. Otherwise, I might pamper my horse Pico, or overfeed him, or — horrors! — use government forage for feeding a personally-owned horse!

What was a reasonable amount of hay for a horse? Were big horses and little horses to be rationed the same way? We didn't know, but Pico and I tried out the office order — eight pounds of grain and fifteen pounds of hay per day.

My hay storage was a big tarpaulin spread on the ground under a Ponderosa pine tree next to the Lodgepole corral. In spite of careful wrapping and rewrapping, we shared the hay with mule deer that ripped the canvas, and with big gray Columbia ground squirrels. They loved both the dry leaves and the seed heads. The rolled barley was stored in a new garbage can with a tight lid. The can was often rolled around vigorously by a visiting black bear. Sometimes he got the lid off. I doubt that the bear gained much from this protein supplement although the jays and the ravens and the camprobbers were appreciative. But it raised hell with our attempts to account for a one hundred-pound sack of grain.

We had no scales. The hay bales were imprecise in weight. On a baby scale our #10 can grain measure held about eight pounds. I gave up on accountability by weight. My job was to keep Pico in working condition. We could check up later on this ration-weight business. Nothing happened, of course. This was my first real experience with an unenforceable procedure.

Pico and I got along just fine. He was a glossy black gelding with four white feet, sturdily built, and short-coupled like a Morgan. He was about fifteen hands high, proud, gentle, an easy keeper, and on the records was listed at almost twenty five years old. This was within four years of my own twenty nine that summer of 1932.

Pico was my preferred mount for my three years of Lodgepole back country patrol work. He greeted me with tolerance and no enthusiasm the day we met. He knew how to lick up sugar lumps or crunch apples and although I carried them for him often he never went hunting for them. He knew every trail in the north end of the park, as well as the short cuts, the "get-bys," and duck routes. He was as sure-footed as a goat, easy riding, a vigorous trailside browser, and generally a quiet and reliable fellow.

Pico and I were successful companions on rescue trips, fish planting journeys, long patrols or when fighting forest fires. He scared me badly one morning as I led him away from his grazing. He lunged at me with his lips skinned back over his big yellow teeth. It looked like he was trying to bite me. But Pico had a problem that day. A yellow jacket was stinging his nose and I was the closest upright he could rub it on.

Fred, a glossy bay, never learned to follow a lead rope. He would stumble along in a pack string right behind the saddle horse. We learned to keep him snubbed up closely as the number one pack animal. As you passed a tree on your right, suddenly Fred would determine to go left around it. If he had enough slack to get his nose around it you were in trouble. There was no rhyme or reason to it. He just did it. And he refused to back up unless you got off and backed him up and led him through the entanglement.

One day we had four pack-mule-cans of eastern brook trout fry — two mule loads — to go into the Silliman Lakes just under the rim rock at Silliman Gap. These are two tiny tarn lakes at high elevation in a barren granite basin. There was no trail to them, but Irv explained that I could reach them by following the south and then the north sides of Silliman Creek, climbing high on the north just before I reached the basin rim rock, and then dropping on down into the lakes. "Pico has been there before," Irv offered "and once you cross the creek there is a duck trail into it." With these guidelines we took off.

At Silliman Creek we left the trail and just kept going along this small brawling stream. We worked our way over the forest floor, crashing through second growth lodgepole pine thickets, jumping over down logs, detouring jill-pokes of blowdowns and clumps of trees and brush. We gradually climbed the hill, working our way constantly higher in elevation. The south canyon wall began to close in on us. After about two miles we were forced to ford the creek. It was a good, open, gravelly ford, and the mules and Pico drank deeply. I climbed down onto the sand bar, sat on a big flat rock, and took time for a pipe smoke.

Ready to start again, I put Pico to the creek and the open side hill, and he willingly plunged in and came right on out and headed in a switchback zig-zag up the hillside. We were on the edge of a long finger of a rock slide from the rim-rock down to the creek. Sometimes we were weaving our way through the forest edge, then we were out on the edge of the rockslide, using its occasional gaps to let us through and onward and upward. It was steep, but footing was good and we moved easily ahead as long as I was certain we were headed the right direction. I didn't know of course, but it matched Irv's fragmentary instructions and Pico felt no qualms about it.

About a mile up the hill we came to an open decomposed granite ridge top at timberline, and began to move along the ridge above the rockslide. Here I picked up the first "duck," a small rock set on top of a big rock so that it was identifiable as a man-made marker giving a point of direction. I stood in the stirrups until I picked out duck number two and then number three and chirped, "Come on Pico. Let's go!" I have no idea who put this trail in, but it was a security point to me. I knew another ranger had gone this way before and had left this marker to help him find his way.

We crossed the rock slide, still headed up Silliman Creek, but at a higher elevation. We crossed more fingers of forest — magnificent giant red fir and white fir, contorted and spiraled huge lodgepole pine, all twisted counter-clockwise. (I am told that south of the equator, the trees twist in the other direction in response to magnetic compass fields.) Alpine fir and small white pine were in abundance, but shrubs and grass were sparse.

I ran out of my line of ducks, but the lower lake was now in sight. I dropped the lead rope for a moment and rode on to the lake. There was a small stream emptying out of it, a few gravel bars, but no evidence of any other break in the bath-tub-looking walls of the lake itself. In fact, this little outlet seemed to be the only access.

The water needed a small bit of tempering, almost all of the fry had survived the rugged mule trip and the climb, and I scattered the youngsters as best I could along the shores of both lakes.

Then I pulled out my collapsible steel fly rod, threaded up the line, tied on a black gnat, and tried my luck. On the second cast I had a strike — obviously a heavy fish — but I missed. I missed the second and third time also. Then I just took time for thinking a bit and realized that these were brook trout with a far different striking pattern than the rainbow and golden trout I had been working on. So on the next cast I simply waited to count to three, and I had hold of a lunker which turned out to be an eastern brook trout. I only knew it was a brookie by the white margined fins, but it was half-starved and an extremely skinny, heavy-headed creature. It had little vigor to make a big fight, so it was soon returned to the lake. It was only eleven A.M., and when I finished my sandwiches and started to fire up my pipe I discovered that I had left it on the flat rock in Silliman Creek. I had worked out a different return route in my own mind, so I did not return by the flat rock that day, and my pipe was still there a year later when I returned with more trout fry to try it again.

Later on I found that the National Park Service had a whole lake full of similar fish at Stony Indian Pass in Glacier National Park; but I felt certain that our Silliman Lakes fish planting was exceeding the carrying capacity of this small tarn lake. I reported this and suggested we leave the Silliman Lakes off our planting plans. After the second trip I did not plant any more little ones just to feed those hungry big ones. In fact, I never went back in again. But I remember the rugged journey, the careful maneuvering with Pico and the pack mules to get the fish planted, the magnificence of the scenery, the wildness of the land and the forest, the blazing wildflowers, the earthy smells, the mountain profiles, the ear-aching quiet of it all. There were occasional red squirrels — the noisy chickaree — to salute us as we passed, the chipmunks and golden mantled ground squirrels were friendly as they looked and scurried about. A marmot might whistle from just ahead of us. The forest edges were black by contrast beside the great granular texture and marbled sterility of the granite. Sunlight reflected from every open rock face. I was the romantic ranger riding through the wilds, the protector of beauty. I was never frightened by this loneliness. The isolation and the impersonal impact of it all someway was a blessing. It was a fulfilling job. A job? It was a way to be fully alive and to overflow with love. It belonged to me; I belonged there. I was the ranger.

Let's linger a while longer in Sequoia. In the summer of 1934, one of my CCC helpers named Gus asked to ride Pico from Lodgepole about two miles to the Wolverton corral. I started Gus up the trail about two o'clock and forgot about it. Al Guttormsen, the blacksmith at the corral, called me about four o'clock asking where the horse was. Of course, I had no idea. Some way Gus had turned onto one of the Giant Forest trails and was then wandering through this wonderland without any knowledge at all of the geography.

Meanwhile, I had other worries. A young lady camping by herself in the Lodgepole Campground had arranged for her family to meet her at 3:00 P.M. at the Sherman Tree. They arrived late from Long Beach. At 4:00 P.M. they were questing around the Sherman Tree and ended at my ranger station. The girl had disappeared. This was a real worry. I had talked with her. She was a nurse, about forty-five years old and obviously on a tight edge emotionally. She had been at the Sherman Tree earlier, and had talked with other tourists who were concerned about her sanity.

Irv had gone to town. The lady camper was gone. Even Gus was gone! A ranger job had some worries! About 10:00 P.M. I was parked in the government patrol pick-up near the Sherman Tree. The gal had been there at 3:00 P.M. The General's Highway was a narrow strip generally north and south — all the rest of the land was mountains and forests and canyons. I wondered where she might seek security and safety in her frightened and confused mind. There were no clues.

But through the trees I began to hear a horse walking in on the trail from the west — clop–clop–clop — and I thought well, here comes Pico, and one of my problems is over, anyway. And it was — into the circle of the car headlights came a patient and indomitable Pico with reins hung loose on the saddle horn. Gus was firmly clutching this security blanket as if it, too, might vanish. He was unable to tell me where he had been except that about 7:00 P.M., in early dusk and completely lost, he had come to a trail junction. The only sign intelligible to him suggested that Giant Forest, near his home camp, was seven miles away, so he went "that-a-way." He had dropped the reins on the saddle horn and said, "Well, old horse, if you know the way, let's go home!" Three hours later they came wearily into the Sherman Tree parking area. I put him and Pico safely to bed after getting that fifteen pounds of hay and eight pounds of grain into Pico. Only that night we gave him a generous bonus and didn't bother to tell the bookkeeper about it.

Large *sequoia gigantea* near the Pillars of Hercules, Sequoia National Park, 1933. The inside of this tree was entirely eaten by fire, yet bore branches and foliage like a normal tree. *National Park Service*.

Author on the farm at Caldwell, Idaho, ca. 1915. *Chapter 1.*

Haines, Alaska, 1930. Chilkoot Barracks in background. *Chapters 2–3.*

Chilkoot Barracks, Haines. The winter school bus, 1929–31. *Chapter 3.*

Lon goes a-courting, 1929. *Chapter 3.*

Lon and Inger, California-bound, 1931. *Chapter 3.*

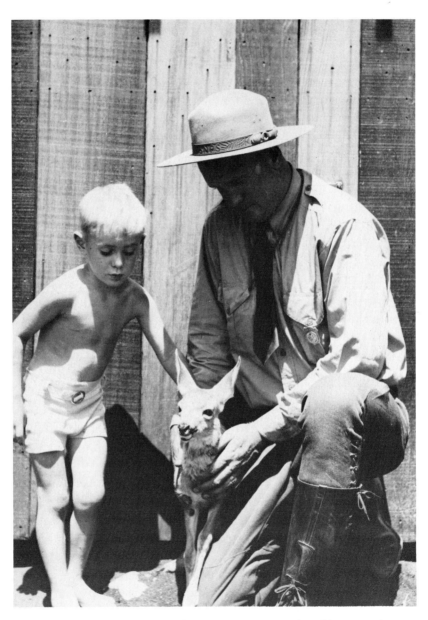

Lon and son Lars with an orphan fawn at Sequoia, ca. 1935. *Chapters 4–8.*

Colonel John R. White, superintendent at Sequoia and Kings Canyon, 1930s.
National Park Service. Chapters 4–8.

The House Group, Sequoia, mid-1930s. *Stagner, photographer.*
National Park Service. Chapters 4–8.

Ranger Billy Nelson, Yosemite, 1933. *Yosemite National Park Research Library.*
Chapter 8.

Birdwalk with Ranger C. H. Harwell, Yosemite, July 1936.
Ralph H. Anderson, photographer. Yosemite Research Library. Chapters 8–9.

Hetch Hetchy Reservoir, Yosemite.
Yosemite Research Library. Chapters 8–9.

Morning in Camp Number Seven, Yosemite, September 5, 1937.
Ralph H. Anderson, photographer. Yosemite Research Library. Chapters 8–9.

Author snow gauging in Yosemite, 1936–37. *Chapters 8–9.*

Badger Pass ski area, late 1930s, Yosemite. "Upski" on right, with Hannes Schroll in middle. (Schroll came to Yosemite from Austria to start the ski school at Badger Pass.) *Yosemite Research Library. Chapters 8–9.*

Badger Pass ski chalet, 1936. Author in center as ski ranger, providing information. *Chapters 8–9.*

Rangers on patrol in the high Sierras, 1930s. *Yosemite Research Library.*
Chapters 4–9.

Lake Tenaga, Yosemite, 1935. *Yosemite Research Library. Chapters 8–9.*

Wawona Road Tunnel Parking area, Yosemite, February 22, 1937.
Ralph H. Anderson, photographer. Yosemite Research Library. Chapters 8–9.

Crest of flood in Yosemite Valley, December 11, 1937, 2:45 P.M.
Superintendent's house can be seen in background. *Lowell Adams, photographer.*
Yosemite Research Library. Chapters 8–9.

Ranger tent, Camp Number Seven, Yosemite, August 5, 1938.
Ralph H. Anderson, photographer. Yosemite Research Library. Chapter 9.

Their Royal Highnesses Crown Prince Frederick and Crown Princess Ingrid
of Denmark, in Mariposa Grove, Yosemite, April 12, 1939.
Ralph H. Anderson, photographer. Yosemite Research Library. Chapter 9.

The missing lady? The Chief Ranger's office alerted the San Joaquin Valley police net and about 9:00 A.M. they found her hiking along in the August heat, wearing a sheepskin coat. I notified her anxious family and another "minor" incident was over.

Sequoia had another memorable steed. Brownie was a youngster about six years old; he was not a rodeo horse and must have been purchased cheaply as a colt. His contribution to my education was vigorous and positive. He expected me to know more than he did and to tell him what I wanted on each occasion. He was so tall and slender that even I must clamber aboard him. But he was a strong and eager self-starter, determined, snorty, twitchy, clumsy, and with tremendous staying power. We kept him rough shod. My anthropomorphic interpretation of his behavior was that he enjoyed the tinkling bell-like sound of his steel shoes and rocks clinking together. When for any reason we stopped in a rock patch on a trail, Brownie would reach out with a front foot and vigorously rattle loose rocks around and listen to their music. At night, these sounds were accompanied by a shower of sparks as the rocks glanced off each other. It was spooky to sit up in the saddle in the dark with an exhibitionist and music-loving horse. Amidst a shower of sparks, Brownie snorted and pawed the rocks happily.

He had mastered a ready-for-action stance that could lead into a sideways jump of about four feet with no warning. Nothing vicious — just a suspicious response to a familiar tree stump. Or an unexpected and noisy chipmunk could trigger one of these sideways leaps which did not seem to bother Brownie. He never even got his feet tangled up, but it could bust an unsuspecting rider's gut in two in the middle quite easily. Riding him was never a relaxed situation. His hair trigger was always set.

He almost unloaded me one morning as we crossed an open hillside near Hospital Rock and passed a single oak on the upper side of the trail. A rattlesnake behind the tree rattled and struck at Brownie's nose as we passed. The strike missed but the snake lost its hold and slid down the trail embankment right under Brownie's front feet. There were no rocks to clang that time as Brownie exploded into a vigorous evasion pattern. The snake was well battered, and ranger Garrison almost got dumped on top of it. Frantic clutching and a stout saddle string kept me aboard while Brownie scrambled away. It took ten minutes to quiet his shakes. It took two pipes of tobacco to quiet mine!

More anthropomorphisms? On another occasion I rode Brownie at sunrise up the trail from Lodgepole toward Clover Creek. It was a delightful, clear August morning, heavy dew holding the dust down as we started up the long dugway across the Marble Fork Canyon wall through the Chapparal — chinquapin, deer brush, and mountain mahogany. It had a special heavy aroma which later in the day became pungent, but early in the morning was just cloying. Just after we crossed the open hillside and before we entered the tree-clad mesa at the top of this trail grade, we came upon a dead fawn stretched out across the trail. It was stiff, but lifelike, in its posture with one front leg folded under, the other extended across the trail. I nudged Brownie up to the fawn but he was suspicious and reluctant. So I dismounted and carried the fawn away and cached the tiny body in a clump of young lodgepole pine.

We swung on up the hill at a good pace; Brownie had a shuffling, fast walk that covered the miles easily. As we topped out onto the first plateau we entered a second-growth lodgepole pine grove. A mule deer doe followed by two bounding fawns crossed the trail ahead of me, beyond a group of trees. The mother and one fawn soon reappeared and bounded on, but as I rounded the next bend I found that the doe had cached the other fawn in a little clearing right in the trail. Again Brownie snorted suspiciously, but kept his stride right up to this quiet fawn. It was stretched out across the trail, head extended, one foreleg tucked under, the other alongside the neck. It looked just like the dead one which had been harmless, so Brownie strode up to it and never hesitated. He put his nose down and snorted vigorously.

A fawn that has been "hidden" in this manner is ordinarily quiescent. It will move only under extreme provocation. Apparently very young fawns do not have any particular body scent (this comes with their first supply of urine), so that even hunting coyotes have been known to pass them by without a glance. But Brownie with his tremendous snort was something else! To Brownie's complete astonishment the fawn exploded in one vigorous bound about three feet high and scampered quickly off into the pine trees. Brownie scampered the other way into the pine trees, giving me a gut wrench that left me sore for weeks.

I always say that the only guy who never fell off a horse has never been on a horse. I have had my share of rough rides, but for sheer explosive vigor Brownie reached a new high for me that day!

THE RANGER JOB

MY TWO PRIMARY JOBS WERE STILL THE BELOVED RESOURCE PROTEC-
TION and helping park visitors to enjoy the park. Rangers lived "next
door" to Mother Nature as they managed Sequoia, and from this
privileged perspective "understood" most of what was going on in her
workshop at the Park. A generation of Harry Yount's rangers forty
years earlier had had a single responsibility — to protect the park from
the hazards they thought were injurious, like forest fire, tree disease,
coyotes, or poachers. But by 1932, when I got into the act, parks had
become playgrounds in the public mind, and people had acquired
"rights," since parks were public land and tax-supported.

One spring day in the Upper Lodgepole Campground two parties
of campers sought me out. The man of party one complained about
the destructive outdoor manners of party two. They had chopped
down some azalea bushes he said. But then the guy in party two told
me about the offensive habits of the female in party one. We had only
pit toilets, and he was pretty specific about people who stood on toilet
seats, had poor aim, and no mop. I was startled. Was it my responsibility to ask the lady to squat down or to use the seat as it was designed? He gave a rueful smile. "I guess we will just drive up to the
other end of the campground and use the toilet there." And they did.
I was still aghast when the messy party packed up and went home.
(Women's toilets are often a mess, I later learned.) And, like most
rangers, I soon learned that such conflicts usually vanished within
twenty-four hours if we could live with the delays.

My ministerial father had often reminded me that "Heaven is
more than playing a harp and sliding down rainbows into tubs of
honey." I also realized that rangers do not always ride white horses
at heads of parades. Dealing with people as a proper part of the environment meant dealing with problems of a serious illness, serious

injury, or even death, which travel with the vacationing public just as they are ever-present at home.

I have written of my travail with Miss Spalding and my seemingly endless trips to Scaffold Meadow. Her record of medication clearly indicated that she knew of her problems and really should not have been there at all. But she had wanted one more trip, and she died amidst the great scenery of Sequoia. We had carried her stretcher the last of those twenty-eight miles, toward the lower elevation for the oxygen she needed. She was apologetic on that last afternoon. But she was also content. Oh, how content she was!

Three airmen were killed as a military plane pancaked into the forest near Cahoon Gap that summer of 1932. I helped carry out the bodies, and I wrote the National Park official reports.

But death was with us. It was part of our job to handle it. Henry was a delightful young fellow — I became acquainted with him in the Lodgepole Campground. He had a charming wife and friendly, responsive kids. Henry hiked up to the Tokopah Ice Cave and sat down in the cool shade. A small section of the roof collapsed on his head and broke his neck instantly.

Vacation turned into disaster and despair for his family. They were away from home. There was no familiar minister or community social structure to call upon to console or to help. There was just the ranger — in this case my Lodgepole ranger station tent. Only I was not at home. Inger got the message and relayed it to Irv. I got into it later. It was my first exposure to the routine.

The crank telephone was a problem. There was only one line out of the park and there were many competing demands. The local switchboard operator was helpful. We called both families. We got the legal processes started — we needed a Coroner's Jury, a death certificate, an undertaker, and a transfer of the body. We got the car back to Oakland, we closed and packed the camp, and handled the final details of mail, telephone numbers, and addresses. And the wife made her unhappy way home, with a reserve of strength most poeple find in emergencies.

In other circumstances, death may strike a temporary employee, or a contractor's employee, or a transient. A different line of responsibility then develops. The ranger must represent the park, Mariposa

County, and the State of California in the formalities. Who is the dead man? Where is he from? Who is next of kin? His wallet cards may tell you, or the Department of Motor Vehicles can come up with an address based on an automobile license plate number. Do you just call the man's home phone and tell the youngster who answers the phone, "Your Dad is dead."?

I always handled this by calling the hometown police department and asking them to break the news. But I learned that I must do something for the family. As the happiness of a vacation was turned into despair, responding to people and their needs brought the good and the rough together. This was the ranger's job.

Ranger responsibilities carried some unpleasant aspects. The hunting law seemed in 1932 to be quite specific on our responsibilities, but our soft, tolerant, friendly, and helpful approach often made real law enforcement difficult. There had to be limits on behavior, and often I had to decide where to draw the line. For example, a hunter parked his pickup along the General's Highway near Little Saddle, loaded up his 30-30, and began spraying bullets around a buck browsing in a roadside meadow. He didn't hit it but he had an audience of other visitors and finally a park ranger — me. I stopped the shooting, and had no alternative but to arrest him. It was a public spectacle, and all summer long I had public inquiries about it. "What ever happened to that fellow who . . . ?"

His alibi was ignorance — he said he thought he was in a National Forest — but I called Walter Fry, the United States Commisioner, set a trial date, confiscated his new rifle, and released him on his promise to return. He was most apologetic, but as I kept reminding him, "Damnit, you did it! I can't do anything but arrest you."

I met him in court, the judge formally confiscated the rifle, and it went into the ranger office supply. The fine was twenty-five dollars, a modest kind of law enforcement.

But suppose — as actually happened to District Ranger Otto Brown and me in Yosemite in 1937 — that a plausible and friendly deer hunter wandering along the Wawona-Boot Jack Road turned out to be on the FBI list of "The Ten Most Wanted Criminals?" Otto had arrested the man along the Old Mariposa Road for hunting in the park. I got into it because I was the relief ranger at the Chowchilla

Ranger Station on that day and Otto stopped by and asked me to go along to the South Entrance. We unloaded the gun, fingerprinted the hunter, called Judge Oliver and set a trial date, collected a $100 bond, and then hauled the hunter back to his own automobile and waved good-bye. We were just two flat-hat rangers with no guns and no sophistication, only good will.

I remember the lurch as my stomach turned over when the FBI got the fingerprints and the telephone rang and rang and rang. "You had him under arrest? You had taken his gun? You just turned him loose?? Unbelievable!" It was. And I was glad that our country cousin approach left us wrong but not dead wrong! It still chills me! Unbelievable! A farm near Boot Jack was soon added to the FBI surveillance points but our hunter friend never returned.

I thought about this a lot — if we had been alert and had tried to capture this character, we might well have died right there. We had no skill in the use of firearms. We didn't even carry guns. I knew that either I must give a lot of time to law enforcement and become a professional, or I had better stay unarmed and continue to be a helpful, friendly park ranger. I chose to remain unarmed.

The controversy over guns (or ranger specialists with guns) was not resolved in my time. I am glad that I was only a friendly ranger boundary patrolman at Chowchilla Mountain, and I suspect that I was a very lucky one.

The rangers split among themselves on this topic of law enforcement. We always had a few like Jerry Mernin and Bill Merrill of the Yosemite ranger force whom we classed as "badge heavy." In varying degrees the rest of us were committed to resource protection through visitor assistance programs.

Bill Merrill — "Two Gun Bill" — was greatly concerned with the routine and the records of professional police work. He kept the arrest records and learned the techniques of arrests and fingerprinting. In fact, if Bill Merrill had not instituted the fingerprint record procedures, it is doubtful that Otto and I would have taken the fingerprints of our one dangerous criminal at the South Entrance of Yosemite National Park that September day in 1937, and put the FBI on the track. Bill was a good law enforcement officer. He was always suspicious. His influence was probably more effective than he realized, as he kept us cautious, too.

(Since Bill retired from his District Ranger job in Olympic National Park he has written a number of successful books, like *Keeping Out Of Outdoor Trouble*. His wife Margaret was also a successful author of *Bears in My Kitchen*. Inger had this same adventure in her Yellowstone kitchen as she was defrosting the refrigerator about 1963.)

Jerry Mernin was another kind of law enforcement ranger. He had been a snow gauger in Yosemite for the State of California, using skis very successfully. He also was with the California Highway Patrol before he joined the rangers. He was the direct, blunt, powerful, and solid cop — six-foot-three inches tall, 190 pounds, crew cut black hair, and a good leader for the temporary ranger crew assigned to Public Order and Traffic. He was great with park visitors, finally moved into administrative work, and retired from an Assistant Regional Director's job (Law Enforcement) in the Southeast Region.

I was as idealistic as the other young rangers. I liked the job but did not want to get involved in politics supporting the Mariposa or the Tulare County Central Democratic Committees. With FDR's election this seemed difficult, since I was a registered Republican. But I was not a fanatic about it. I just changed my registration to Independent and otherwise ignored it for the first years.

On that July morning in 1932 when Irv Kerr and I had sat under the fir tree at Pattee Meadow Creek and explored procedures for converting my zeal into permanent status of some kind, we had talked about political influence in ranger jobs. In spite of the fact that Irv had left Detroit for a political park ranger job in Sequoia, he did not feel that politics made much difference. But that was before FDR.

I could not convince myself that rangers would be exempt from political intervention. The jobs were too inviting. The National Park Service had been established through a political process, although I had no real concept of the pressures and the publicity which must have been involved in the event. Certainly the Secretary of the Interior and his key people — politicians all — controlled budgets, dollars, jobs, hiring, and land use such as grazing, logging, water power, and dam building. The machinery was working so that I got a pay check. More politics?

As a novice I decided that I had better leave that end of job hunting alone and concentrate on being a ranger — the best damn ranger in America! I was in the right place to work on that. My political goals were all in-house. I sought the support of the staff I worked with. I knew I must always do my share and a bit more. I must not only be an able patrol ranger, I must try to understand the broad pattern of ranger responsibilities. I joined the American Civic and Planning Association. I joined the National Conference of State Parks. (Steve Mather, recognizing that the National Park Service needed assistance in meeting the park needs of America, had helped form this organization. I became its president in 1974.) Were we competing with the U.S. Forest Service in our campground operations? Were city parks and recreation part of our responsibilities? What about state parks?

I was always eager to meet people with interests similar to mine. Sequoia Superintendent Colonel John R. White had served with the British military in Macedonia. He had gone to Alaska, where he became involved in the labor movement on the White Pass and Yukon Railroad in Skagway. He had joined the U.S. Army and later was Provost Marshal in Paris. He had joined the Philippine Constabulary. He was a National Park leader. In some way the romance and the charisma of the red-headed Colonel sparked with mine, and his friendship became helpful.

Larry Cook, the dynamic Chief Ranger in Sequoia, represented the new breed of park rangers with professional training. Larry was a great fire chief. My Alaskan background and training in forest fire management fit in with his own convictions. He too became a supportive friend and fellow worker.

I had a great affection and respect for Irv Kerr. His examples of industry and creativity guided me in my most formative years. Irv was a fine naturalist. He felt that visitors to Sequoia had a right to know everything we could teach them about the flora and fauna, as well as the simpler questions of camping, distances within the park, and geography.

My analysis of priorities convinced me that I was still on the course of my career plan, and as nearly on time as politics permitted. My period of qualifying would end about the time FDR's ceiling on new jobs would be lifted. It was a good prognosis.

Our Sequoia years wound down rapidly. For most of the four

years we had lived in a tent with a baby. The first summer's living
had centered around the baby's laundry and the outdoor fireplace on
which we heated water. My morning chores began with filling the
wash tub out of the adjacent Marble Fork River and splitting enough
wood for three fires. By the third year, we had a tent-cabin combination. Living was much easier, but it still centered around the woodpile. For Inger, the firewood was also handy to throw at marauding
bears if needed.

I wore the ranger uniform daily, and required one clean shirt a
day. I had only two shirts, but Inger had a sad iron. We always
seemed to make the schedule, although at that time the uniform shirt
was a very light Oxford gray. Rough work and dust were disasters,
as there was no fatigue uniform at this time. I also wore the choke-
bore breeches and field boots. The hard-brimmed Stetson hat was distinctive, and no problem except in a high wind or rain. If it got wet
the brim would either droop or curl up, so that a hat rack was essential for storage. (By the mid-1940s, when the Park Service uniform
committee recommended an option for straight-leg, forest green, elas-
tic trousers, breeches and boots vanished completely from our wardrobes. But even in 1977 the Stetson was so attractive that a group of
female Superintendents opted for this hat as their distinctive uniform
crown.)

I rode Pico on trail patrols to assist visitors, and on boundary
patrols during hunting season outside the park. I fought forest fires,
but we had only small ones. I put up park boundary signs along great
wilderness sections of the north park boundary. I carried a doctor
with a broken leg out of the Middle Fork Canyon and another one
out of Dorst Grove. I marvelled at the number of overweight hikers
who got into trouble. None of the skinny ones nor any pretty girls had
to be saved. I rescued a rim-rocked climber off Moro Rock, patrolled
campgrounds, salvaged stranded trout from the stream in Crescent
Meadow, wrote nature notes and wildlife observations, talked with
park visitors constantly, and explored most of the back country in
"my district." I marvelled that I could get paid $117.50 a month for
doing all of these wonderful things.

Suddenly my career plan worked out. In October of 1935 I was certified to Yosemite National Park to fill a special ranger job at Hetch Hetchy (which I remember happily as "the place that is so nice that they had to name it twice"). The city of San Francisco, under the Raker Act of 1913, had built a storage reservoir at O'Shaughnessey Dam on the Tuolumne River in Yosemite. In 1935 the city was making the dam higher. They financed two park ranger positions with "cop" duties in the 500-man construction camp. The jobs carried all of the standard park ranger descriptions — FCS 8, which simply meant Grade 8 in the Field Classified Service — with a salary of $1,860 per year. By this time, the 15 percent Economy Act reduction had been restored. The job description carefully specified that this was an extremely hazardous situation, because 3.2 beer would be available in the camp store.

I came to Hetch Hetchy dam in Yosemite National Park as a permanent ranger. There were no ranger quarters at Hetch Hetchy. Inger and Lars went to San Jose, where she began to pick up her academic work again. I lived in a small shack at the dam right next to the blacksmith shop. Mechanics arc-welded and hammered out truck bodies all day and all night. Vernon Lowery, the other cop-ranger, shared the cabin.

Now I was expected to be a policeman. I had not met the Ten Most Wanted Men yet — I was just a traditional "Let's behave ourselves" friend of the workmen. I acquainted myself with the construction job. I ate and played pool with the men. Vernon and I had good visibility. And I acquired a stool pigeon! Carl was clearly in violation of the fishing laws when I caught up with him, but since he seemed truly ignorant of the rules, I let him go with a "sin no more" admonition.

Two weeks later when Carl came off the midnight shift, he came by the cabin and scratched on my back window screen. He informed me of some planned mischief and went on his way. I anticipated the events in timely fashion and there were no bad experiences. Several times he appeared in the dark at my back window, and so we quieted down incipient events. We looked good with our secret source.

He came one evening after dark to tell me about a professional gambling ring. Two professional gamblers had labor jobs, worked just enough to get by, and turned on the heavy artillery each payday evening in a no-limit poker game. Their winnings were substantial, which outraged my stoolie friend. His morality was fully traditional. He hated to see the workers with families get fleeced, and hoped I could do something about it. Should Vernon and I have called the Chief Ranger, only thirty miles away by air but a full day by automobile travel? We elected to try to handle it ourselves.

Carl would play poker briefly tomorrow evening. This was also payday. His goal was simply to learn the location of the game. At 9:00 P.M. he would leave the game in anticipation of work on a 10 o'clock shift, and come by the Bull Cook's apartment. The Bull Cook, Hiram Tate, was a housekeeper-janitor, and his room was an informal gathering place. Without conversing with anyone, Carl would leave a piece of paper in the ash tray with the room number written on it. A few minutes later I would come by and in the general conversation check the ash tray unobtrusively.

Then Vernon and I would pay a call.

This chicanery worked out very smoothly. My initial admonition to the nine players, was adequate: "Keep your hands on the table — all of you. Let's see how much money you have." One by one Vernon and I counted and returned the players' money and sent them to their rooms. Then, one by one, we called on the fellows with a warning that there were professional gamblers in the game and for them to watch their step. The two pros were given different instructions — we suggested that they would enjoy their jobs more if they did not play poker. Both of them drew their time the next morning. There were no reoccurrences that I ever knew about.

Under present thinking, Vern and I probably were out of line about one hundred miles. I chuckle to myself about it sometimes. We were moralists, too! We were cops and judge and jury — but nobody lost any money. Neither of the professionals objected; several of the farmers thanked us. Our law enforcement image was pretty good!

We handled the legal aspects of several deaths on this construction job. We kept the camp quiet just by being there. The 3.2 beer was like dealing with Clancy in Alaska — "the problem" never happened.

My Hetch Hetchy ranger appointment was "vice Oscar Irwin," which simply meant that I replaced Oscar Irwin. His job number was vacant for two years until I was appointed to it. I did not know him — he had returned to Arkansas before I got to Yosemite.

Then Yosemite asked for another ranger register to replace ranger-patrolman Billy Nelson, and Chief Townsley decided to transfer me into that job and get a new replacement for Oscar. This game of tag went on later with Vernon, so that he too came over to Yosemite Valley as a permanent ranger. We were close friends.

I was pleased to have my appointment read "Vice Billy Nelson." Billy was a genuine old-timer, best remembered in Horace Albright's book, *Oh Ranger*, in which Billy, traveling on a pack trip with the King of Belgium, informed the King that he could not remember all this "Your Highness" stuff, and he would just call him King if the King would please just call him Billy, which he did!

Billy was the Yosemite Valley campground ranger aptly described as the short ranger riding the big white horse and smoking a big black pipe. He was a jewel — one of those who created the original image for the national parks.

I found my transfer to the Yosemite ranger force rewarding — I was first at the Mariposa Grove of big trees, then at Chinquapin Ranger Station. When I finally moved to Yosemite Valley and became the campground ranger, I really did replace Billy Nelson.

My six-month tenure as "the Ranger cop" in the construction camp at Hetch Hetchy was not all that different from subsequent positions. This was deep in the Depression, and jobs were scarce. Unemployment was high, and the massive relief programs were not yet in effect.

(In 1931 I had not attended the Stanford University graduation ceremonies to receive my long-delayed diploma. It had blood, sweat, and tear stains on it by that time! But I was picking apricots at Mountain View at a wage of $.15 per hour; I would lose $1.50 if I walked across the platform to get the diploma. I could not afford the cap and gown. Inger was very pregnant. The university would mail the diploma to me, and I did not need the actual paper then or for the next forty years. Inger and I are still the only ones who have ever seen it. So I picked apricots for ten hours.)

In 1935 I knew those hunger pangs and I understood the concern of the local men who had gotten Hetch Hetchy jobs at the fabulous San Francisco union wage rate of $.75 an hour. To them, this was the most important function of a National Park — jobs. They were not about to jeopardize these by any action which might get them involved with the "law" (which in this case meant Rangers Garrison and Lowery and a poker game). The law enforcement task was a park resource protection problem. The decision had been made to build the dam at Yosemite. I was to keep order while they did it.

Vernon and I occasionally needed some visibility to control speeders through the construction area. We could reduce the noise level in the bar room just by being there, but besides the breakup of the gambling we had no problem with law enforcement. During the six months I held that job I made no arrests and had no court cases. Our "court" was the United States Commisioner's Court in Yosemite Valley. It was a six-hour wintertime drive over there. We used a lot of what is contemporarily labeled "jaw bone" to keep the camp peaceable and get the dam built. We just tried to use understanding and common sense.

As always, discussions on visitors and resources end with the probable meaning of the basic 1916 legislation. What had Mather-Albright-Yard meant as they wrote this legislation? During my discussions with Meinike in 1932, I had reached the conclusion that with increasing numbers of visitors, the most important thing we must do was to preserve the resources. This, in response to the changing background and habits of these visitors as they became more and more urban and less and less rural, with increased mobility, better highways, and improved automobiles.

But these resources did not seem threatened in 1935. And in reality (coinciding with the great conservation theme which the rangers and the park leadership shared), much of the park management favored *not* developing protective skills, but establishing ways and means to welcome and to serve more and more people.

I could accept that. It was my management pattern for many years. The supposed number of tolerable visitors always seemed to move higher in response to the actual numbers. Controls like the Lodgepole Campground road barrier stones and the Yellowstone geyser basin boardwalks were for use and protection. Inviting campgrounds, or participative interpretive programs like the Yosemite Field School of Natural History or the Junior Nature School, welcomed everyone. It helped if there were more understanding visitors. We could take care of them.

I was later told that in 1938 the summer of the World's Fair on Treasure Island in San Francisco Bay, that the Yellowstone ranger force had geared up to manage a fantastic crowd of over 500,000 visitors — a whole half-million! Ranger Frank Kowski commented that there was great pride in handling this overload, but the rangers could now relax and anticipate more normal and moderate visitation. (By 1941 there was another increase of 60,000 visitors, and the numbers have accelerated from there to over two million.) But in 1941 there was no serious thought to limiting visitation. There was plenty of room. Roads needed some changes to improve traffic flow, but the American people loved and used their parks. This built political and budget support.

I was thinking like a superintendent very early. We bragged about increasing park travel. We reported to travel councils and neighboring Chambers of Commerce that this great travel bonanza was right on track and growing happily to help them. All we needed was more money for rangers, for planning and building roads, campgrounds, water and sewer systems, hotel rooms, museums, campfire circles, exhibits, and signs. A happy Congressman could get them for us.

The three "A's" (American Automobile Association) used our travel figures to promote more highways. It went on and on. The justification was that to preserve these great scenic places, and to provide access to them, evidence of visitor use was required to convince Congress that more operational money was needed. It was an endless circle, and park rangers were the most fortunate of men to help in preservation and interpretation of these great and beautiful places. You could not wear parks out by looking at them!

We did not call them "resources" in those days. We made it more personal and we all knew our euphemisms and superlatives. Morning Glory Pool, The Great White Throne, Carlsbad Caverns, Spruce Tree House, Cadillac Mountain, Bryce Canyon, The Grizzly Giant, and Mount Rainier: it was a shining and glorious galaxy. Our jobs were healthful, natural, and in the public service, and we served a great select and social purpose in our custodianship and management of these "national jewels."

We would have thirty more years of this evasive thinking before we really began to face up to the reality of people, highways, cars, leisure time, social pressure, and politics, and spoke openly of needing more National Parks just for recreation space. In 1937, I was with a group of civil engineers from Spain visiting Glacier Point. We surveyed the firmament before us. What magnificence! What glory! We faced first toward El Capitan and Yosemite Falls and then eastward to the far horizon of a world full of lofty peaks. The first exclamation of the engineers, of course, was "What a great place to build a dam!"

Only we could not. The great valley was already in intensive use. Those black ants scurrying around down there were people. There were hundreds of them. The valley was protected from the greater and total spoilation of a dam simply because it was already serving people constructively.

At that time we were not concerned about people management as much as we were about some aspects of resource durability. We began to ask questions of ourselves — never aloud — about the fuel buildup along the western boundaries of Sequoia and Yosemite. The growth of brush, chaparral, and deadwood below the parks would provide fuel for very hot forest fires. We would need the blessings of heaven and the weatherman to come out of that one alive! But our leaders did not worry about it. It would be threatening "someday." The political forces were all directed towards increasing use, and hence funding facilities for more use. It was like Mr. Finney's turnip, which ". . . grew and it grew and it grew behind the barn and the turnip did no harm. . . ." "Parks are wonderful!" we cried. "Come out and help us look at them!" And people did. This was our heritage. People must enjoy the parks so they could tell their Congressmen about them, and then the parks would get bigger appropriations to serve more people.

I was a brand new permanent ranger — an inquisitive one! In Yosemite there were twenty-one of us. The most junior above me was Duane Jacobs, who had been a ranger for over five years. When I transferred out four years later, only Vernon Lowery from Hetch Hetchy was junior to me. Most of them thought I was nuts. "Transfer? You already have *the* job! Where can you do better?" The job stability was tremendous. We were a proud fraternity with love for the parks, high ideals for public service, and contentment for our-selves. And the blazing idealism of Mather and Albright kept us all enthused on matters of park management and conservation defense. They must have had to compromise on many procedural issues, but their major victories were heartening and preserved resources.

Looking at their record, I have realized that those two leaders were tremendously effective battlers. Modesty in expectations and requests was not part of their makeup. They were active idealists, recognizing that if you made a proposal which was less than you really needed, you had started with a compromise and you could only end with one which was less satisfactory.

For the ranger, Halliburton-quality experiences were almost daily events.

When the Crown Prince and Princess of Denmark visited Yosem-ite Valley, I was assigned as their special night guard. When the Chief issued me a gunbelt and revolver to wear for this "hazardous" duty, my first action was to unload the revolver. I trusted my physical prowess more than I did my marksmanship, and I did not want any malefactor grabbing my revolver and shooting me with it. The night was uneventful. There did not seem to be any foreign national ene-mies who might attack the royal couple. However, precaution was necessary. An African potentate had previously been threatened with assassination. Where easier than in a resort hotel like Yosemite's, with only park rangers as the police force?

Bert Harwell, the park naturalist and bird specialist, reported joy-fully the next day on the pleasure of the companionship of the royal couple on a bird walk. Bert was a great ornithologist, and his bird song imitations were correct in melody and could literally charm the birds to him.

Bert and I were on the tennis court for some relaxation. "The Princess is lovely," he said. "Did you get to meet her?" I could not resist the opening.

"Yes. I spent the night with her," was my ungentlemanly response.

During Spring vacation at high schools and universities, many student groups visited the National Parks. Yosemite was a favorite. Usually such groups arrived with reservations made for any needed services, but occasionally groups showed up which gave the rangers problems. A Redwood City High School sneak day program left a lot of kids roaming the Valley, begging food and stealing it from unwary campers. Boy Scouts were required to file travel plans and programs. Sometimes a derelict or lazy scoutmaster neglected this. A northern California group of thirty boys were left on their own for a day with no program and no money while the scoutmaster went hiking and swimming. Unfortunately the hungry kids soon fell afoul of the patrol rangers, and we blistered the lazy scoutmaster. I had been a "lone" scout and was proud to see a "good" scouter program using the parks as I thought they should be used. I was still the moralist!

The summer of 1936 found me stationed in Mariposa Grove. One of my patrols was on Sam, a big-footed but docile bay horse, along the roads up towards the Grizzly Giant, the Wawona Tunnel Tree, and Wawona Point. This was the year a lot of drivers learned about vapor locks. A modern driver would have no idea what this might be. The earlier generation didn't either, but with a heated motor and hot summer sunshine, high-test gasoline flowing to the automobile gasoline pump through exposed tubing would occasionally vaporize right in the gas line. This would block the gasoline flow.

The ranger's cure was fast, simple, and miraculous. I carried a gallon canteen of water and a dish towel. As drivers fumed or joked about swapping their car for the horse, I would open the hood, wrap the dishtowel around the gasoline pump and a section of tubing and pour water on it. In just a few minutes the coolness of the evaporating water would condense the gasoline, and the driver could restart the car and drive away. It was magic! I insisted that I would trade Sam only for a Cadillac — we had a lot of fun out of it that summer.

Sam had one practical trick — he had learned how to drink from the continuous bubbler drinking fountain near the Grizzly Giant. While he enjoyed it, it was a sloppy procedure. He chewed and slobbered and licked away in the flowing water, but I noticed that after Sam got a drink all of the humans lost their thirst. We had to wait for the immediate group of visitors to leave before others would approach the bubbler. So Sam enjoyed the bubbler only when we were alone!

In 1936 at the Wawona Tunnel Tree I was approached by an elderly gentleman from a successful San Francisco janitor supply firm who related his visit just fifty years earlier. He had been mustered out of the cavalry at the San Francisco Presidio and before he got a job he had decided to see Yosemite National Park. He bought a light team of mules and a spring wagon and drove cross-country to Yosemite and Mariposa Grove. The Tunnel Tree had been carved through in 1882, and he commented "Do you know that in five years tourists had completely covered the inside of the tree with carved initials and hearts and dates. It was disgusting. So I drove the mules through and dropped the traces so the wagon was right inside the tree. I stood up in the back and with a broad axe I slabbed off a whole layer of this carving. I got it all nice and smooth and then on the ceiling I carved my own name and address. I even put a flowery border around it. I was looking for it today, but do you know that some SOB had carved it off!"

I had no comment. Vandalism was an established behavior pattern. The vandal does not feel guilty. This gentleman would not have understood my real attitude, but his has made a great moral fable.

Seasonal ranger Bill Felkner, a graduate biology student from the University of Oklahoma, was the ranger in charge of Yosemite Valley Campground Number Seven when I parked my patrol car, a 1931 Pontiac roadster with the top down, in front of his tent one August morning in 1938. At his front table Bill introduced me to Johnnie, about three years old, last name unknown. "Johnnie, this is my boss."

But Johnnie was starting on an ice cream cone Bill had purchased for him from the campground supply truck which was still parked nearby. In spite of his aplomb and the twinkle in his eye, Johnnie was a lost youngster. He had just been deposited with Bill by an empathetic camper who had found him crying in front of a rest room.

How could we get Johnnie and his family back together again? Probably the family was nearby or at least near a rest room. But where? There were probably two hundred cars in this unmarked area. Bill was experimenting with a new identification interview procedure and was just about to give it a try. Johnnie had mentioned Oakland to the camper who found him, so Bill started there.

"Does your daddy live in Oakland, Johnnie?" asked Bill.

There was no hesitation. "Yes," responded Johnnie.

Most of our campers were either from the San Francisco Bay area or from Southern California. Johnnie's geographic identification told us that we would probably be looking for a car with California license plates with the initial license letter between "C" and "H." California license plates were that way in 1938.

"Is it white, Johnnie?" Always give Johnnie a positive statement to react to. His color perception was good. He said it was black. In fact, most automobiles were black in 1938.

"Does it have two doors on each side?" This involved numbers and a choice, but Johnnie was equal to it. It was soon resolved as a four-door, black sedan. So Bill added another dimension.

"Does it have a spare tire behind the truck?" All cars had visible spare tires. Where was it? Johnnie suddenly remembered that he had dropped a nickel in the side fender well last week and it was still there.

"Does your daddy have a trailer?" The answer was negative.

So we would be looking for a tent camp with a black, four-door sedan, side-mounted spare, East Bay license plates. It was time to make a quick patrol. Families had been known to inadvertently abandon youngsters as they drove away, discovering their loss an hour later at the next rest stop.

The ice cream cone was under control. Bill wiped Johnnie's hands and face. I drove and Johnnie stood firmly between us on the seat, with Bill's hand giving him a good anchor. The roadster with the top down was great for this kind of eyeball survey.

There were only a few official location posts in the campground and one paved loop road with many informal intervening loops. It was still an "open" camp without established campsites. Campers were free to move in wherever they found room along the sandy tracks and among the lodgepole pines. In the friendly sharing of amenities as many as three tents were often tied to the same tent peg. Whoever went home first created a disaster for the others. Of the two hundred vehicles in camp, some were just entering with the drivers making a preliminary reconnaisance of open space; some were packing to leave; others seemed to be settled in for the day.

I drove the car and we looped in and out and around very slowly to cover major areas, but saw nothing of a black four-door with the proper license plates and running board-mounted spare tire. So we returned to the ranger tent to regroup.

"Johnnie," Bill began, "we don't see your daddy's car here at all." Johnnie was quick with the explanation. "Of course you don't. My daddy's car is in Oakland. We came up with Uncle Joe."

So we really regrouped! The camper supply truck was still there and we got another ice cream cone.

"What color is Uncle Joe's car?"

The answers were less precise, but our second patrol was in search of a brown car with a camper trailer. There were few house trailers in 1938. (In fact one young couple who were supplying information on camping equipment frankly amazed us by stating that they were taking a tent camping vacation from regular life in a house trailer. This required a new column in our statistical records!)

We started around again with Johnnie firmly anchored in the middle. Soon we saw a brown car with a trailer in the middle of a group of agitated people, and as I paused nearby, Johnnie bailed out over the side in an instant.

"Mama!" the relief in the tone of voice!

"Johnnie," and equal relief as mother swept him into her arms. "Where have you been?" The squashed ice cream cone was abandoned — Johnnie could only point mutely to ranger Bill Felkner. Mama, however, suddenly remembered that Johnnie had disobeyed orders about staying near the car even if he did have to go to the bathroom. She suddenly reversed her grip so that with his rear bumper in view she whacked him vigorously, but lovingly. Whack-whack-whack. "Don't you go away from camp again!" Whack-whack-whack. Dust flew for a minute, but suddenly all was loving joy again. This lost kid business was highly important and had top priority, but it was just normal routine.

On the 4th of July in 1938, we had thirty-four such incidents at the Yosemite Valley campground. Bill's technique worked well, but Johnnie's case was relatively simple — one lost youngster, one ranger. If we had not been able to return him promptly we would have called the Chief Ranger's Office — CRO in our code — and they would have added him to the log and alerted all valley campgrounds and ranger patrolmen. If, by chance, Johnnie had wandered across the road into Campground Number Fifteen and they had picked him up, we would have had three ranger alerts — Felkner in Number Seven where he had disappeared, Number Fifteen where the ranger had one extra youngster, source unknown, and his parents at the CRO, which would try to put it all together.

My concept of my job included this helpfulness to visitors, and I recall a delightful story about another "Johnnie" who, with his barely mobile younger sister, was found in Camp Number Fourteen one July morning. It took several hours (including volunteer baby sitting by a ranger's wife, and frantic worry by the distraught parents), before we returned them to Camp Seven. The kids had vanished with the salt shaker right after breakfast, determined to catch a friendly robin which had shared their table.

My crew of six campground seasonal rangers were mostly unmarried. They tackled these situations alone and I would admonish them that, since we had no social services facilities, I simply expected each of them to keep these lost youngsters until they got them returned. However, I ended the season myself with an encounter with a comely young lady of about eighteen who hailed me when I was on a road patrol up near Mirror Lake. She frankly admitted that she was lost, and knew that she should ask a ranger for locator assistance. There were no family groups there looking for her and she seemed badly confused, so I finally returned with her to Camp Fourteen where my campground rangers were having a coffee session that morning.

She was somewhat startled by this array of young and friendly rangers. After we worked a while with the telephone and the CRO, we learned that Louise was an instructor with a campout group from a school for retarded youngsters registered at Camp Twelve. Her adventurous journey began as most of them do by taking the wrong turn on leaving the washroom, so she walked on and came to Mirror Lake! Meanwhile, Bill and Gene and Bob were asking me innocently, "Will you keep this one, Mr. Garrison?"

Fortunately, the locator system worked, and the ranger banner of "helpful visitor service" continued to fly proudly.

Another bugaboo was our lost-and-found department — mainly remnants from the camp washrooms. An ornately-decorated and very dirty wrist watch looked like a treasure from a box of Cracker Jacks but turned out to be a platinum, jewel-encrusted keepsake valued at about $5,000. It was picked up off a nail in a Camp Fourteen washroom wall after two days and turned in to the CRO, where it was promptly identified. Towels, soap boxes, shoes, dentures, and jackets are an anonymous lot by themselves, particularly if the owners couldn't remember where they left them.

Good fortune continues to reward those who give it a chance. On my very first day of Yosemite duties, I was sent to the park hospital to have a physical examination. As I returned to the CRO for further instructions, I was intercepted by an impatient visitor. His urgent and blunt demand was for immediate directions to find the park hospital.

And truth has a strange way of exceeding any possible fiction, so that during one stormy mid-summer afternoon with wind squalls and bursts of rain I stopped to assist an unhappy visitor with a pile of wet canvas and ropes. To lighten the situation I quipped, "Did you come down in a parachute?" His startling reply was simply, "No, I went up in a tent."

In October 1938, Chief Ranger Forrest Townsley sent me and Jim Skakle, who had transferred from the Border Patrol, to take all the horses from our part of the park — Wawona, Chinquapin, and The Valley — to the lower Tuolumne country for winter pasture near Mather Ranger Station. We used one of the horses as a pack animal, carrying our light camp outfit, our sleeping bags, extra ropes, and an extra tarp in case of rain. Most of our twelve horses were in two head-to-tail control strings, but two ran free with Swiss bells. They came right along with us faithfully. The magic was cheerful. We left the Valley by the trail up the Merced River, past Vernal and Nevada Falls, and on to Little Yosemite Valley and the Merced Lake Ranger Station. There were two horses in the corral here to add to our string. We converted four gunny sacks into feed bags and gave each horse a small bait of grain and then the fifteen pounds of hay. They were hungry, but also strange, so after we had removed the nose bags and put them in the corral they fought and ran all night. We identified the bad actors so that next day we could tie them at separate locations. In the morning we skipped a grain feed and gave them another hay ration while we fixed our bacon and eggs on the ranger cabin range. We belled another horse that seemed particularly trail-wise, and by

8:00 A.M. we were on our way over Vogelsang Pass towards Tuolumne Valley.

We paused briefly at Vogelsang Pass, for this was the intersection with the Half-Dome trail, and neither Jim nor I had ever been there. But the fourteen horses were impatient and we didn't want to take the time to tie them and then sort them out again. So we went on to Tuolumne, arriving about 4:00 P.M. Duane Jacobs, the District Ranger, was waiting for us and had the corral gate open.

We took a five-day layover here and on the first day went fishing. Archie Thompson of the Yosemite Fish Hatchery had asked us to get some golden trout for spawning stock. The Chief was glad to oblige, and we were too. We took one day riding to Fletcher Lake and back. Fishing was fantastic! I had a new popping bug I wanted to experiment with on my fly line and it worked fine. However, we had a problem with the weather. The lake was not frozen, but it was windy in a formidable winter fashion at this 8,000-foot elevation. Ice formed in the fly line guides between casts. One moment of melting ice was all bare fingers could stand, so we soon had a warming campfire beside our fish-carrying cans and the tethered mules. The scenery was grand, the company was excellent, as we three rangers caught golden trout.

We had taken five mules with us to Fletcher Lake with ten fish planting cans. We put seven or eight gallons of water in each can, then added five or six ten-inch fish, and before noon we were filled. The packer hustled back to Tuolumne and quickly got the cans into a hatchery truck with an air compressor. The venture was highly successful. I visited Archie Thompson's fish stock ponds that winter just to say hello to our proteges. I had seen golden trout in Sequoia — they really are beautiful.

Returning from Fletcher Lake, I made a poor selection of a saddle horse. Dude was ordinarily a pack animal; he was a big, rotund, complacent, scenery-loving horse. I always rode with a very dull set of spurs. (I had acquired these from Everett Ruess, a very interesting and talented young artist and painter, in Sequoia National Park. Everett's later disappearance while roaming the southwest Indian Country with a burro was a great mystery.) It seemed safe enough to ride Dude loosely and tolerantly, kicking his ribs from time to time to remind him where we were and why we were there. Each such nudge startled Dude; he was always hungry, browsing as he walked, and he always had his mouth full and had to take time to masticate the load before he reached for another one. Meanwhile, he would forget. I would interrupt the sequence and Dude would be startled and glare accusingly back at me. I had insulted him! I gave a brisk nudge and he lunged ahead briefly with a prodigious fart, only to immediately lose his place in the process and reach for another trailside clump of grass. Kick-twitch-fart was the travel sequence Dude preferred, until I gathered the reins in tightly, got Dude's full attention with my spurs, and we started on briskly for Tuolumne Meadows. Dude's attention span was short. He would lapse immediately unless I nudged him again and again. We reached Tuolumne Meadows about 5:00, but Dude was suspicious of me from then on and I did not try him again as a saddle horse. Faithful Sam from Mariposa Grove was my best selection.

We reminisced that evening around the stove at the Tuolumne Ranger Station. Jake had Texas cowboy yarns, Skakle put in some about the Mexican border patrol, I told of my Alaskan days and my Sequoia experiences. I first heard some old Yellowstone ranger yarns that night from Jake, but they were all second-hand, and I was more interested in Yosemite and its traditions. Gabrielle (Gabe) Sovulewski was one of the subjects. He was with the troops in Yosemite and transferred to the park to run the back country trail patrols and horse herd. Gabe's name was everywhere in the back country. He had been a regular participant in Tuolumne Meadow's history. He was still living when I moved to the Valley in 1937, but very old. Upon his death, he was buried in the Yosemite pioneer cemetery just behind the house where we lived in the Valley.

Duane (Jake) Jacobs had the stuff rangers were made of in Zane Grey's adventures. Tall, blonde, able, and dependable, always youthful looking, he became a great friend and companion. We lassoed a bear one day and then had to figure out how to release it in a cage to transplant it into a national forest in the Coast Range. (In later years we worked together again in Omaha where I was the Regional Director and Jake was the Assistant Director for Ranger Affairs; we called it Resource Management by that time. He retired about the same time I did, but in 1938, Jake was senior to me and he was a helpful companion.) That night I was just a visitor at Tuolumne, but it was a happy circumstance. Skakle and I were going on in a few days to deliver the horse and mule herd to Mather Ranger Station. This was next door to Hetch Hetchy, where I had started in Yosemite in 1935.

I was instructed to look at as much of the back country as I could. Hence the five day layover. The next day I rode Sam up the Lyle Fork of the Tuolumne River and topped out at Donahue Pass on the Sierra Crest. The trail was scenic all the way, climbing across the endless gray granite above timberline and traversing slopes of granitic scree across to the 12,000-foot pass. Here was a superlative view of the fall-off to the eastern edge of the world; I could see forever across a world filled with mountain peaks. But it was only briefly inspiring as the chill winds of the 12,000-foot elevation in mid-October cut through my denim coat and jeans, and I did not linger.

The next day it was warmer. I took the Gold Rush Days trail from Tuolumne, up Return Creek to Virginia Pass on the eastern park boundary, just above Saddlebag Lake east of the park. The mine here was active in the late 1800s and the owner-operators often wintered in, although transportation was cut off after the first deep snow. It had been more convenient during the big snow months to get to the Saddlebag Lake mines by skiing down the California side from Sonora or Jamestown (Jimtown), into the Yosemite country, crossing this same mountain pass enroute to the mines.

The famous mountain man-skier, Snowshoe Thompson, was one of the winter suppliers for the mines, crossing right at Virginia Pass, where I was, with his very long and wide skis, often called snowshoes in those days. He used one long pole for a pusher and straddled it for a downhill guide. Snowshoe and his brother apparently made the mines in about three days one way, traveling light with one pot for oatmeal and another pot for tea. Their single blankets were enough shelter in case of bad storms, when they would hole up under a canopy of trees, behind a rock, or in an overhanging cave. Their freight and mail rates of one dollar per pound did not seem unreasonable. The load limit was about one hundred pounds and was mainly groceries or small parts for the mines. This was a historic place, and I relished it!

I found a sheltered rock on the boundary, out of the wind with a bed of needles and moss, and loosened Sam's saddle and let him browse close by for a while. With my binoculars I scanned the country on east into Nevada carefully. The Snowshoe Thompson legend was not the only one pertaining to this pass.

Joaquin Murietta, the famous early California "Robin Hood" outlaw, had passed here and cached a cargo of silver-mounted saddles and bags of gold which were never recovered. As I dozed quietly in the sunlight, the trail was repopulated for a moment with miners, mountain men, trappers, packers, gamblers, adventurers, dance hall girls, teachers, and even one unlikely minister, all part of my own background reading of gold rush history. It was a great delight; something in me welcomed all of these travelers. They were an adventurous and optimistic lot. "Welcome to Yosemite!"

Suddenly a chickaree barked overhead, Sam shuddered in a giant stretch, and I was a Yosemite Ranger on an orientation trip again.

I took time to borrow a car and drive across Tioga Pass to Mono Lake. I drove around Tenaya Lake and the campgrounds. Finally Jim and I again departed to Mather via May Lake and Ten Lakes Basin, across the fringes of the forested Tuolumne River canyon. We missed many delights we knew, but we now had eighteen head of horses, some loose-herded and some on leads. The loads were light, the air was clear, and the sky was blue. The only noise was our own clatter and an occasional jay or squirrel investigating us.

We tethered most of the horses individually that night and slept lightly; we kept one eye on the horses and one ear cocked to the tune of the bells wandering in the nearby meadow. A rope gate blocked the trail below us. The moon was helpful and friendly. Early daylight found all the horses clustered around our informal campsite, begging for barley. We could not accommodate eighteen head with only four nose bags, so we fed the last of the hay and grain to our saddle horses. They were carrying loads; the others were traveling like tourists through this wilderness landscape.

We dropped down to the middle elevations and entered the Carlin sugar pine tract. This was named for Tim Carlin, an early stockman who owned some of this gorgeous land. His magnificent tract of sugar pine had just been sold to the park. We traveled through it for about two hours. The array of forest giants, with their occasional fire scars which we called cat-faces, was impressive. They are one of the tree species that creates its own forest environment, probably by some type of exudate from the needles which is harmless to little sugar pine trees beneath them, but fatal to other species. For miles we traveled through this cathedral array of forest silence. The deep needles, the open and park-like forest floor, created a sense of reverence as we entered. Even the horses and mules were quiet!

I showed Jim the depth of some of the fire scars. Deeply burned, the glossy black charcoal in its innermost recesses has a different kind of exudate and life pattern. The slowly oozing tree sap, collecting in the innermost crevices, forms small lumps of resinous gum which weather from dead black to a pure granular white, becoming the legendary sugar for which these mighty trees are named. I had experienced this before so I could not be tempted by the sweetness of the sugar, for I knew that it was not only delightful, creating a craving for more, but it was also a· violent cathartic. Jim simply could not believe that anything so good could be harmful and his first taste led to more and more. But alas, the last two hours of our journey were misery for him. He was interrupted constantly by his rueful and spasmodic response to the various cramps and wretchings which occasioned his frequent stops.

Meanwhile, I was struggling with eighteen head of horses. We jingled into the Mather Ranger Station corral that night by moonlight, and our great journey was over. It created the kind of memories which never fade. In fact, I suspect that memory may have become more colorful, as my empathies have encompassed a few adventures I wish I had had, but probably didn't, for there were not enough days on the trail to really do all of the happy things I have mixed into it. My medicine opened wondrous adventures before me.

My year at Chinquapin Ranger Station was really a demanding one with its great variety of ranger duties. Road patrols were the most time-consuming — Chinquapin south to the Wawona Tunnel; Chinquapin to Badger Pass, Bridal Veil, and Glacier Point. "Patrol as much as possible; at least once daily." It is surprising how often you "just happened" to get there at the crucial moment following an accident, or a visitor flagged you down for information, or you could talk with visitors who were stopped to look at a doe and twin fawns in a roadside meadow. For the ranger, visibility and availability were important.

Accident investigations were unexpected and had high priority. An Elderly widow from Iowa and her twenty-five-year-old Marine Corps grandson were driving just at dusk from Chinquapin to Glacier Point near Badger Pass and on a very sharp curve met a motorcycle coming towards Chinquipin, traveling flat out and clipping the corners on every curve. The Model A Ford windshield was somewhat pitted and the motorcycle headlight hit it full beam just in time to confuse the driver. He swerved and hit the motorcycle head on. The driver of the motorbike ended on the car hood with a multiple fracture of his leg. The charming University of California co-ed, riding behind the bike operator, flipped over and wiped out the Ford windshield with her butt-first slam into Grandmother's face. I was almost on the spot when it happened.

I was the investigating officer. I knew them all. They had visited with me at Chinquapin that morning and I had called the Glacier Point Hotel for room reservations for them that night. The fine young Marine was uninjured. He was enjoying taking grandmother on a vacation trip. They were just on their way. The motorcycle rider was the harum-scarum son of a research professor. I had met the delightful girl. The Marine helped me and we got the injured people laid out as comfortably as we could. There was no dangerous bleeding. I flagged the first passing car and got a message to Inger at Chinquapin to call CRO for help and an ambulance from the Valley. I put out warning flares and flags. The Marine flagged traffic around the debris, another ranger stopped to help, and we waited for the ambulance. Nobody died, but the paperwork, police reports, and insurance statements went on all summer. This, too, was part of being a ranger.

A happier business was my musical discovery at the upper end of the Wawona Tunnel. I stopped to call the dispatcher from the phone just inside the tunnel, and while I was waiting for the telephone operator to come on the line I idly hummed a tune. Suddenly, I realized that this 4,000-foot smooth bore, concrete-lined tunnel was an incredible sound amplifier. I experimented with it.

If there were no cars in the tunnel, I could step out into the middle of the road and belt out a simple "Do-Me-Sol-Do." In about four seconds it would reverberate back to me. The initial lower register "Do" would come in like a concert basso. The baritone "Me" would blend in, the second tenor "Sol" would harmonize, and the higher "Do" gave a four-part chord. I was a full male quartet, singing all four parts myself! The other rangers thought this was a frivolous kind of resource interpretation, but I loved it. In fact, I occasionally forgot to telephone. A chord with the dominant seventh was tremendous — a great organ-like harmony.

I caught a few speeders with my road patrols. Occasionally, a tourist would recognize the ranger pick-up and flag me down to ask if he was on the right road to Fresno. If he discovered that he had taken the wrong turn at Chinquapin, he would curse, whip the car around, and head back for Wawona and South Entrance. Always in a hurry! I suspected that this travel would be above the speed limit, but I knew that old "2000" — the license number of my Model A Ford pick-up — could not overtake him, so I just wished him well and quit chasing.

CHAPTER IX

MORE RANGER JOBS

James McCauley was a pioneer who built the first Glacier Point hotel some time before 1900. The road to the point was simply a set of wagon tracks. The four-mile trail was the popular one, mostly traveled by horseback. The ledge of one-and-one-half miles was for more vigorous and youthful travelers. McCauley was an active and imaginative fellow involved in the beginning of the famous Yosemite fire fall.

Every summer morning about 8:00 A.M., he would trot down the trail and visit the overnight establishments — Desmonds and Camp Curry. He would converse with the rocking chair guests on the front porch facing Glacier Point and ask about their interest in seeing a fire fall that evening. He would point out the spot on the Glacier Point rim high above them from which the fire would flow. He would sing wondrously of its beauty. "All those who would like to see it, please contribute."

"Yes Ma'am, I will dedicate this one just for you, Ma'am," he would cajole a prospective donor. Five to ten dollars would be his usual total collection.

Then he would trot back to Glacier Point and bring in a cartload of red fir bark, which was the most desirable fuel. Old timers call red fir bark "the Scotsman's wood," for it will ignite and glow and swell up, but without a blaze. It will glow and glow in the dark. It worked beautifully for McCauley's fire cascade. Promptly at nine o'clock, McCauley would slowly feed the bed of coals he had prepared over the lip of the cliff. It was highly spectacular and incredibly beautiful as it trickled and then cascaded in a stream of fire for about 800 feet down to a great rock bench across the face of the cliff.

Then McCauley got together with David Curry, who had founded Camp Curry as a transient wagon train camping site about 1890. He developed a pattern of great evening campfire programs for his guests,

between eight and nine o'clock. They agreed that the fire fall would
be a great finale. A hush would fall across all of Yosemite Valley as
the magic hour approached and everyone searched for an open view
of Glacier Point. Just at 9:00 P.M. Curry, who had a magnificent
voice, would end his program with a recitation about the Senator of
ancient Greece who had kept the home community informed of news
events by his public announcements. Then he would lift his face towards Glacier Point and bellow "Hello Glacier Point!" To the campfire audience, it was truly stentorian announcement. Faintly and trem-
ulously the thin reply would return the salute. "Hello Camp Curry!"

And Curry, in emulation of the true Stentor, would command the
heavens — "LET THE FIRE FA-A-A-LL," and it would! The tiny
campfire glow would enlarge as it was stirred and then slowly creep
over the edge in a trickle which quickly became a stream of fire hundreds of feet long as the glowing coals fell and fell only to disappear
on the dark face of Glacier Point.

Eight decades of firefall — daily in summer, weekend specials the
rest of the year — had eliminated the nearby supply of red fir bark.
Foraging trips were necessary. By the 1970s the conservationists got
into the picture. This was an unnatural event. It was in the pattern
of gilding the lily or perfuming the rose. So, although it was beautiful,
it was artificial, and Director George Hartzog cancelled it.

McCauley had a small flock of chickens which dodged coyotes and
foraged over the open expanse of Glacier Point catching grasshoppers
and competing with golden mantled ground squirrels and chipmunks
for visitor-supplied peanuts. He would start a conversation with a
group of visitors by casually asking if they thought a hen could possibly fly from Glacier Point down the 3,500-foot wall to the Valley
floor. If there were interested onlookers, McCauley would pick up one
of his hens and march up to the fence guard rail and prepare to launch
her over the rail, only to draw back reluctantly. "I just can't afford
it," he would say. If visitors were interested enough to offer to pay for
the hen, he would collect one or two dollars and then with a grand
swoop launch her out into space, headed down the canyon.

The hen would set her wings and sail away. In a few seconds she
would vanish around the first bend in the canyon wall. "Poor thing!
There she went," Mac would say, but the hen almost immediately

sailed into McCauley's barnyard and onto the upper end of the four-mile trail. In a few minutes, she would be back on Glacier Point chasing grasshoppers!

I was in the Glacier Point parking area late one summer afternoon just leaving for Chinquapin when a squabble erupted near me. A teen-aged boy and his father disagreed to the point that the youth leaped from the car and screamed that he was not going to ride with his dumb dad — he was going to walk back to Camp Fourteen. He dashed away through the parking area while Dad just started the car and drove away.

I was not disturbed — the kid had started in the right direction to hit the Ledge Trail down to the Valley. So I drove on home, but unfortunately Junior did not know the trail to the Valley. He turned and ran behind the Glacier Point Hotel into the short hanging valley underbrush and headed downhill — directly towards the Happy Isles Fish Hatchery, 4,000 feet below him in one long step!

He tried to slow down as the ground suddenly got steeper and steeper, but he was still mad and out of control and he slid down about three hundred feet right to the very edge of the cliff. Fortunately, he slid right into the last small white pine growing out of the very last ledge at the top of the cliff. One step aside either way and he would have been on the big toboggan. No one saw him — he was beyond the swell of the granite rim and could not be seen from above. It was impossible to return, and he found himself looking almost directly down into the road beside Campground Number Twelve. There were people on the road and in the campground, but it was almost a straight mile down to them.

"Help! Help!" yelled Junior.

He kept on calling, and surprisingly, a camper in Camp Twelve heard the recurrent SOS and set herself to locating the source. She did it with a pair of binoculars, and she alerted the campground ranger. I got the call as I arrived at Chinquapin. With tennis shoes and jeans, I headed back to Glacier Point, where CRO would provide assistance.

As I looked down from Glacier Point, I could tell from the line-up of people along the road between Camp Twelve and Happy Isles roughly where Junior would be. But I could not see him. I worked my way down through the brush in the general direction I needed to go. I could even hear him calling once in a while. He was getting hoarse.

I tried to maneuver around to hear him more clearly, but every time Junior yelled, two or three loud-mouthed onlookers down at Camp Twelve would respond, "Hang tight!" or "Jump." I don't know if Junior was confused or not, but I was.

Ranger Duane Jacobs and Ross Cecil, a red-headed, local cowboy, packer, and mountaineer, drove in with the climbing ropes. We knew approximately where Junior was. The noise from Camp Twelve continued; Junior was losing his vocal power. It was getting dark and we simply were not going to make any exploratory trips down our 300-foot rope. We had to know exactly where he was; then we would risk our own lives getting this idiot out of the jam he was in. We didn't know who he was — we just knew we had to try to get him out, which we would do, but only after taking security protection for ourselves.

I worked down to the nearest point and got Junior's attention. "You will have to spend the night there, Junior. We will come for you in the morning as soon as it is light," and we left him there. We slept on the Glacier Point Hotel lobby chairs, had early coffee and doughnuts with the chef, and before sunrise were back over the edge again trying to locate Junior. The Camp Twelve roadside audience was gone.

When we located him, we selected a belay point. I volunteered to go down the rope to take the hitch on Junior, but Ross and Jake both vetoed it promptly. "You are just too damn heavy," was their decision. "If we've got to haul a ranger out of there we want a skinny one."

Jake elected to take the trip over the side. I got the major belay and Ross was standby. I snubbed my belay line around a convenient white pine and away Jake went, dragging our extra rope. Our idea of lowering a line to Junior just didn't work out. The cliff appeared to be straight down, but it wasn't, and the rope simply would not slide on it. We kept Jake snubbed up, but not tightly, and in just a few minutes he hollered that he had arrived.

Junior was in a frame of mind to come out hand-over-hand, but Jake gave him no option. Jake tied him on the extra rope and then Ross and I kept the line snug as Junior climbed out. Before we could get him untied, Jake had taken advantage of the freedom of action, and using the firm belay I had made in his line, came climbing out alone.

Success! We embraced Jake warmly! There was no audience. We loaded our gear in the pick-up to return to the Valley. I called CRO. The log later showed that we had our job done by 7:00 A.M. Junior was not contrite. He looked around airily. "Where is a good place to go fishing?" he asked. We gave him no help — just blasted him about his idiotic behavior. Lives had been risked to salvage his — was he worth it?

"You sound just like my dad," he said.

We had breakfast at the Glacier Point Hotel. Junior had no money. It cost the three of us $1.75 each for four breakfasts.

When ranger training classes started the next spring, we held climbing and belay lessons down in the Indian Caves near the Ahwanee Hotel. It was obvious that mountain climbers from the Sierra Club or from other National Parks such as Grand Teton or Mount Rainier should be used if we needed them. So this was my last rope climbing experience.

I worked with Jake off and on for the next twenty-five years. We were supportive friends. I always remembered the surge of warm admiration I felt for him that early morning on the Glacier Point cliff.

One morning a clatter on the front porch of the Chinquapin Ranger Station drew me outside to meet Mr. Louis Miller. He was about five feet-four inches tall, a broad and husky fellow, with a big handlebar moustache. He was caretaker in Spider Meadow, just below the west boundary of the park. His domain ran west, down to the South Fork of the Merced River between Wawona and El Portal. This great block of cut-over land, probably 4,000 acres, had been logged 20 years earlier. The old Yosemite Lumber Company had made a trade to do some logging in the park up towards Deer Camp. This was a trade-off, so that the park road from Alder Creek to Chinquapin and on to the Wawona Tunnel ran through an unbroken block of primeval forest. Much of it had been private land, and this exchange for Yosemite trees brought it all into the park and retained the beautiful corridor. Visitors never knew the cut-over land was behind the roadside forest wall. It had been skillfully handled.

The Spider Meadow tract included logging railroad grades which were now primitive roads, several mill sites, and a great logging chute above El Portal called Incline. Logs were hauled to this slide and then skidded down to a mill near El Portal. The slide was a very steep one, lined with straight, heavy logs. It must have been exciting to watch the big ponderosa or white pine logs slam down the chute into a bumper, with a great roar and crash. The employee responsible for keeping the chute open had carried a shovel and bucket of axle grease and a big swab. He kept it well lubricated. He was called the Pig Greaser!

Louis Miller was an ex-logger and, among his other avocations, he was a trapper. Much like the Idaho and Alaska trappers I had known, he had made a coyote set and caught and killed a great golden eagle. He brought this in for me to admire and to add to the park museum collection. It was an enormous bird.

Louis' ski equipment greatly intrigued me. I had heard of this kind of primitive "snow shoes," as the Scandinavian skiers had dubbed them. It was the same kind of equipment that Snowshoe Thompson and his brother had used between "Jimtown" and Saddlebag Lake. I had never expected to see any of it, but here it was, authentic and in actual use. The skis were four-inch-wide pine boards about ten feet long with toe strap bindings. The shovel, or upcurve, of the ski toe was made with a wire twisted in to lift it. He used a single ten-foot hardwood pole instead of ski poles. This was his pusher, used as a double-ended paddle for uphill going. Downhill, Louis did not need Arlberg technique. He would point the skis directly downhill, shove this single pole deeply into the snow between the skis and just ahead of his feet and then sit on it. By waggling the ski pole and adjusting the depth he could steer easily or even come to a complete stop.

Louis' extra equipment was equally as interesting. For a base wax on his skis he would get an old cylindrical phonograph record and melt it down. This was done with greatest caution, for it was highly inflammable material. Melted and then painted onto the dry and heated skis, this was a superb base wax. He didn't call it that — it was just his ski wax and he added various kinds of grease to it for special purposes. The dressing for drive belts in machine shops was great for cross country skiing; for real super-duper "slickum" wax, paraffin was the best. I often used that myself. It wasn't very durable, but it sure was fast. For real sticky, chewing-gum snow, Louis used salt. A Bull Durham sack full of rock salt was poured full of bacon grease and the package kept in a snow bank. I tried this one — it worked just great! We just rubbed it on in emergencies. It didn't last long, but it was a handy gadget!

I noted in various California ski meet reports that there were occasional events for the old timers. Their ability to schuss and maneuver quickly was unbelievable. I could believe the reports of eighty miles an hour for a straight schuss downhill! "Just let 'er go!" said Louis.

I had to learn more about skiing!

I was a competent snow shoer — it just took a lot of leg muscles.

I had done it in Alaska. I carried a stick to whack the snowshoes at each step to keep the snow cleared off them, but this was no preparation for being a skier!

First, I had to get the equipment. In 1937, the clumpy hard boots were just becoming important. The Yosemite ski shop finally got a pair of Chippewa, size thirteen. They were awfully big! Heavy, too, but striding around in them someway made me feel about a foot taller and more vigorous. The Park Service issued me a pair of solid hickory Northland skis, eight feet long. They had a simple clamp binding, which went okay with the boots, but the skis were "kinky." They had been left standing on end in shallow snow so that the last four inches of each had warped about an inch. They were murder for ski travel! The edges of the skis were rounded off, too. I was not a very successful ski ranger! I looked good either standing with the skis on, ski poles in position, or with the skis over my shoulder, but I couldn't get anywhere. I finally went to the ski repair shop and found that occasionally people broke skis, so within a period of about two weeks I was able to get two single Attenhofer skis so nearly alike that they looked like a pair. My Attenhofer six-foot nine-inchers were a great bargain! I got a pair of Bildstein heel springs calculated to break away in wrecks without tearing my legs off. Then all I needed was to know how to travel on them. I never was very good at it, but I traveled a lot of miles. The skis are now in the Yellowstone Museum collection of old ranger equipment.

I was wearing them one March night in 1938 when Otto Brown and I got lost in an equinoctial blizzard. We were in the second day enroute to Buck Camp for snow measurements. We had climbed out of Deer Camp early in the morning on hard crusted snow, leading our skis and crunching along with no problem. A pine marten played tag with us in Empire Meadows, wrapping itself around a ten-inch lodgepole pine tree with its fluffy tail visible on one side and its inquisitive nose stuck out on the other. It would watch as we passed, and then suddenly disappear, only to appear watching us again from a similar perch just ahead.

About noon, we came to Chilnualna Creek Valley and turned up towards the Johnson Lake junction. The hard gray skies began to squeeze out a few snow pellets. In about half a mile, we put our skis on as the snow began to accumulate. The weather warmed enough to turn the sleet storm into soft and clinging snow flakes. We ate our sandwiches along the trail without stopping, crowding our pace to reach the trail turnoff, but suddenly we were in a howling blizzard with zero visibility. Otto knew the land and the landmarks. We knew we must keep going up Chilnualna Creek for about two miles and find the Johnson Lake-Buck Camp trail, coming in up a valley from the south on our right.

These old Yosemite trails had had blazes chopped into trees along them but they were put in by men on foot, and consequently were only about three feet from the ground. These were too low in snow to be seen by a skier. The Army scouts had had no illusions — a blaze was to guide somebody, and needed to be big enough to blazon out at you. It was meant to be seen twelve inches on a side. But these blazes were grown over and hard to find. A more discreet Park Service trail crew had kept in mind the esthetics of park protection, and added occasional blazes of a more modest dimension. In the blizzard these were invisible also.

We could sense the uphill nature of the terrain and were able to keep a true course along the creek bed. In an occasional lull, the fog of snow flakes would lift and we could see the neighboring hillsides. But the Johnson Lake turnoff eluded us. About 2:00 P.M. we concluded that we had overshot it and were just slogging up Chilnualna Creek through a blizzard into wilderness country. Actually, from the turnoff it was only a short half-mile up to Johnson Lake, where we would take a snow course reading, but we couldn't find the trail junction. Our landmarks were firmly in mind, but the whirling snow gave it all a different perspective. Even after we turned back to try again, it was still a game of blind man's bluff. We missed it again. And now it was snowing so hard that in five minutes the tracks we had made going up the creek were drifted full of new snow.

We recognized the Empire Meadows turnoff, but elected to try to find the old Chilnualna Creek cabin just above Chilnualna Falls, about three miles on down the creek. At early dusk we found it, but the roof had blown off, there was nothing but bare walls, and we decided to look at the trail down to Wawona. In fact, the snow suddenly lifted and we could see the Wawona CCC camp just over 2,000 feet below us. A quick inspection revealed that the trail was drifted full of snow and was almost invisible. The oncoming darkness and return of the howling snowstorm turned us back into the forest, and we found a huge split rock with an overhang. It shut off the falling snow and deflected most of the wind. It would be our bivouac.

We tramped the snow down, stuck our skis in a row, hung our packs on them as a further windbreak, and addressed ourselves to the problem of getting a fire started. A nearby yellow pine log that was partially decayed gave us a supply of the pitchy residual these trees leave as they decay. I kicked the remaining limbs loose with my boots. We crawled around through the deep snow, digging under covered bushes, and came up with handfuls of dead and almost dry twigs, a couple of dead limbs we could wrest from an oak tree, a few semi-dry leaves, and pine needles. We hoarded this collection together, sheltered it with one of the packs and with cold-stiffened fingers, and whittled a few shavings from a small pine limb. We curled around it in the snow as I fumbled a match from my Marble match safe and tilted it under the edge of our brush heap. I burned my fingers quickly — in fact, I was on the third match and success seemed imminent when a sudden wind squall screamed down on us and scattered our precious fire starter.

We remembered that Otto's ski wax kit included a cake of parrowax he used for downhill travel. We sliced it up to reinforce our feeble kindling heap. With this encouragement, the fuel caught fire. A canteen cup was put to use melting snow. Our tiny triangle enclave — two granite walls and the third side leaky — was surprisingly cozy and snug. Otto soon curled up in the snow, cocooned as best he could with mittens, fur cap, and coats, and went to sleep. My ungainly six-foot-three was oversized for the living room. I got to sleep but managed to stick my foot in the fire and burn off part of my pant leg. In fact, it was the smell of burning wool that awakened me just before the blaze really started on my pants. End of siesta.

End of adventure. At daylight the storm relented and by 8:00 A.M. we were at the ranger station and the phone was ringing. It was Chief Ranger Townsley calling Otto. Were we okay? A well-wishing neighbor from the upper Wawona community had just called the Chief to report two drunken rangers hiking through the community. Everything was normal again.

We each had a good shot of bourbon and Otto cooked breakfast. A pound of bacon, a dozen eggs, and half a loaf of bread were the main ingredients.

A week later we went back to Buck Camp. Ranger Frank Givens went with us. I never knew whether we were showing Frank the country or he was to be our guide. Either way, we made it.

We skied all the way. The pine marten was not waiting for us at Empire Meadows, the Chilnualna Creek turnoff was familiar, we could even find the blazes for the Johnson turnoff. The snow course was carefully measured — ten to twelve feet of snow, which our scale converted to equivalent inches of water. It was about twelve to one — a foot of snow equalled an inch of water. San Joaquin Valley farmers could expect to have irrigation water available until the last of July.

We started for Buck Camp, climbing out of the Johnson Lake basin onto the divide. From there it was a long, steep mile down to the cabin. The topography was such that we always reached this pass just as the sun went behind the ridge, and the snow immediately froze. It was icy all the way. Otto and Frank had gone ahead and I worked down the hill with short switchbacks and kick turns until I was just above the cabin. I could see it. It was just another hump in the snow. The sun was still shining around it. I optimistically aimed my skis for the sunshine and started down the last one hundred yards. This was a mistake.

The skis leaped ahead of me — I was almost sitting on them. I caught up abruptly as they hit the sunshine. That surface was still melted and very sticky. In fact, it was what we called "chewing gum" snow. My dream of stopping in a tremendous Christie went glimmering as I fell headlong over the ski tips and made a fast roll to one side. I was suddenly about two feet under, my pack sack on top of my head, and a squinty-eyed look revealed a nearby ski with a foot in the binding. It looked like my Chippewa boot. It was. Frank's comment to Otto did little to soothe the situation. "This would be a good time to take his temperature!"

But they lifted the pack off, unclamped the skis, and I rolled over and up again. No broken bones, no broken skis — I was stretched into a new shape, but still mobile. I think of the ski maneuver as "Grandma's Churn" and have watched a few other novices do it inadvertently. It is risky for wilderness skiers.

By contrast, an eight-inch snowfall that night left the entire forest blanketed with a soft, fluffy cover. From Buck Camp to the pass it was easy climbing. From the pass down to the lake we could fly! Any ski turn worked. My right Christie, which had been almost impossible, came through easily. We made excellent time all the way home.

Somehow all of the "hard" trips are easier going home. No matter if on horseback or skis, the last day home was always the distance covered the first two days out. So it was with this journey — it was fun! Deer Camp by noon, a quick lunch on the hillside above the cabin. I saw unexpected dark spots in the snow and discovered a small group of live mosquitoes in the fluffy snow, an unusual find. They seemed intact and healthy, but slow-moving in the cold. I emptied the matches from a small cardboard box, put the mosquitoes in the box, and tucked it into my shirt pocket to take to the park museum.

The last leg of our journey was through the cutover land of the Yosemite Lumber Company, along an abandoned railroad grade, then back into the forest strip protecting the South Entrance road. We were almost home — and safely.

At Chinquapin (my ranger station) I related the strange incident to Inger and took out the box to show her my catch. My body warmth had revived the mosquitoes, however, and as soon as I opened the box they flew briskly away. Subsequent inquiries, however, revealed that this was not a completely unusual situation. Overwintering mosquitoes were occasionally found in snow banks.

In the winter of 1936–1937, Badger Pass had just over 33,000 winter users. Some were just on-lookers. These sightseers usually sat in the lounge near the window, overlooking the "up-ski" and the nursery slope. One outgoing lady was watching an amateur skier as he bobbed unskillfully along across the nursery slope. Every dip, swoop, stop, and start the skier made, the dear lady made right with him. Finally he picked up a bit of speed, and as he slid out of our picture one ski tipped the other and he went head-first into a five-foot ridge of snow. The only remaining trace was the bottom of his skis staring blankly at the open sky. His friend clasped her hands in delight. "Isn't it lucky he had those skis on," she exclaimed. "They could never have found him!"

Lars, our Sequoia-born son, was now five years old. The Yosemite Park and Curry Company, personified by our friends, Dr. Don Tressider, the company president, and Mary Curry Tressider, provided every child in the Yosemite school group with a Christmas present of skis and bindings.

Inger took skiing lessons. I did too, but informally. At age five, Lars would join me on the old Chinquapin road, which was now a primitive, but delightful, ski trail, and bob along with me the four miles down to Chinquapin for lunch. This took some maneuvering with cars so I could get back to my duty station, but it was worth it!

Every Sunday morning the number one parking slot at the Badger Pass ski lodge was always used by a Merced, California family. They apparently had a food market; their spread included corn-on-the-cob, special fruit, and the like. The first Sunday they left a real mound of debris in their parking place, so I spoke to them helpfully—I hoped—about their responsibility for cleaning up. They were abject in their apologies. The site was never cluttered again. It was a model of tidiness. In the spring when the snow banks receded, however, their entire winter's garbage was revealed, carefully packaged and stuck in the snowbank in front of the car, even though a trash can was right next to them. I still think skiers are great people, but . . .

Was skiing just a transitory fad? Certainly the colorful costumes, the invigorating exercise, the clean fresh air, the rosy cheeks, the bite of the crisp, winter air were positive factors. Ours was a day-use program at Badger Pass. Rooms and meals were limited to Yosemite

Valley, and to the Yosemite Park and Curry Company. This concessioner also provided bus transportation, the ski school and instructors, the ski shop, and the equipment. Skiing was a park-like activity, limited to those who could afford trips to Yosemite. But 33,000 people in a ski season were impressive, particularly to a park ranger! They used roads and services already available. And skiing was not physically destructive. It met my conditions, particularly because a number of the Yosemite runs were practically touring journeys.

How safe was it? That winter we lost only one skier. He had started for the Ostrander Lake winter cabin. It was not really a cold night; we found him shivering but unharmed at daylight. His complaint was that the search was not well organized. Using electric headlamps, a number of searchers had whizzed around him during the night, but he could not yell loudly enough to stop any of them.

Skiing was more work for the rangers, since the accident rate was high compared to other activities. We established an emergency first aid room with the special splints, tapes, heat devices, and stretchers needed for these leg-twisting injuries. Dr. Avery Sturm, head of the Yosemite Medical Service, became an excellent skier himself, and his skill in treating mangled muscle and bone was amazing.

Skiing was "off season," when the concessioners and the National Park Service were seeking additional visitors to use otherwise unused facilities. But these concessions were losers in mid-winter. They had been designed to accommodate the summertime visitor loads. I was particularly interested in camping and in campgrounds. These were summertime problems.

The Yosemite Valley campgrounds probably have the unenviable distinction of being the first in the National Parks to which the terms crowding and overuse could be applied. This situation developed while I was there. It sneaked up on us. Suddenly the impact of highway improvements, better cars, special and more sophisticated recreational equipment, tourism publicity, and specifically of Yosemite advertising, converged on the Yosemite Valley campgrounds. We weren't ready for it. We were exactly in the position Colonel Richard Lieber, Director of State Parks in Indiana, had described: "The automobile manufacturers and the equipment manufacturers and the highway engineers have done 90 percent of the thinking for the National Parks

for the last ten years." Our acres and wonders were free! "Come and
enjoy them!" we seemed to say. The public did come, using the manufacturers' new equipment.

Yosemite was the place to go. My young friends camped in the
Valley, and loved it. My niece and her husband camped in the Valley,
and loved it. So did thousands more. Early 1930s' attendance figures
showed that over half of the Valley campers were repeaters, and their
average was slightly over three visits per year to this mountain idyll!

The Valley campground consisted of five numbered campgrounds
managed as one unit by a campground ranger (a new one, me), five
seasonal rangers, and a relief man for days off. The land was — and
still is — 116 acres of sandy, open valley floor with occasional clumps
of second-growth lodgepole pine or black oak. A few large pine or fir
were still surviving. This campground illustrated exactly the environmental impact that Meinicke reported in his 1928 study of dead trees
in National Forest campgrounds. Indiscriminate driving gouged tire
ruts deeply into the soil and exposed tree roots. Oil drips mixed with
the sand to block water absorption. Roadside trees, especially "key"
trees in clumps, were skinned and battered, exposing others which were
in turn skinned up. Charcoal and ashes were scattered everywhere;
and while restrooms had wastewater sinks, the air was redolent of dishwater slung out in every direction to "settle the dust."

Yosemite planners dubbed it "The Yosemite Slums." A normal
midsummer night had a population of 8,000 to 10,000 campers and
July 3rd or Memorial Day would often double this. In 1938 I counted
campsites by a cruising patrol with my 1932 Pontiac roadster. With
the top down, creeping along in low gear with a "talley-whacker"
firmly in my left hand, I cruised the oiled loop road in each campground counting campsites — *clackety clack*. I returned to check every
side loop and nook — *clackety clack*. I stopped and stood on the car
seat to see around tents and into places screened by all those other darn
tents — big tents, little tents, campers with no tents at all (mainly
young folks) — *clackety clack* again — and then a few luggage trailers
which had gotten mixed in. My combined total was well over 5,000
campsites on the Third of July. I did it again and came out with the
same total. I checked records of previous campground rangers, Billy
Nelson and Harry During. They had the same totals. At 3.5 people

per campsite, we had nearly 20,000 people in our five-unit campground.

The campgrounds were friendly places — really little communities. Camping was open to anyone who could find a place to pitch a tent or unroll a sleeping bag. Whoever got there first had priority — if he could find a place to park his car. Two, three, or even four tents might be tied to the same tent peg. Our tent city stretched horizontally in one bubbling layer. I checked the National Almanac population statistics for Pittsburgh, Pennsylvania. It had a population density of only 50 percent of our "wildlands" campsites!

Often the seasonal ranger in charge of a campground would have a complaint from an early-arriving camper who had found a charming spot against the boundary log next to the Merced River, only to have an interloper park his car and set his tent right across Number One's front entrance. This kind of flap usually happened in the evening, and my ranger crew had a firm guideline that after 5:00 P.M. I was not to be disturbed except for major emergencies. "Let them get supper to quiet the crying children and then a night's sleep." I would call in the morning to adjudicate the problem. I did this, but each crisis had always resolved itself. The kids would be playing happily together as they tried to catch a chipmunk; the women planning a museum visit and then a bridge game; the two men fishing together. They had discovered mutual friends in Alameda. It was quite agreeable.

This suggests the range of camper activities — the whole family could be occupied pleasantly. Naturalist programs were educational as well as fun for the youngsters. Deer mooched morning pancakes. A bear prowled the camp in the evening, preceded and followed by a gang of wary observers. But Bruin was only checking garbage cans. A robin lit on the table to share dinner.

Earlier Yosemite administrators had learned that on a busy summer day, about 60 percent of the daily crowds milling through the Valley were campers. They were mostly long-term campers, staying all summer. Dad would move the family, tents, sleeping bags, and kitchen utensils onto a Yosemite campground site in May or early June and leave them there. He would return on weekends or holidays or for his own vacation. The Park Service had responded by establishing a thirty-day camping limit. This created outcries, Congressional inquiries, and newspaper publicity, but these had cooled down by the time I became campground ranger in 1938. Changing visitor habits as well as camping equipment and better roads offered greater options for summer vacations, and we had so few of the thirty-day visitors that the limit was dropped to fourteen days without complaint. In fact, it soon became evident that the average camper stay was less than seven days. *Pro forma*, the limit was set at seven days. It still is. Really, no limit is needed, in all probability, but a few of us kept remembering the problems of those summer vacationers!

Many of the rangers believed that the great variety of optional summer activities was taking park management away from the job of preservation. We could not limit the number of visitors, but could we reduce the pressures on Yosemite Valley by moving the crowding problem to less fragile sites? (This is like the salt distribution formula that works so well in manipulating range utilization by livestock. The herder puts the salt where he wants the stock to go.)

We would reduce Valley camping, and at the same time give everyone a more meaningful and rewarding park experience. Which activities could we move? Were there alternate, less critical sites? Obviously, just asking visitors "Why do you camp in Yosemite Valley?" was too general a question. Could we approach it indirectly and ask, "What did you do during this visit to Yosemite Valley?" This is where I came in. With my psychology background, I could be presumed to know something about techniques for this kind of investigation. I talked with the Chief Ranger; I talked with the Park Superintendent. With their encouragement, I visited Stanford and talked with two of my psychology professors. They did not go into it deeply, but their general reactions simply suggested that we establish a list of activities and then a method of counting the number of users. A 2 percent sample would probably be adequate if it were carefully collected.

In each of the summers of 1938 and 1939, I distributed just over 2,000 questionnaires. The basis was calculated on records of the five campgrounds, the popularity of each day of the week, and the dates of holidays. For example, information about California campers might be collected on any weekend. However, visitors from the East or Midwest were presumed to have started for Yosemite on Saturday morning to reach the park on Thursday or Friday. In the fall of 1938, I sat down with 1,572 returned questionnaires — 2 percent of the 1938 campers — to calculate their interests and activities.

Fortunately, my winter ranger job was as night watchman for the utility and residential area in Yosemite Valley. This was a highly repetitious task. I had a night watchman's clock and every hour made my round of fifteen stations with keys to punch my clock at each location. It was a brisk walk of about fifteen minutes. Then I would return to the radio room and fire cache office on the third floor of the hose drying tower. I had a telephone so the night phone operator could reach me. I had heat, electricity, lots of space, and a typewriter.

I reviewed my statistical methods course and then started converting the material into useful data. The forty-five-hour week gave me eleven consecutive days on duty and three days off. I needed that kind of free time and isolation to keep the project moving. Chief Townsley kindly offered to exchange my time with other rangers so they might share the inconvenience of my night time work schedule, but to his surprise I asked him to leave it alone. I was getting my own chores done quite satisfactorily. My final report on *Camper Activities in Yosemite Valley* was published in the June, 1939 (Vol. XVIII, No. 6) issue of *Yosemite Nature Notes.*

(I might add that I had time also to develop a successful series of juvenile articles for *The Open Road For Boys* magazine, *Outdoor Life*, *Desert Magazine*, and other outdoor publications. I sold them all — rates modest, but at least I got paid and had something to show for my overtime schedule. In fact, my little pot boiler articles were rewarding enough that I seriously considered making outdoor writing a complete career. There were many things to write about — there was an eager audience for the adventures I reported. Finally, I decided that it would be great to be a ranger and write about it. This plan was not successful — the ranger soon became a superintendent and my outdoor, wildland touch faded.)

This progress was amateurish, but it was "hard" data that planners might use if they wished. Unfortunately, no one seemed to need the information. I use the simile of the abrupt disappearance of a hard-boiled egg dropped into a bowl of soft mashed potatoes. The information stayed in the bowl until I revived it as part of the Mission 66 National Park Service study sixteen years later.

We did spend some weeks trying to influence camper movement at Bridal Veil Falls campground between Badger Pass and Glacier Point, but it was ineffective. This campground was simply too remote. I got back on a regular schedule of ranger duties, became acquainted with Inger and Lars again and was ready for the next adventures.

As I pass this milepost, I must make a Yosemite campground ranger observation: Camp Seven was one of the more pleasant campgrounds along the Merced River. There were a few peripheral large ponderosa pine and incense cedar, lovely vistas across the river, and a single ranger tent at the entrance. The campground was comfortably stuffed with California campers, including many families with children of school age. About half were from the San Francisco-Oakland area, and their schools always opened in mid-August. Consequently, on August 10, I viewed Camp Seven as an experimental project. A lot of the campers would have to leave, and I wanted to see how the residual half behaved. They would have an inadvertent experience in open space camping they probably had not anticipated.

My predictions were correct. On August 13, the exodus began. On August 14 many more left. August 15 found about half the campground empty in a comfortably scattered pattern. It looked good, but August 16 found almost all the campers together in the west end of the campground. The others had taken their tents down and moved to join the crowd. We had the same confused jam all over again. The campers liked it. They were unperturbed about my philosophical discussions of isolation and loneliness and crowding.

Crowding? What crowding? They just liked it! All that open space gave them a problem. They were frightened to be sleeping in tents with nobody near the outside walls. The open space must be enticing to bears and other varmints, they thought. It would be easy for looters to slip up to an unprotected tent wall, rip it open, and steal the camp equipment. It was too quiet away from the crowd. Besides, the whole Valley program of camper activities was still in full swing. Car pooling, baby sitting, and planned fishing excursions were all simpler to arrange on a neighborhood basis with the close community ties.

We didn't want to believe it, but most of those campground enthusiasts liked Yosemite as a beautiful backdrop. They found the open meadows to be inviting sites where they could run and holler. The scope of family activities was great. Space was adequate, and there was no great drive to develop more facilities. Camping was an experience with friendly people. But it could happen anywhere. It did not need to be Yosemite Valley.

I like to think that John Muir's Valley of Light, as I knew it in 1935, has survived relatively intact without a great deal of the nibbling which erodes natural scenic and recreational resources so subtly and surely. There were crowds, but the basic geography and the forests and the waterfalls are still there today. Muir's ideals left glowing embers which I blew upon, and they warmed anew. The courageous Steve Mather trumpeted his dream of conservation against the negative forces about him. The practical Horace Albright could take this philosophy and articulate it in programs and deeds. They must have had lonely moments and questioning periods of introspection, but Yosemite in its majesty speaks for them. Two generations of lesser followers have met the same opponents and held the line. I think of myself as a part of that parade. For Garrison, the Yosemite years were a success story.

In the fall of 1937, Lars was ready for the first grade. His birthday nearly coincided with my park beginnings — July 3, 1932, for my first seasonal ranger job; July 10 for Lars' birthday. I was transferred from Chinquapin to Yosemite Valley in October 1937, and we were assigned quarters. (Heavens! How quickly we pick up vernacular!) Assigned quarters? We were lucky to be offered a house in Yosemite Valley rather than an apartment!

Before we made this significant move, we decided that we would have a community party. The Otto Browns co-hosted it with us. By hosting a barbecue at Chinquapin, friends from Wawona, South Entrance, Badger Pass, Glacier Point, and the Valley could all make it. I had read in *Sunset Magazine* about an open pit barbecue with a kid or lamb on a spit. We had lots of oak wood. It took off from there.

A park neighbor near Nipiniwassee had a kid — dressed weight around forty pounds. I dug the pit in front of the house, keeping in mind the prevailing wind and time of sunset in late September. I bent a length of one-half inch pipe into a spit and crank handle and drilled holes in it so we could key the carcass to the spit and they would turn together. I made a cross-buck rack at each end to support the spit, got a length of two-inch-wide corrugated tin roofing to partially reduce the intensity of the heat, and we had at it.

It was our first experience with this kind of cookout. I started the oak wood fire at eleven o'clock and by one o'clock it was a great bed of coals. I started an auxiliary bonfire for the dutch oven and to provide extra coals from time to time as needed. We skewered the kid to the spit, tucked garlic cloves into the meat, made a basting compound of olive oil, wine, and salt, and swabbed the meat thoroughly. It was a leisurely process: Every five minutes a quarter-turn on the spit; prop it into place; wait five minutes; another quarter-turn — I cut the shoulder blades loose so heat could penetrate behind them, used the heat shield to protect the thin flank section, basted it often, and just waited it out. At six o'clock, I moved it onto a trestle table to carve and it almost fell apart. A little beer, a washtub full of corn-on-the-cob, an endless supply of dutch oven biscuits, a great skillet of fried potatoes, a supply of coffee, and ice cream cones for dessert. It was great eating. The skin of the kid was crisp and crunchy, the meat was juicy and hot — I had all the good fortune in the book on this endeavor. We fed about sixty people.

We learned that it was fun to entertain informally and traditionally as I knew that both Steven Mather and Horace Albright had done. Inger and Ardeth had a miracle kind of meal. We had extra logs for seats, wood for a final blazing campfire, campfire singing, and impromptu skits.

This was my last field assignment on the ranger force. Someway I sensed that once I moved into park headquarters life and tasks would change — as they did. So memories of this happy occasion are warm and refreshing. The lessons of the barbecue were transferred to many other places — Glacier, Grand Canyon, Big Bend, and even Yellowstone. We had a pattern to follow, a level of quality to meet. Inger and I had no hesitation about jumping into this kind of *al fresco* entertainment. We did it together.

We met wonderful people in Yosemite. Visiting scientists from the Yosemite Advisory Committee, staff people from the National Park Service, distinguished foreign guests, the Governor of California, a Congressman, and a Senator. Politics was a no-no, but it was important to meet these people. The growing recognition of Ansel Adams as a great photographer gave a special sparkle to knowing him. He was a music student who moved to photographic art when he found out about it. We were young together. This friendship has persisted.

Other avenues of growth opened. I filled in as part of the park interpretive program during the winter, giving my first illustrated talk on "The Role of the Ranger," describing the four seasons in Yosemite. I went to a Forest Service ranger training school at the Feather River. I was the National Park representative for the San Francisco World's Fair on Treasure Island in 1939.

The 1937 early December flood was a big one. Early snow had accumulated and was piled up above 5,000 feet elevation. A sudden warm rain up to 9,000 feet peeled off this layer of snow with the added three inches of rainfall. I was relieving at Arch Rock. The Merced River came up over its banks and I watched many of the Valley road signs float by as well as parts of buildings from the Cascade Creek CCC Camp. The 200 enrollees came walking out wading the water down the road, single file, holding hands as a security measure. The water was deep enough that I stood on a floating log and rode it down the road through the entrance station gate. We extended a rope and a chain from our dry-foot entrance station booth over to the hillside and anchored it to big trees, so that in case our station was swept away we had a firm escape anchor. The electricity was on; the radio news had little about our flood. By telephone we could keep the Chief Ranger's office informed of our status. The entire valley was under water, six feet deep in the store and the Superintendent's home . Later there were sales of canned goods whose labels had soaked off in the flood. Every meal a surprise!

Inger was marooned in the Valley. Electricity went out in our all-electric home. She had ample grocery supplies — a custom we learned in Alaska, and on outpost ranger stations. There was no crisis at home.

After three years' experience as a permanent ranger, I took a long look at the career potentials. It was a great job! I loved the whole setup, but was there potential for promotion? It didn't look as enticing from that angle. I had come on board in 1935, the first new

Yosemite ranger in at least five years. Jim Skakle came by transfer
from the Border Patrol in 1937, but was already making noises about
returning, which he later did. Vernon Lowery came in, as I had, via
the Hetch Hetchy cop route. Lawrence Merriam, the new Superintendent, was concerned about the stereotyped ranger image and the
salary squeeze. He put through a pay raise of $5.00 a month for each
ranger who had been without a salary increase for three years or more.
The entire force of twenty-nine rangers qualified. We were glad to get
it! We were particularly pleased with the recognition.

Meanwhile, I was questing a bit. I had the beloved job. I had
permanent status. I had finished my campground questionnaire on
camper activities.

I had been involved in wintertime interpretation programs for
park visitors. I had made several hundred dollars by free-lance writing. Inger and I liked the social status and the park companionships.

I was ready to try something more. I talked with our Yosemite
Chief Clerk, Russell Sprinkle, whom I knew had been a Yellowstone
ranger some years before. He loaned me the civil service books on
position classification and I learned about the scope of federal jobs and
the interesting dimension they just called "the impact of the man on
the job!" I felt that I had had some impact.

"What do I do now?" I asked Sprink.

His frank comment was positive. "Get the hell out of the GDR's,"
he said. I knew the "R" would stand for rangers. I presumed the rest
of it. I didn't agree, of course, but I had asked the question and was
in no position to argue. I knew that Yellowstone had three Assistant
Chief Rangers. Each one expected to become Chief Ranger. They
refused other promotions or alternatives because "If I move, one of
those other S.O.B.'s will get it." This was a no-win proposition. Chief
Townsley looked good for many more years at Yosemite. What were
my alternatives?

Suddenly, I received a letter "through the Superintendent" asking
if I were interested in becoming the Superintendent of the new Hopewell Village National Historic Site. I could not get much information
about it, except that it was an old iron furnace in Pennsylvania which
had probably made munitions for George Washington's Continental
Army. I did not know that Secretary Ickes was having a ruckus with

the local Congressman and had sent for a "western ranger — preferably a big one" to take over. I knew that my earlier mentor, Colonel John R. White, was the Washington Chief of Operations. It was a handsome promotion; one that would take a decade to achieve in the ranger ranks. So Inger and I decided to accept.

CHAPTER X

PROMOTIONS AND POLITICS

THERE WERE MANY THINGS TO COMPLETE BEFORE OUR MOVE. Most pressing was the Park Service's information booth at the World's Fair. We were not well organized. My booth had a sign which stated that I represented the Yosemite National *Bank*. After this was straightened out, I still had no exhibits and little literature, but I met a lot of nice people! By visiting the exhibits of business corporations and other government agencies, I developed a report on what we might do the next time, but there never was a "next time."

By mid-October we were back in Yosemite. My last campground questionnaire report was finished. The lovely fall scenery with its riot of color had just peaked. Acorns from the great black oaks above our house were rattling day and night on our roof. The sleek mule deer bucks were aggressive, necks beginning to swell, almost ready for mating season. Yosemite was a magnificent place to live, but we were going to move out of it.

My letter accepting the profferred transfer to Hopewell Village was like the start of a countdown to a million. I had a lot to learn about government transfers, travel orders, account numbers, personnel actions, position descriptions, and the like, but I took the first step into the maze and we went on from there — always by mail. The ready use of long distance telephone was unheard of.

I had had an experience with a government travel order in October a year earlier when I was sent to a Forest Service training session for new Junior Foresters who were becoming forest rangers. I later used parts of it for Yosemite Park ranger training, but one lesson I learned was not to monkey with one's travel schedule once it was approved. I was like "The Admiral." I learned hard but I remembered.

I was authorized to receive four dollars per day for travel. I was driving a Yosemite ranger pickup. I noticed on a road map that if I returned to Yosemite by east side forest roads to Mono Lake and into the park by Tioga Pass, I would see a lot of new country and would save some mileage.

Only I ran into a snow storm and had to spend a night in Nevada. Trouble? Deep trouble! My travel order did not authorize me to go to Nevada. I was to travel only in California. My Chief Clerk friend, Russell Sprinkle, took me severely to task about it. He was sorry, so sad, but so damned adamant. "You should have known better!"

I enlisted the aid of the Superintendent, Lawrence Merriam. Sprink explained my derelictions. Sorry, but he would have to "disallow" about $6.00 worth of Garrison's Nevada travel. Lawrence knew more about authorities, budgets, audits, and such than I did, and Sprink finally agreed to certify the voucher — this meant he told the accountant to pay it, but he would leave a note in my personnel file that if this were audited, I could expect to repay the $6.00 of illegal travel money. Sprink was a good clerk. (I learned later to love these old penny watchers, as they kept me out of trouble.) He was a nice guy, but he didn't want his record loused up because he was a good Joe in helping a dumb ranger. I've been waiting for that audit since 1938.

Ranger gossip was also informative about the technicalities of having a signed travel order in hand before you spent any travel money. There were horror stories of rangers who found themselves arriving at new locations where they were not expected, with hundreds of personal dollars expended for moving expense because somebody changed plans and forgot to tell them.

I did not realize the full impact of this first actual official change of station. We had moved by ranger pickup truck twice a year in Sequoia, and thought nothing of it. Our initial assignment to Yosemite was at my own expense and I just hired a neighbor's dump truck for five dollars and bought the gas. Our accumulated plunder did not even require padding or packing. I got it all into boxes and lashed down with clotheslines.

Hopewell was a formal move — the first of fourteen subsequent changes in location. Of course, we didn't know that yet; I thought it was exciting. The great vans for moving furniture were seldom used in 1939. We moved by railroad, authorized to ship 4,000 pounds plus the tare of packing material — in this case, lumber, as the park carpenter built crates for all of our beds, barrels, dressers, books, lamps, and the like. As an LCL shipment (which just meant that it was less than a carload) the crates would be moved from one boxcar to another as they slowly made their way across America to Birdsboro, Pennsylvania, in about six weeks.

As we unloaded the boxcar at Birdsboro, parts of equipment like our treadle sewing machine, the legs of the dining table, and parts of our day bed were leaking out of the boxes and were thrown into the truck with the crates. Adjudication of losses was difficult, discouraging, and costly. (We realized that the adage of "two moves equal one fire" was valid after move number three, Washington to Glacier National Park.) The havoc wrought by the packers was thorough. It put us into the moving protection business, as we began saving barrels, padding, crates, original cartons, cardboard shields, wardrobes, shredded paper, and the like. I actually got very good at packing dishes. We never broke a dish after our first disaster.

(Once the furniture was on the way, the neighbors gave us a great going-away party at the Ranger Club. This club was a legacy from Steve Mather, intended for use by Yosemite rangers on their off-duty hours. Mather had not always been consistent on this, for at one time he is reported to have cancelled an appropriation to build an outpost ranger station at Hamilton Lake with the judgment that he did not want rangers to sit in a ranger station. He wanted them to ride the park trails, helping visitors and protecting wildlife. He authorized the Superintendent to buy another good horse and saddle instead of building the house. The Ranger Club, however, became an imposing center of Yosemite hospitality. We had a wonderful party!)

We did not know much about Hopewell. Even the usually reliable underground telegraph system, which kept us informed of anticipated National Park moves and policies, did not bring us any scoop on the new National Historic Site. Historic Sites were an innovative venture, anyway. Our Yosemite farewell M. C. labored as best he could with the toast, "Whatever it is, we Hope Well For You!" We said, "Amen!"

We were suddenly focusing on new levels of work, both as a Superintendent and in embracing American history. Inger and I were both confident that history would be equally absorbing for us — as of course it was.

We sold our snappy 1932 Plymouth convertible and bought Lawrence Merriam's 1937 black Buick four-door sedan. (This conservative and lovingly pampered member of our family went with us to Hopewell, to Washington, D.C., and through the years of gasoline rationing to Glacier. We finally sold it in Grand Canyon for only $50.00 less than we had paid for it. Meanwhile, we had pushed it over the 100,000 mile mark and up to 20,000 on the next circuit.) Through the Automobile Club of Southern California and their cooperative tourist information program in Yosemite, we knew about available tourist maps and information aides, so we left well-counseled and with great expectations.

Lars — now seven — left school with no visible reluctance. He was a good traveler. Erik, our Yosemite baby, was just six months old — a good-natured youngster who gladly slept all the first day as the great car rocked and rumbled along. Then he wanted to stay up all night. We changed the sequence the second day. We were a stagecoach heading east for new discoveries; we were Santa's sleigh as we sang and looked for white horses or hay stacks — only we learned that the southern California and northern Arizona desert country was not much for hay stacks.

We followed a National Park tradition, although we didn't know it, by visiting as many National Parks as we could along the way. At the Grand Canyon, Acting Superintendent Jimmy Lloyd gave us a special tour. The Petrified Forest Chief Ranger Stan Dinsmore gave us a welcoming greeting and a tour. We loved it. Our National Parks were really superlative.

Our side trip to the new Regional Office of the National Park Service at Santa Fe paid good dividends. Herb Maier, the Acting Regional Director (and a great architect and planner whom I worked with many times later), was most interested in my Hopewell assignment. He had just returned from the NPS Washington headquarters and he knew of a "plan" to move a western ranger to this National Historic Site, but he did not know who it was.

"Did the Washington Office tell you anything about the job?" he asked me.

They had not.

"Did the Regional Office in Richmond give you any special information about Hopewell?"

They had not.

Herb thought it over a while. Obviously he viewed my new assignment as something like throwing Daniel into the Lion's Den. He suddenly told me about the flap which had developed at Hopewell over the selection of the Superintendent. The local Congressman, Danny Koch, was determined that this was a patronage job — his. He would select the new man.

Secretary of the Interior, Harold Ickes, the "Old Curmudgeon," was adamant. He wanted a professional park man at Hopewell Village. Agreement was completely lacking, so Ickes made the decision.

"I'm going out to the western parks and I'm going to pick a great big park ranger and transfer him in as the Superintendent of Hopewell Village."

End of message. Select the ranger!

Between my old Sequoia Superintendent, Colonel John R. White, the Chief of Operations for the National Park Service; Lee Ramsdell, the Personnel Officer; Park Service Director Newton Drury, a former member of the Yosemite National Park Advisory Board (whom I had met several times); and Lawrence Merriam, the greatly respected forester, conservationist, and Superintendent of Yosemite National Park, the big arrow pointed in my direction.

I was convinced that this was really a reward for excellence! I had wanted to be the "best" ranger, and to become involved in national events for the National Parks, and this obviously meant becoming familiar with the historical branch of our outfit. I was on my way!

Suddenly, thanks to friend Herb Maier (and I was greatly indebted to him for his concern) a lot of the air went out of my balloon. But I still was Superintendent of Hopewell Village National Historic Site. I certainly had solid political backing! Inger and I talked it over; we were right where we thought we were. I had better come through — keep my mouth shut until I found out whom I could trust. I was serenely confident that this job was just what I wanted, and I could and would do it!

The Buick ran smoothly and well — twelve days and over two thousand miles later we reached our target, but we couldn't find Hopewell. We reached nearby Readings. We reached its close neighbor, Morgantown, but not Hopewell Furnace. We found David

Kurtz, a congenial garage proprietor. He thought a minute and said, "Oh you must be looking for the CCC camp." And sure enough, we were. There were other iron furnaces reasonably close, but this was the only one with a two hundred-man war-veterans' CCC camp. Man-made Hopewell Lake was nearby. It had been constructed by the CCC camp crews and was now the center of a considerable recreational development. Its full name was the French Creek National Recreational Demonstration Area Project, a Pennsylvania state park. Hopewell Village National Historic Site had been created from a part of the French Creek land.

I dressed in my full NPS uniform and called at the camp. The uniform was recognized. I received a most friendly welcome.

Charlie Shearer, the CCC Camp Superintendent, was away, but would return the following day. I met Lincoln (Linc) Murdough, a landscape architect; Christian (Chris) Eben, a civil engineer; and Paul Koch (no relation to the Congressman), an architect. This was the normal complement of professional overhaed staff for a CCC Camp, and they looked like a competent outfit. Company strength was about 90 percent of the authorized quota of two hundred. Work projects were centered on the French Creek State Park Recreational Demonstration Area group camp buildings and a new lake at Sixpenny Creek.

Besides the CCC Camp, there was an Emergency Relief Administration Center (ERA), also working on French Creek recreation projects. I called there next. Their work strength was about three hundred men. The professional staff was Arthur Silvius, a forester (what an approriate name for a forester, particularly a graduate of the old Vanderbilt Forestry School), and Frank Kelley, an architect with great interests in historical architecture and Hopewell Village. These two were competent, eager, willing, and communicative, but I did not hear a word about the Congressman! In fact, I never met him.

This was beautiful, forested, and hilly country. We were right at the end of the fall colors. Roads were all narrow, crooked, and paved, with farm houses often tight against the road. Barns and support buildings were mostly in excellent condition. It was a new scene and it was lovely! Governor Pinchot's roads had indeed gotten the farmers out of the mud.

A month earlier I had been an FSC-9 ranger at a salary of $2,000 a year. I had been promoted to that level just one week before I left Yosemite. Now I was over in CAF — Clerical Administrative Fiscal, grade seven, at $2,600 per annum. I was in charge of nearly six thousand acres of land in the Recreation Demonstration Area, a four hundred-acre historic site, a two hundred-man CCC Camp, and a three hundred-man ERA project, all with a regular budget of $6,000 per year, $2,600 of it in my salary. There was no Hopewell "staff" at first, but I found it either alarming or amusing to write my former ranger peers describing the scope of my new duties!

I still did not know about my duties. National Park Service Regional Director Minor R. Tillotson in Richmond, Virginia, was a perceptive fellow. He convened a conference of Southeast Region National Park Service officials in Richmond and sent me a travel order which I gratefully accepted. It was timely, taking me out of the local picture until I could learn more of the ground rules. Staff-wise, I needed to be oriented; program-wise, I seemed to have many job priorities, all number one! I had an excellent Coordinating Superintendent in Herb Kahler at Morristown National Historic Park in New Jersey, but I had not met him yet. I had a CCC State Park Inspector I would meet in Richmond, but if I hollered for help, who would answer? Tilly got me off the hook. I met him in Richmond. (I later knew him at Grand Canyon and at Big Bend.)

The conference mainly dealt with planning and with the technicalities of various work funding programs. The professional standards were obviously high, and accepted routinely. The historians and interpreters were provocative and sharing. They took me on a tour of Richmond and its environs.

I was surprised that there were no blacks on the leadership staff. My awareness of the minority problem, as I had met it in a CCC camp in Sequoia, was not reflected in Richmond, Virginia. There was more togetherness here, but no measure of equality. How readily the inequities were accepted! Many of my concerns had been with American Indians. Here it was all black. We were too unconcerned. I was certain that as a Superintendent I would work with blacks both as employees and as park visitors, but right now I had too many other new things to think about.

It was exciting just to be in Richmond. I learned about grits, duck pins, the problems of a one-inch snowstorm in Richmond, and three new kinds of high-low poker! I met men from historical parks, from Shenendoah, the Skyline Drive, the Blue Ridge and Natchez Trace Parkways, the Everglades, and Mammoth Cave. The "new" National Park Service was startling, but for real. I had homework to do to keep in step.

The French Creek Recreational Demonstration Area had been the beginning at Hopewell. This was Resettlement Administrative submarginal land. The Pennsylvania State Parks administered it, but meanwhile the National Park Service would assist in planning, financing, and construction of the extensive recreation facilities. At French Creek, this was hundreds of thousands of dollars and many years' work with professional staffing. It built Hopewell and Sixpenny Lakes, and it also developed recognition of the serendipity treasure that was Hopewell Furnace. The State of Pennsylvania agreed, and the Secretary issued the proclamation creating Hopewell Village National Historic Site on August 3, 1938.

This is where I came in.

The CCC Inspector, Emil Heinrich of Harrisburg (whom I met in Richmond) was the most competent supervisor in the outfit for CCC and ERA work. I depended on him to handle this, and things went well. He had excellent rapport with the regional office staff, the project supervisors, and the State. He knew the money management needs. He was responsive to policy requirements. We got the jobs done.

For Hopewell Village, I began to assemble the National Park Service reports and convert them into work programs. I established local contacts with the Berks County Historical Society and state officials. Previous planning called for an archeologist to be added to the staff in the first year. Money had been allocated for the position, and our man soon arrived. Fortunately, it turned out to be John Christian Fisher (Chris) Motz, who brought Harvard degrees in both archeology and architecture, plus a serenity and competence which were a delight.

My other task was to communicate with Superintendent Herb Kahler of Morristown, my direct supervisor as a Coordinating Superintendent, so we could move ahead together. Actually, we had no problem, but I wanted to know his ideas for Hopewell. Mel Weig on his staff had done the preliminary research on Hopewell and was a continuing, dependable resource.

After returning from Richmond, I looked up the early French Creek Citizens Advisory Committee. The chairman had been Mrs. Hazlett Hoopes of Reading, who still lived there. I got in touch with her and we talked about French Creek and Hopewell. She provided strong community support; she was a great civic leader. With her help I embarked on a series of National Park Service and Hopewell Village lectures during my first winter at Hopewell. I had color slides and presented a story of the great scenic National Parks of the West — I wore my full ranger uniform, including breeches and boots, to make it completely authentic. I also spoke of the great places of American history which the National Park Service managed. I ended with one of these places of history the government was preserving, Hopewell Village in Berks County, and told how we planned to do it. It was a simple tale, but highly successful. I gave thirty-seven lectures on this subject between mid-January and the beginning of June. I tried to give us an identity — I spoke to service clubs, schools, churches, garden clubs, women's clubs, anyone who would listen. I think we made a few converts. At least there was a sizable group aware of the role of the National Park Service in this community beyond the activities of the CCC Camp!

On May 9, 1940, I hosted an open house for Hopewell, inviting the local citizenry to come out and see what we were doing in both the recreation and historic fields. Captain William Cooper, in charge of the CCC Camp, was eager to take part in this. He arranged a great turkey dinner at the CCC mess hall. I arranged a schedule of events and places to see, and Connie Wirth, Assistant Director of the National Park Service, agreed to speak. We had music, campfire singing, endless food, and fun.

I had labeled the event as simply "A Community Leaders Day — An Open House at Hopewell Village." We sent special invitations to about five hundred political office holders, bureaucrats, businessmen, scholars, and teachers. About two hundred of them accepted. With Mrs. Hoopes' help we got our names in the papers! (I used this "Community Leaders" theme again on other occasions.)

For Ranger Garrison, Hopewell was a great lesson in political focus, and how it was viewed locally. I have already discussed Secretary Ickes direct role in my selection. Six months later, Undersecretary Elbert K. Burlew made a point of calling on me for a brief visit — ("How was I getting along?" "I loved it!" "Great! — Goodbye!"). In spite of all the grumbling about Harold Ickes, he was an honest and courageous fellow, and he stood behind his men. He had gotten me into this. He was just checking up. George Clouser, one of my CCC Camp foremen, was a member of the Berks County Central Democratic Committee. To his surprise, he liked me! We had a fire school and he found that I really knew what I was doing. He told me one morning that his committee chairman was determined to get me fired and have my "big ranger hat nailed up on the horse barn" but it did not happen. Then one Sunday morning George and the chairman called on me at home to "bury the hatchet" and otherwise get things back under control. In their political machine, all patronage jobs had a price. My job was worth $100. If I would pay this, all would be forgiven and the war over.

I was astounded! I explained that the newly passed Hatch Act prohibited my paying for a job! And I was certain that the Hatch Act also established penalties for those who solicited money as the price of a job. I believed that it was a felony. I would look it up and let them know. George promised to call me again. I didn't look it up; he didn't pursue it further. I was secure again, but he had one request that I thought was a great idea, although I did not handle it exactly as he had envisioned. There was to be an election very soon, and I was expected to get the E.R.A. troops registered — hopefully as Democrats. I was to be certain that they had job time to vote. I was to advise them who their "friends" were in this uncertain period.

My response was hearty. I called a "safety meeting" for the entire crew of E.R.A. workers the next Monday morning at eight o'clock. All three hundred of them assembled in the work yard and I climbed into the back of a dump truck to address them. In my speech I made three points: "*One*. There is an election next week. It is your right of franchise that makes America great. Use it! Get registered. *Two*. You will have two hours off to vote. Take it any time of the day you wish, but get there and VOTE! *Three*. When you are in that voting booth there is no hand on your shoulder, and no one telling you how to vote. If I were there I would just tell you, 'Vote, Damn it! Anyway you want. Just Vote. Let's use this franchise.' "

We then had our safety meeting. This was the end of my direct political involvement on the local level, for National Parks or Historic Places. My original decision to be non-partisan and apolitical was the only one that could have worked for me. Today we speak of "political realities." We mean direct confrontation, such as I experienced at Hopewell. We also mean that those of us who work for an agency have an advocate job to do. We have an obligation to be faithful to our park preservation trusts and to the Congress and the citizens who worked to establish it. At the same time, we must be honest with users and politicians about our judgments and decisions. We cannot always win, but we can keep our own integrity and honor.

This was my first major lesson from Hopewell. The second major part of my training at Hopewell was learning the great lessons of history in America. This began with an attitude of appreciation and respect. Pride in ancestry is a normal attribute. I have long observed that civic interest in community history is in direct ratio to the size of the city cemetery. If it is an old town with a large cemetery, many citizens have ancestral ties to the community, and historic values are appreciated.

CHAPTER XI

THE HOPEWELL LOVE AFFAIR

I LIKED HOPEWELL BECAUSE OF ITS HONESTY. The men there had taken raw earthen materials and built part of America. They had made their own lumber with whipsaws in saw pits. They had cultivated family gardens and ground their own meal. Each working family in the tiny industrial plantation had kept its own cows, chickens, garden, and flower beds. There had been a school and a church. The housewife's part of the furnace record book might record credit for occasional sale of eggs, butter, woven or knit cloth, and purchases of simple things like salt or sugar or spices. When the furnace page for A. Lincoln (Abraham Lincoln's grandfather, who had worked at Hopewell and had lived nearby) was turned, it revealed barter and self-sufficient living. The miner, the "Collyear," the school mater, or the housewife had contributed to the American way of life which grew here. One thing had been sold in the great markets — iron or iron products. Tradition has it that because Hopewell's chilled steel took a smooth face that was long prized in making wheels for railroad cars, these cold-blast charcoal-burning furnaces persisted for decades beyond their normal obsolescence.

Inger enjoyed it all with me. We became craftsmen in our minds, and through our appreciation of the grooved stone base for the lye barrel, the peel for the bake oven, the whorled glass for the six- and nine-pane windows. We loved the homespun coverlet, the honest glazed red pieplate or butter crock, or the lovely majolica jug. Our own dining room now displays a cherry gateleg, arrow-back and half-spindle-back chairs, and a cherry sideboard. It sounds unreal, but our conversion to antiques, at that time was because prison-made rug runners were cheap. And the cherry gateleg table cost less than a conventional one. That was the market in 1939 and 1940.

We had read carefully the history of the Iron Master's house at Hopewell. We knew the dates of the Bird and then the Brookes families. We had seen the records of 1770, and of the general remodeling about 1800, and that of the bathroom about 1860. One Sunday afternoon, much to our delight, Chris Motz, Inger, and I conducted Dr. Fitze Kimball, art historian from Philadelphia, through the Great House, and like an open book he read the historic dates of the house in the wood turnings, the hardware, the moldings, the glass, the degree of wear on drawer runners, the kinds of wood, and the furnishings. It was a fun experience for him — for us a heartwarming love story, as he revealed through his discerning eye the tales of design and beauty of the people who had lived there.

As I tell my story now, it is difficult to leave Hopewell. It clings and warms and refreshes in my memory and in the few personal symbols we have which recall it.

I was asked by the Masonic Lodge of Coatesville, George Washington's one-time "Masonic home," to give a talk on Hopewell. This was after I developed my love affair with the place. I was honored to recount in that place some of the beauties I saw in Hopewell. The brethren were most attentive, and, when I departed after the Lodge was closed, the Master slipped an envelope into my hand. "An Honorarium — a gift for you to do with as you please. May it bring you good fortune!" It was a $20 bill.

I called on my friend the antique dealer, Walter Wittman, and related my search for a charcoal wagon of the 1780 period.

The original Hopewell Furnace land holdings of William and Mark Bird and the Brookes Family were about 6,000 acres. On a thirty-year cutting cycle they would "coal" about two hundred acres a year. The collyers — or colliers — or coalers — would cut the wood into four-foot billets. These were later stacked for burning in a fifteen-foot conical pile called a "pit." The entire pit was covered tightly with earth and a center flue-hole was ignited. The smoldering fire would eat out into the covered ricks of hardwood. The settling of earth in the dirt cover was patched by the collyer. He would open and control draft holes. He had a broad, flat pair of wooden slab shoes with toe straps for climbing to the top of the pit. He could not stay long in any one place, but he kept the fire directed into the unburned portions and then smothered it at the proper time so that it did not reignite the charcoal and burn it up. This process took about ten days.

Teams of horses would then bring in a charcoal wagon to load up the new fuel. It was a high-wheeled, narrow-tired wagon with dump board floor slats for unloading. The sides were flared to reduce the pressure on the friable fuel. Sometimes an eager collier or teamster would load live coals — these could then ignite the wagon load and ultimately the whole wagon. One celebrated driver at Hopewell, after a tavern stop, was reputed to have let a fire in his wagon get such a big start in the floor boards that he could not dump it, which was the usual cure. Instead, he whipped up the horses and set two miles of forest on fire enroute to French Creek one fall day!

The "coal" would be unloaded at the charcoal shed, a great stonewalled building near the furnace. It was then transferred to wheelbarrow-like carts, with a small amount of limestone for flux, and dumped into the furnace.

Various local wagon makers had made charcoal wagons. In 1940, when Chris Motz and I searched, we could not find one wagon, even in museum collections of farm equipment. We found a wagon maker north of Reading with a family wagon works still in business. He mainly repaired buggies and farm equipment for the Amish, but in his desk he found the 1840 sketches from which his predecessors had built such charcoal wagons. For $800 he would build one for us.

We did not have $800, but it was intriguing to contemplate! We kept on looking, and on a chance visit to Principio Furnace at the head of Delaware Bay, we found one. This was a pre-revolutionary furnace, and one of the founding owners had been Augustine Washington, George Washington's father.

In 1940 it was owned by a Wheeling, West Virginia iron company which was farming the furnace lands. The charcoal wagon bed with thin rolled sheet-iron sides had been stored in an unused stone barn with a metal roof for over one hundred years. It was in excellent condition. The running gears had recently been put to use on a hay wagon. The narrow tires and high wheels made it an ideal unit for hauling hay through stumps in a hay meadow. It was completely authentic down to the linch pin wagon wheels.

"Yes, you can have it for Hopewell," said the manager, "but I need the hayrack outfit. Can you replace the running gears?"

This is the problem I took to Walt Wittman. Walt often generously took me to the farm sales held on the neighboring farms. "I have twenty dollars from the Coatesville Lodge," I told him. "How expensive is a wagon?"

"I'll price them," he said.

That Saturday evening he telephoned me, and his clipped, brusque diction said, "Mr. Garrison, I got your wagon!"

"Wow! How much is it?"

"To you it is twenty dollars."

I never knew how much it cost him. He often shared specialties with me, like the hand-made drill bits I was seeking for the Hopewell blacksmith shop. Usually, they were casual parts of a "lot" he might have purchased for anywhere between five cents and fifty cents. I felt certain that at twenty dollars our wagon was a "bargain!" We drove out about three miles to look at it.

He had acquired a real prairie schooner freight wagon from an old Amish farmstead. It looked just like the type which the Studebaker Wagon Company patented and made famous before 1900. It was complete with the sway-sided bed, double tree, two single trees, linch-pin axles, tool box on one side, and a leather tar bucket hung under the rear axle. It was a museum piece by itself, but I had one thing in mind — I needed a charcoal wagon for Hopewell Village. Thanks to the Coatesville Lodge and Walt Wittman we now had trading stock in this Conestoga schooner. I got our Hopewell W.P.A. crew to drive over and haul the Conestoga home. Then Lawrence Kayzor, our genius blacksmith, went to work on it. He set the tires, tightened all of the iron parts, replaced a broken slat, and then painted it a glorious wagoncart red! It was a shame to hide it that way but I still wanted a charcoal wagon. Now I was ready to trade. I wrote to the Wheeling Iron Company manager at Principio. His family home was at Elverson, near Hopewell. He drove over to look at the wagon and wrote that he was content with the exchange. So I sent another crew down to Principio with the new red running gears — I kept the schooner-type bed for trading stock for Hopewell — and we made the exchange.

Kayzor then worked over the original, but I would not let him paint it. It was a beauty sitting there on our charcoal shed dirt floor!

Lawrence Kayzor had learned his trade as an apprentice blacksmith while a youth in Hungary. His five-year term ended with the construction of a full set of blacksmith tools—tongs, hammers, flatters, punches, cutters — which then became his graduation gift.

He could build anything you could hand-weld. His ancient log-weighted drill press and clumsy steel brace were polished jewels. The hand-made bits were scaled, marked, and sharpened. He had rebuilt our ancient leather blacksmith bellows. He confessed that as a student he had been vigorously whaled by his master because he tinkered with the shop bellows and succeeded in getting it to suck in smoke and thereby burned a hole in it. His training thus included construction of a new set of bellows. Fifty years later, he took me with him as he inspected and selected sheepskins for our bellows.

They must be tight and even and smooth. He insisted that the leather be stitched and double-stitched entirely with an awl, a bristle, and waxed thread — a needle would double the size of each hole, leaving a string of pinhole leaks which made for an inefficient bellows.

At his little shop at home he carefully selected drill steel stock to make me a full set of cold chisels, angles, and punches. I still use these occasionally with a warm memory of a great artisan.

As you must surmise, Hopewell Village, with its charm, historic integrity, humanity, and completeness, was as much a "grabber" as Yosemite or Sequoia had been in the natural history field. In the two years I was there I also became acquainted with the Abraham Lincoln ancestral home near Reading. I later selected a small box of acorns from the family yard to send to Superintendent Al Banton at the Lincoln Boyhood Home Site in Indiana. Al is a professional historian, but he turned out to be similarly enthralled by the tales and legends of the human side of our historic treasures. Professional historians often jeered; we were characterized as infatuated with legends rather than statistics and historic facts, but park visitors did not complain. I never learned if the Indiana acorns grew. But it appealed to my sense of fitness to move germ plasm over three generations from Hopewell and an earlier Abraham Lincoln, to Dale, Indiana, and finally to Tom Lincoln's boyhood home of America's Abraham Lincoln. For "Abe" had shared the pioneer farm life until he was twenty-one and had moved to Illinois.

Our E.R.A. work program became mixed in with W.P.A. — the Work Progress Administration — and I hired a stone mason named

Daniel Boone, whose ancestral home was also in Berks County, near Reading. Here I had a confrontation with bureaucratic technicalities.

Our Daniel Boone had no birth certificate. He was unquestionably of early American ancestry, but it was almost a year later that the W.P.A. watchdogs accepted Dan's U.S. Army recruitment and discharge record as proof of citizenship! We had a lot of scholarly and political interveners in that one. This type of monstrous insensitivity provokes a fighting response in me.

We replanted portions of the historic Hopewell flower garden at the Iron Master's house. We received tremendous assistance from the University of Pennsylvania horticulturalists who, even in 1940, were concerned about preserving a "gene pool" — the true species of historic flowers, trees, shrubs, and vegetables. Fortunately, we were able to use their services. They grafted from our ancient and gnarled fruit trees in the orchard to restore the pattern of the family orchard. Nearly thirty years later, we used the same procedure to restore the historic farm crops — like yellow dent flint corn — for the Tom Lincoln farm in Dale, Indiana.

Hopewell had been a forge from 1743, and became a furnace in 1772. The Bird family controlled it until the mid-1780s when Mark Bird's patriotic loans to the new United States government were not repaid in the "milled coins" he had specifically pledged, and others, ending with the Brookes family, took control. The furnace finally closed about a century later. The Brookes chain of ownership remained from 1800 until the Resettlement Administration purchased it in the early 1930s.

In 1940, I learned that the Brookes family (who still had considerable holdings, including another Iron Master's-type house in Birdsboro) were offering to sell some of the original Hopewell Great House furnishings. Fortuitously, ninety-year-old "Nanny" Care, an ancient family retainer, was still available. She had been a maid in the Hopewell Iron Master's house in the 1880 s, and had a sharp memory for identification of the furniture and where it was used in the home. It had apparently been a summer residence for the Philadelphia family.

There were two lines of Brookes ancestry. The maid had been with the Hopewell branch. She examined the two households of period furniture stored in the barn and the mansion in Birdsboro. She spent hours with our archeologist, Chris Motz, selecting the pieces she remembered. There were four-poster beds, occasional tables, a dining room set of twelve cathedral-back chairs, gold-framed portraits of the Brookes family, a sewing stand, a night stand, rosewood sofas, wardrobes, and the grand piano which was still at Hopewell. Nanny recalled taking girlhood piano lessons on this great instrument.

There was also a set of nineteen horse-drawn carriages, including one with a ballbearing axle, a road coach, a sedan, a phaeton, a dog cart, a cutter, and an Irish jauntingcart. In addition, there were coachmen's uniforms and tally-ho horns, and many carefully maintained sets of harness. All of these treasures were from Hopewell, although admittedly some of the barnyard equipment was post-1880. Could we acquire them? In the spring of 1940, this select inventory was appraised for the magnificent sum of $2,900.

I called on Mr. Brookes, suggesting that the family might wish to donate this equipment as a Brookes Family Memorial, a permanent legacy of their Hopewell involvement. There was little humanity in Mr. Brookes that day. The furniture had been appraised. The carriages were a rather complete collection. For $2,900 we could have it with no strings attached. I asked if he desired to consider it and respond later. "No." His answer was final.

We didn't have $2,900, but our altruistic park archeologist, Chris Motz, had recently come into a small personal inheritance, and he bought the "lot" from the Brookes family. I made the commitment to Motz that it would all go to Hopewell as a permanent collection.

Herb Kahler, who had moved from Morristown and was now the Chief Historian of the National Park Service, had reminded me about what he called "year-end money." I had learned about year-end money at Yosemite. I even had about $100 at Hopewell. With about one hundred Park Service accounting offices, each one operating independently, each superintendent and chief clerk protected themselves against any accidental last minute overdrafts by deliberately holding back a little reserve — just in case you forgot something, or coal had gone up two dollars a ton, or you had to make emergency pump repairs. All of this penny-pinching in total amounted to several thousand dollars each year, and Herb Kahler suggested that I ask our Associate

Director, Arthur Demaray, if we could use this residual to pay Motz for the furniture.

With Herb's prodding, my importunate letters, and a bit more in the extras than had been anticipated, Arthur okayed my purchase order! In fact, he came to Hopewell and we looked it all over together! He was a knowledgeable artist, antiquarian and park manager, and he was enthused about the opportunity to have original furnishings for this great house.

The result was that soon after Chris formally donated the furniture, we paid him $2,900 and notified Mr. Brookes that the park now had full title to it. In the few weeks that Chris had owned it, he was able to find a neighbor who hitched up a team of horses to the road coach, and we took a trip to the Lloyd place, the 1797 Bethesda Baptist Church, and a few other delightful points. The kids — ours and Chris' daughter, Keela — all rode "shotgun" to help the driver. I had not harnessed a horse for many years. I had forgotten the hazards of roadside trees scraping a carriage top! I doubted that I would like to ride it to Philadelphia (which the Brookes family had done periodically). The tires were loose, and we didn't want to have to ask Kayzor to rescue us!

I called Morristown one day to ask the Chief Clerk, Bill Coles, about writing a purchase order for some needed supplies. I had never written a purchase order, but I had $2,500 for Hopewell supplies. I needed to get busy. "Are there any items that are mandatory somewhere?" I asked Bill. "None that are apt to bother you," he replied. So purchase Order Number One of my career was for one dozen whisk brooms for Chris Motz to use for his archeological work. They were seventy-five cents apiece. I bought them from Stichter Hardware in Reading.

The phone rang the next morning. It was Bill Coles at Morristown. He had gotten a copy of my purchase order.

"Sorry Lon, brooms are mandatory from the industries for the blind. I can't pay for them." It was no use arguing. I went out to the spring house. "Chris, how many whisk brooms do you have left?" He had used four. So we drove back to Stichter Hardware in Reading and returned eight whiskbrooms for credit. I paid three dollars cash for my initiation — and the incident was over except for a certain amount of conditioning about chief clerks! I soon learned to protect myself in this kind of situation. I just hadn't taken the time to read my own manuals. A $3 lesson was cheap!

I think some of my Hopewell lessons are important because they became my guidelines for management and maintenance of other historic places. The park staff recognized that honesty with park visitors and integrity in our standards and stories was rewarding.

I had a thing about pianos. In 1965, for example, when I became Regional Director located in Philadelphia, our historic properties in the Northeast Region included fourteen pianos. I do not have perfect pitch, but nonetheless at every site I visited which had a historic piano, I sat down and picked out a few bars of some simple melody. Did it sound right? When was the piano last tuned? I had a horror of a split sounding board, a strings bank filled with mouse collections. You had better believe it!

My other passion was clocks — all clocks — particularly grandfather clocks. They must be operational, on time, set regularly, kept clean and neat. I imagined a successor park official opening a well-polished clock case some day and finding the clock machinery as a pile of rust on the floor.

These two idiosyncracies were indicative of the level of maintenance I expected. I felt that all historic equipment should be kept to this level of excellence. This started in Hopewell in 1940.

One of my disappointments was that the water in the beautiful spring house, which splashed and flowed in rocky basins through the two half-cellar rooms, was a no-no by Public Health Service standards. We could only cool closed jars or cans. We never found the underground source of the pollution. We just could not use it.

Our outdoor bake oven was typical in appearance, but Chris had dug through the ash pit cleanout one day and discovered that the oven itself had an inner set of flue and draft channels which responded excellently to hot air circulation during baking. One of the service technicians with "expertise" in standardized military bake ovens was recruited to "repair" our Hopewell furnace. Chris and I got so riled over his attempts to rebuild "our" oven in "typical" style, thereby destroying the original hand work, that the expert went home in a great rage. We never got the oven rebuilt. In fact, it was difficult to get any of the historical technicians to do any work for us at all. But for us a "typical" bake oven would have been a travesty, when we actually had the real one, requiring only cleaning to be operable.

M. R. Tillotson, the Regional Director, talked to his staff about it. "You aren't going to do it your way," was Tilly's decision. "The superintendent's way isn't changing anything. Just leave it alone." That was a good guideline for an incipient Regional Director, although I was far from that level of dreaming about my future, and the oven worked well just like it was.

While at Yosemite I had begun writing for various outdoor magazines. The *Open Road for Boys* was a favorite target for my articles on campfire, cooking, skiing, use of the compass, and the weasel family. I was doing very well as strictly an amateur, but, I had concluded that I should retain my ranger job so I could write about it. I was now on the other side of the desk — I had few daily experiences which contributed to good outdoor writing. I wrote speeches both for myself and my boss.

One of the great women of the early National Park Service was Miss Isabel Story, who had been a "wheel-horse" worker with Mather and Albright in the 1916–1917 era. She was still with the National Park Service in 1940, with the title of Editor-in-Chief. She handled the National Park Service newsletter — an early house organ — the press releases, the photograph files and records, and the composition of policy letters or articles. It sounded like a fascinating job. She had spent some time with me in Yosemite so she knew me. She asked suddenly if I would be interested in becoming her assistant in Washington. This was the focal point of a lot of activity. Newton P. Drury was the Director of the National Park Service. Harold Ickes, the "Old Curmudgeon," was Secretary of the Interior. I use this title for him by preference, for I have a great admiration and respect for him. He was the Head Honcho — life could never be dull with him around.

Isabel took me in for an interview. He had said he wanted a ranger in this job. My part was mainly listening to a couple of grunts as she extolled my ability for the job. He wanted to talk about an Interior Department problem; he felt that she had gone off on a tangent. She was a quick-tempered lady and she had opinions too, mainly about the drones in the Interior Department office who could not recognize either news or policy. She felt they had fouled up by their erroneous political evaluations of Interior functions. People and the outdoors were Interior programs, and this meant the National Park Service should be getting more helpful attention. We could do him a hell of a job if he would just let us!

His secretary bounced in. He had a phone call from the White House. "Goodbye" not even "good luck." I have a thing about "good luck" as a salutation, anyway. It implies that you need it! Only by the most fortunate breaks can you make it, but I had no doubts. I could work with him if I could learn to work with Isabel. Her volume and flow of rhetoric had snowed the Old Man! He didn't have a chance to interrupt. Besides, this must have been a familiar tune. It gave me a guideline to Isabel's thinking, courage, and competence. Suddenly, I knew it could be very good duty to be her assistant! Besides, salary was clear up to G.S. 10! $3,200 a year.

I cannot leave Hopewell Village without one final report. Where did William Bird come from, and why did he name his forge and furnace Hopewell? There are many "Hopewell" communities in colonial America. This one is on French Creek near the Schuylkill River in Pennsylvania. What are its antecedents? To my surprise, Charlie Montgomery and I found out by a serendipity adventure that led us to the right fountain head in New Jersey by way of Indiana.

To a scientist, serendipity is a normal kind of opportunistic discovery of "values not sought," but you have found them anyway. I had had natural history experiences in this sense, such as the discovery of golden trout in Clover Creek in Sequoia, or the overwintering live mosquitoes in the snow bank in Yosemite, but I had not seen any reports of serendipity as a benefit to historians. I had had little opportunity to encounter it, but during my two years at Hopewell Village I suddenly found myself in the midst of a great event, which rose from several small events and ended with unusual new knowledge. I will tell you about it. We answered three big questions which had bothered Hopewell historians since the "village" was discovered. First, who was William Bird? Second, where did he come from? And third, why did he name his French Creek forge and furnace Hopewell?

Our discovery began when we issued a press release about Hopewell Village being open for visitors on August weekends in the summer of 1940. One Sunday afternoon, while we had a small group of visitors, one of our maintenance men asked me to look at the floor of the second story of the old furnace office building. This two-story, whitewashed field stone structure had developed a "soft" place in the floor boards right at the head of the stairway. One of the wide floor planks was obviously in trouble, so we closed the upstairs until we could investigate. This was serendipity point Number One.

The ceiling of the first floor was of pine board. So was the second-story floor. Obviously, the joists supporting the second floor were logs supported on sills, and one of the log joists had slipped out of place, loosening the floor board. The ceiling/floor combination was about fifteen inches thick, so a major repair job might be needed.

I was neither a historian nor an architect, but I recognized that the building and all its components, its furniture, its paint, even the tool marks on the wood were sacred property. To repair the floor we could not telephone the lumber yard and get a load of two-by-fours and have at it with a crowbar. I was fortunate in having Chris Motz as a staff assistant with both archeology and architecture degrees from Harvard University. We had often discussed the special challenge of historic building maintenance. So we proceeded very cautiously as we worked the bad end of the floor board loose. It was a whipsawed board about twelve inches wide, fastened with a combination of nails — some were the old "L" head stamped nails, a few were the older up-set-head nails, and there were several of the more modern cut nails which Chris had determined had come into use in Berks County about 1782. So the construction date was obviously after 1782.

It was also obvious that a shim used to level the supporting joist had worked aside. Our increased foot traffic had just moved things around. This was easily corrected, but Chris was an inquisitive soul and he was puzzled by several bits of paper in the void beside the joist. He retrieved several. They appeared to be mouse-chewed bits of record pages dealing with early furnace operations. By judicious probing, we then discovered that the entire space between the log joists was stuffed with furnace records, all near the date of 1785. This was fascinating stuff! Serendipity point Number Two.

I notified our regional office in Richmond. I also called to report it to the curator of the Berks County Historical Society at Reading,

Pennsylvania. He was interested, but he wanted Chris and me to meet Mr. Charles Montgomery, who happened to be with him in his office that day. This was my third serendipity point, but I didn't know it yet.

Mr. Charles Montgomery had been the curator of the Berks County Historical Society until failing eyesight had recently forced his retirement. He was greatly intrigued by our discovery. He was working part-time on Hopewell Furnace books in various Pennsylvania historical archives in Philadelphia. Could he come to Hopewell and catalog our find? We soon knew him as Charlie Montgomery.

By chance I next met Mr. Walter Streeper, the director of the Berks County WPA program. We had about three hundred WPA workers on the Hopewell Recreational Area jobs for the State of Pennsylvania. I asked Mr. Streeper hopefully if there were any way I could hire professional help to further our furnace research and get it typed. I learned that the WPA did have a supplemental phase of work for planning and research. For every one hundred WPA workers, I could have one researcher for twenty hours a week at ninety cents per hour, which was far above the subsistence scale. We soon completed our formalities so I could seek this kind of professional assistance.

Further conversation with Charlie Montgomery established that his eye sight was adequate for this kind of part-time work. He was bored. He wanted a job. The wage rate was satisfactory. He had transportation. I could hire a typist to transcribe his notes. It was a dream world for both of us. This, then, was serendipity point Number Three. I hired Charles Montgomery.

He did not work at the Hopewell Furnace office which, incidentally, was in the old barn. He worked in various depositories and libraries, and turned his time sheets and his notes over to me. We realized that twenty hours a week was all we could pay for, but we were eager and for the first week we reported honestly on his actual time — about thirty-five hours. This was not only an error, it was illegal. I could get fired quickly for working Charlie in excess of the approved twenty hours. I was taking advantage of his poverty. The WPA bookkeepers had a field day.

Streeper came to my rescue. We retrieved all copies of Charlie's "erroneously-prepared" time slips and redid them showing exactly twenty hours of duty time. Some way his first exploratory set of time sheets vanished from my desk. Charlie Montgomery and I were both back in good order. Point Number Four.

This kind of serendipity adventure was rewarding! We were getting the job done to bulwark future restoration and operating plans. It was great, but it was just beginning. The big break, point Number Five, came when Charlie arrived one Friday afternoon with a letter from a friend in the Historical Society in Sandusky, Ohio. For many years, Charlie had been a valued member of the American Association for State and Local History. In fact, Charlie had been an officer. The Association was having a drive to establish all possible information about the contributions of Polish immigrants to the settlement and growth of the United States. This was one of the early programs in ethnic awareness of American immigrants.

One of the prized examples of Polish enrichment of American life was in Mr. Anthony Sedowski. He was a Polish immigrant peddler who had been centered in Harrisburg, but had become a friend of Mark Bird at Hopewell Furnace. In fact, Sedowski had married Mark Bird's sister, Marie, before moving west to Ohio to found the settlement later Anglicised as Sandusky. Charlie Montgomery had told me about it.

The inquiry from Sandusky introduced a new aspect of the picture which led to a new uncertainty. In completing his vital statistics, Sedowski had stated that he had indeed been married at Hopewell Furnace, but to a Miss Maria du Bort who had been born at Raritan, New Jersey. The full records would be found in the local church. Could Charlie Montgomery elucidate on this, or better yet travel to Raritan, New Jersey and get a record for the Sandusky historian?

Charlie and I read and reread the letter. There was no question about our willingness to respond. I squeezed the Furnace accounts and got fifteen dollars for travel expenses for Charlie. But he could not go until Monday. This was still an active house of worship, and the records would not be available over the weekend. They were all in Dutch, and the pastor would be needed to translate them.

The suspense was terrible! Who was William Bird? He was an enigma. There was no information about him in the early records. One author, recognizing that most iron masters were English, had described William Bird as "A rosy-cheeked Englishman," but this was without historical support. Had all the researchers been looking in the wrong places?

We could hardly wait! Charlie left early and returned joyously the same day. He revealed that the Bird name was indeed a mispronunciation of du Bort. The entire Bird family, as we had known it, was faithfully recorded in the Raritan Church archives as du Bort. This was my final serendipity landmark.

It is the story of one day in America, and I have contributed to one footnote on one page of Pennsylvania history because of the Polish–American search for roots in early America, particularly in Sandusky, Ohio.

This is serendipity. For nearly forty years I have had a love affair with American history. It is a great experience, full of serendipity.

CHAPTER XII

WASHINGTON-GLACIER AND THE WAR YEARS

WE LEFT HOPEWELL IN SEPTEMBER 1941. This was our first move by van. A Reading trucker offered to move us for one hundred dollars. I looked at the options in taking bids, the red tape, and the problems of railroad shipments, and I asked him if he could accept $99.99 to keep it under the open-market limitation of $100. He could; he was careful in packing and handling the furniture, and we left Hopewell for Washington.

I have made it a rule that when I leave a place I do not try to run it by long distance. The new man would have his chance, just as I had had mine. We did visit Hopewell as often as we could, however, because we loved the environs and the people. It was here that I had established my measures for public relations, for the integrity of resource management, the relevance of interpretation, and the quality of goals. I bemused myself that these would not be retroactive only to Hopewell. They would guide me on my next assignment!

Isabel Story wanted me to make a quick tour of the Southeastern parks. It was a beautiful three weeks — Yorktown, Jamestown, Fort Fredrica, Kings Mountain, St. Augustine, Santa Rosa Island, Talahassee, Mobile, New Orleans, Natchez, and Vicksburg. All great historic shrines. Inger and I "lived off the land," trying native foods, and I returned with a gallon of sorghum, a bushel of apples, a jar of honey, a twist of tobacco, sweet potatoes, pralines, books, and, from the Great Smokies' Pi Phi shop, two children's rockers. I also have a sad memory of the taste of Blue Ridge homemade white mule whiskey!

I was delighted with the French Quarter of New Orleans, the Great Smoky Mountains, the Blue Ridge and Natchez Trace Parkways, and Natchez under the Hill. The NPS staff were continuously helpful and outgoing. I was proud that the parks attracted and kept quality managers.

My first job in Washington was to pitch into the photograph file.
A problem in values immediately developed. We had a tremendous
scenic photographic file, much of it historic in content. We had constant requests for pictures, mostly for publication or for teaching. The
Interior Department photo section was determined to lump ours with
all the construction-level photo files from Reclamation, Mines, Lands,
and Power. They seldom had interpretive and artistic photographers,
and the Park Service conversely had consistently retained outstanding
craftsmen such as George Grant. Should we give in? I joined Isabel
in composing a response. We pointed out our specific need for pictures
and interpretive services, and the time and knowledge that went into
our program.

On December 7, 1941, this all became academic. By chance we
had our radio turned on and listened to the Pearl Harbor news. Sleep
was troubled that night! The marble halls of the Interior Building
were unreal on Monday morning. So many things were going on as
usual — could Washington be sabotaged? What could I do? I applied
for Navy OCS, only to be informed that at age thirty-nine I was too
old. "You understand that you're a good old man, but you're too
damn old for us."

There was a controversy about parks. A few politicians suggested
that we ought to close them all! They took up valuable government
time, land, and Washington office space. At least, what programs
could the National Park Service reduce or eliminate? I was the last
man who had moved into the Washington office. Could I be the first
one out? I made it!!

I served a one hundred-hour training period with the Washington, D.C. fire department, and became a volunteer fireman for building fires. I stood regular watches three or four nights a week. I conducted special building fire training schools for the National Park
Service in Georgia and in Pennsylvania. I worked springtime fires
along the Blue Ridge Parkway. We had two fire seasons: the first, as
the snow melted and exposed the residual of last summer's vegetation;
the second, in early fall, as another crop of grass and weeds ripened.

I wrote the 1941 park travel report. I wrote press releases about
parks' wartime recreation uses, primarily for military recreation. I
wrote the last issue of a National Park Service newsletter. I wrote

articles for now-defunct encyclopedias — Colliers, and Funk and Wagnalls. These carried Director Newton Drury's name. I had known
him when he was on the Yosemite National Park Advisory Board. He
was a courageous leader in protecting park lands. He opposed raids
against spruce forests in northwestern parks. (This wood was wanted
for airplane construction.) Spruce was plentiful elsewhere. He opposed opening the parks to grazing; he defended them against mining
and prospecting. He was in the true mold of Mather and Albright.
But he was politically unpopular with the Secretary of the Interior,
Harold Ickes.

By that time it was obvious that the park office was to be moved to
Chicago. Meanwhile, Ray Vincent, the Assistant Superintendent at
Glacier National Park, had been recalled to active military duty as a
Captain in the Military Police. I was draft exempt and available.
Would I be interested in his job? It was a great kind of briar patch
in June of 1942! Anyone who looked around Glacier soon recognized
the destruction caused by past forest fires. I had a good fire fighting
background. I was a natural for the job.

Moving required a few wartime preliminaries. First, I had to get
gasoline stamps because fuel was rationed. Second, I had to get the
Buick off the blocks I had put under it six months earlier when I had
joined a car pool. Third, I had to get the car towed to an inspection
station so I could get an operating sticker on it. Fourth, I needed
extra tires. New ones were out of the question. We ended with a
pyramid of used tires on a cartop carrier. They were never needed,
but it was comforting to have them.

Our little clutch of three youngsters and Mr. and Mrs. Ranger
made a good travel group. We started in early June. In western
Nebraska we stopped to admire a small turtle which seemed lost in the
center of the road. It was so appealing that we put it in the back seat
with the kids and drove on. Suddenly a yell brought us to a halt again.
The turtle had a firm grip on Lars' drawing pencil — fortunately not
his finger! This was our first exposure to snapping turtles. The young
one was rapidly returned to its roadside habitat.

We crossed Marias Pass and drove down from the Continental
Divide to Belton in a driving snowstorm. Through the snowflakes we
had our first glimpse of this magnificent country of big mountains, big

sky, and lots of trees and water. It was a good whirling snowstorm, but it did not pile up and the road surface was clear. This was indicative of our weather. We were snowed on somewhere, somehow, in every month of our four Montana years.

I understood the park enthusiast who commented that if he had only one day to see one national park, he would select Bryce Canyon's brilliantly colored red and white columns; or he would go to Grand Teton's magnificent front range; but if he had a week he would want to spend it all in Glacier. It would take the entire week to become acquainted. You can't just off and look at it. Its mountains and forests and wildlife and lakes and rivers enfold you. It reaches people with its ineffable sense of wilderness and distance and belonging. It has many faces.

One afternoon from Matt Brill's guest ranch at Trail Creek, Glacier was the blue wall of the Continental Divide that excluded all the world except the pocket of trees and sunshine and dappled water as the North Fork of the Flathead River moved quietly beside me. On another day, Glacier was a herd of elk materializing in the drifting January snow at St. Mary ranger station as my midnight car lights swept suddenly across a bend in the road. Glacier was also Logan Pass and the neatly piled and tilted rock strata which are vertical or crossways, or even whorls of fossil algae in places. Mother Nature was neat in planning this scenery, but her housekeeping has been terrible. Glacier has a constant timberline of about 6,000 feet; a hard and brutal rock world above that elevation. Always in winter it held the hazard for humans of high wind, low temperature, and frequent snowfall.

It was a challenge. Could we accept and readapt to the natural controls of bleakness and raw nature? We had three youngsters now. After our Alaskan adventures, it really was not a frightening prospect. In fact, it was very comfortable. Our home at Belton, now West Glacier, became another time of enjoyment with work. This time the ranger was the Assistant Superintendent, practicing the broader aspects of conservation and management.

I had had a brief year in Washington, D.C., following my two enjoyable "school" years at Hopewell Village as the superintendent of a small gem of national history. I had tried to apply my natural park standards to the mix of American history and a recreation area serving primarily urban visitors. It had worked smoothly. Now I was back home — I was in Glacier.

This was a time of testing for the entire program of the National Parks. There were plenty of "practical" men and politicians who saw this as their opportunity to eliminate many parks altogether. They wanted to open the land for more mundane and traditional uses, like logging, mining, or grazing. However, support in the Congress and among park advocates was great enough that the National Park System remained on a solid basis for the war years. It was a time for holding the line, catching up on record-keeping, and for thinking.

I entered the job with eagerness. Park Superintendent Don Libbey welcomed me. Organizational structures were very flexible. Men were being drafted. We anticipated this and used our remaining people to fulfill several responsibilities at once. We gave high priority to park protection, mainly against forest fires. We put maintenance on a bare bones basis. We gave special attention to wildlife and to protection from poachers, particularly fur trappers, along the international boundary. This was a great expanse of uninhabited wilderness, and fortunately the fur market was low.

Visitor services, particularly interpretation programs, were deferred. We did only what the rangers could do — helped our few visitors. All our programs were strictly "maintenance-based," and there were no new jobs filled. As we might transfer a ranger into Glacier for a special job, we had to recognize that the organization that lost him to us would probably have a vacant position until the war was over. Which one of us needed him the most? Regional offices were faced with many Solomon-type judgments!

We hired women as seasonal rangers for the first time in Glacier. We found that it worked very well. An irritated visitor might respond belligerently to a brusque ranger, but not to a charming female with the ranger hat. Margaret Ness, wife of Assistant Chief Ranger Elmer Ness, was one of the first. She and her sister Julia Arthur, a school teacher from Great Falls, made two gracious and charming rangers.

We recruited sixteen-year-old kids, we put honeymoon couples on fire lookout, we rehired and retrained retired folks. Money was scarce in all accounts and limitations imposed on many functions. Gasoline supplies and tires were tightly controlled. Our long distance telephone allowance was twenty-five dollars a year. This was actually okay except during forest fires.

In early July 1942 we had a telephone call from a housewife in the park community at Apgar. A drunk had collapsed in her front yard. Could we do something about it? We would try.

Fire Chief Dick Nelson went up to investigate. The stranger seemed a reasonably articulate and able fellow except that he was a little confused. He had bought a bottle in Belton and then lost contact with Highway 2. Apparently he was trying to hitchhike to the west coast. This was no sin, as I remembered my own youth, but he was 4-F according to his draft card and unemployed. He had a normal complement of arms and legs. Maybe a fire lookout job for the summer could help him resolve his own uncertainties. He thought it might, and after he dried out a bit in our headquarters' bunkhouse, we sent him in to Belly River with an escort. We did not want him to get lost again. The lookout was forty miles from the nearest bar and that was in Canada.

Still headed for the west coast, he bid us goodbye in mid-September. He had done a good job; we used this kind of recruiting to get our work done.

Superintendent Don Libbey and I had many conferences about our priorities. We held maintenance and resource protection programs (such as forest fire control) to a high standard. What few visitors we had were usually military personnel with travel orders. Our office accounts, records, and reports were continued. Building and keeping high staff morale was another priority. Don and I both worked at it, but it was my special task to keep it moving. Our park headquarters staff at Belton was about thirty-five people, fluctuating with the military demands. This was beyond our control and we accepted it readily.

Our park headquarters community was two miles from Belton and its general store, service station, and school. It was thirty-five miles from either Kalispell or Whitefish where doctors, druggists, movie theaters, clothing, and specialty stores were available. Because gasoline was rationed closely, evenings in Kalispell or Whitefish were rare and then usually combined with trips for many other purposes. Amenities such as piano lessons were particularly difficult. Tires were rationed, too, and new ones required special permits. Meat was rationed through "red" points, vegetables and fruit through "blue" point tokens.

The local Flathead County Ration Board consisted strictly of local citizens who were very conscientious and able in adjudicating their point allocations. It was a thankless task, and I thought they did it well. On the Curley Bear Mountain fire, our trucks used two months' tire ration for the entire county. The ranchers were unhappy, but somehow we all got tires. The Ration Board learned about deficit point financing, and they carried us with it. Fortunately, we did not have to face the same circumstances again!

The United States Forest Service devised a special fire lookout package of groceries. The cook book was based entirely on the ration issue of one-man, thirty-days. If a ranger or a fire lookout didn't eat all of the canned peaches the first day, he could survive the thirty days well-fed and with only a can of spinach left over. Nobody liked spinach very much.

This deluxe cuisine cost thirty dollars plus the cost of a small fresh food supplement, and it could be handled by payroll deductions so that a lookout could start eating the day he went to work. It took five days' work to pay for the grub, and our youthful work and fire crews loved it. It was a great adventure with exotic food such as canned butter, canned fruit, ham and bacon, and cans of Boston brown bread.

One enterprising young fellow signed up for a job and the thirty-dollar ration and then walked off the job with the groceries, the only time we got stuck. We became suspicious quickly!

I went elk hunting in the fall of 1943 with most of the community. I used a borrowed rifle. On the Flathead National Forest, thirty miles from the park up the Middle Fork of the Flathead River, I killed a fat elk cow. Butchered, packed-out, cut up into serving size packages, frozen and stored in a Kalispell locker plant, this was the equivalent of 3,000 red points — a real bonanza!

We butchered a whole pig we bought from a farmer, manufacturing a small supply of ham, bacon, lard, and sausage. We stored eggs in water glass.

Four of the women went on a foraging expedition one day and visited a large Flathead Valley farm with the single crop of seed peas.

The Flathead Valley soil was free from spores of blight, which normally necessitated an expensive sanitation process. Flathead Valley potatoes were in the same category. Many storage shed owners refused to admit "foreign buyers" who had visited other potato storage regions and might have blight spores on their shoes.

Our foraging team got permission from the owner of the fields to pick peas for home canning. The peas could not be sold because of seed pea contract pledges, but the "Pea Queen," as our gals labelled her, gladly shared the harvest. When I returned for dinner, we were up to our ears in pea shelling.

I had read of a new process in *Sunset Magazine*, so we optimistically prepared the peas for the washing machine wringer. First we dumped the gunny sacks full of green peapods into our bath tubs, washed them, and added all the ice cubes we could find to chill them. We then put the cold pea pods through the wringer one at a time. By holding a cold pod on edge, it would be sucked in and popped open. The peas would jump out behind the pod. The empty pods went on through and dropped into the tub. We formed a bed sheet into a tube for intercepting the flying peas, and in a surprisingly short time we had converted sixteen bushels of peapods into four buckets of green peas.

These community ventures were delightful. Usually, as with the pea shelling or the chicken cooking, one of us would cook hamburgers or hot dogs for the "crew."

The Glacier National Park staff had organized quite a successful employee union — The National Federation of Federal Employees. The social committee wanted to support a community social program, but our park plumber, Ray Conine, absolutely refused to belong to the union. He was vigorously and loudly opposed. He would not even take part in social events the union might sponsor. There might be others who felt the same way, so we followed the principle of creating the "greater ring" to include him. We revitalized the former Glacier National Park Social Club. Ray joined this one!

We called an employees' meeting, solicited ideas, and then supported the organization proposals by providing meeting space, lights, heat, and the like. We were in business. It was important that we create our own special program since our people could not reach outside the community for social life. We already had examples of incipient cabin fever. After working with people all day, you didn't necessarily want them for bridge partners that evening.

Our Social Club included all the park community from headquarters and the outposts. All were welcome, although those from the outposts could often not attend. We made it a point to keep them informed by telephone, and arranged special headquarters assignments for them. Our committee planned two social evenings a month in our great recreation hall — an abandoned dance hall which had been moved into headquarters and converted into a training center. (We didn't plan parties for the busy work months of July and August.) We included every family at headquarters in the leadership. The committee (and we were careful that it was a committee and not an administrative arm) arranged many kinds of events: dances, square dances, canasta, bridge, a "formal party" with old college tuxedos or rarely-used dark suits and long dresses, a white elephant card party, a "bad taste" party, a party of kids' games, a "backwards" party, a valentine party, and many more. It was all great fun. Our crew accepted the challenge, took part, and closed ranks in support of each other. They had superb morale.

The most successful part of any program was the refreshments. These were served at a cost of thirty-five cents. The "bad taste party" cooked corned beef and cabbage, carefully scorching enough to smell up the place. At the white elephant party, we carefully rewrapped a chamber pot that Gene Sullivan, our very practical joker, brought bundled in a newspaper. We converted it to a devastatingly huge parcel, and Gene chose it for his gift! This was a belly laugh for us all winter.

Inger and I combined a trip to Kalispell with a stop at a farmhouse where there often was ranch-style separator cream at thirty-five cents a quart. We made a huge batch of cream puffs which promptly vanished. We carefully filled one cream puff with a dill pickle, and another with a wad of absorbent cotton, both stuck shut with tooth picks and put on the serving tray. They disappeared with the others. We have never found out who got them. Someone reversed the joke by keeping quiet about it!

In early January we drove in caravan to a party with our east side crew at St. Marys. This was an eighty-mile drive in sub-zero temperatures, over the Continental Divide on U.S. Highway 2, to East Glacier and then to St. Marys. Those bunk house beds were comfortable, but golly, it was cold! A steak dinner, dancing, stunts, the East Siders kept it lively! We made a moonlight tour to see the elk in St. Mary's Valley before we drove home, returning with a warmth of feeling which continued to crackle across the Divide. We brought men in from outpost stations for temporary jobs at headquarters ("Bring your family!") to get them involved. In turn we sent headquarters people to the outposts to complete inventories, or for special studies.

We did not have religious services regularly, although occasionally a minister from Kalispell would hold Sunday afternoon services. On several occasions we knew of family illness or special hazards of military service. Dick Finch, our Chief Ranger's son, heroically landed a training plane after he had collided with a target kite. He broke one shoulder badly and was hospitalized. Miner and Callie McPherson's son was with an outfit publicized for special bravery and heavy losses in the Battle of the Bulge. A month later they learned that he had been transferred three days before the big action. All were lonely and concerned about family members away in the service. Frequently we would quietly pass the word that we would have a brief prayer session at the Community Hall, and without real leadership except our common plea to the Lord to protect our loved ones, a few families would gather, pray together, and return home comforted.

My job? Yes, I took the morale problem seriously. I worked at it. In many situations we learned more about our staff people than we were really interested in knowing, but I had learned to accept this as part of my job and to keep my mouth shut about it.

Our conveniences were primitive. Our "refrigerator" was a kerosene-burning Servel — we were delighted to have it! Electric outages were frequent; our standby equipment consisted of an Aladdin kerosene mantle lamp and Coleman lanterns. We had a gasoline iron, but we donated it to the military. Nurses were moving into areas without electricity, and these irons were excellent small sterilizers.

Our Servel always held frozen fish, a brace of ducks, or a frozen wild meat roast ready for any social situation. All of the men foraged in this way for their families. Wives and children joined in hunting, fishing, and berry picking.

All these activities brought back memories of my days on the trails in Sequoia fifteen years earlier. Now I was an assistant superintendent, overseeing many of these same tasks, and I loved it. For me the great charm and spell of Glacier lay in the flowers and forests, the wildlife, the valleys and passes, and the endless peaks of the Continental Divide. In their majesty, magnitude, dignity, serenity, force, and impassive beauty, I became enraptured by their spell. I purged my own emotions just by being in this overwhelming crush of grandeur. "The Glaciated Mountains," the geologists called them. "The Land of Shining Mountains," the Indians called them. I would stop atop a trail pass, or turn an abrupt corner on the highway and stop quietly. "Gee Whizz! Just look at that!" was my feeble and humble note. For I was at home among these mountains.

I enjoyed saddle trips again. One early October I joined Chief Ranger Elmer Fladmark and District Ranger Don Barnum for the drive to winter pasture. We would gather our west-side horse herd, trail it across the Divide to Many Glacier, and down to the Blackfeet Indian Reservation. Wives Margaret Fladmark and Grace Barnum, both experienced mountaineers, accompanied us. They were good company and able hands for camp chores and for controlling fractious horses.

We trailered our headquarters stock to Logging Ranger Station. We then took a side trip by truck to Polebridge Ranger Station and on to Kintla Lake to stock the cabin there. This beautiful lake — together with Middle Kintla Lake and Upper Kintla Lake above it — is tucked between the North Fork of the Flathead River and the Great Divide near the Canadian border. It is one of the loveliest places in Glacier.

We returned to Polebridge Ranger Station, collected the horses there, and rode down to Logging Ranger Station to join the herd. From here our route lay through a dream world. The long forest trail along Bowman Lake led into the Hole-in-the-Wall country. We continued to Brown's Pass, where, even in October, last winter's snow was still deep beside the trail. The last of the "spring" flowers were now covered by new snow. We were up near the Fifty Mountain region and the recently-abandoned high mountain camp. We dropped down to Goat Haunt at the head of Waterton Lake for an overnight.

Waterton Lake straddles the boarder between Canada and the United States. It is a great, long, cold finger of water, exceptional in clarity and reflective beauty, rimmed by towering cliffs, peaks, and mountains. Goat Haunt was the name given to a high mountain chalet on the east side of the lake, closed for the war years. The next day we rode up to Stoney Indian Pass and Stoney Indian Lake, down to Glenn's Lake and Crosley Lake, and stayed with ranger Joe Heims overnight at Belly River.

From Belly River we took the trail to Many Glacier, climbing along a small brawling stream which soon faded away entirely. The trail continued in a series of switchbacks to the foot of the rimrock above the narrow valley.

It began to snow and blow, and my great heavy-footed, fearless, and strong white horse, Eagle, led us through a blinding blizzard. Our ledge trail now filled with drifting and blowing snow. It even snowed straight up as the wind whooped and yelled and whirled around us and crammed our scarves, our earflaps, our collars, our noses, and eyebrows, and even our pants pockets with the sifting fine snowfall. Suddenly Eagle's lunging leveled out and he was traveling smoothly. I took a quick peek at his feet. I discovered that he was walking on top of the dry rock wall on the outer rim of the trail! I put him back into the snow, and we continued lunging, resting, breaking trail, shivering inside our snow cocoons as we were first suffocated and then plastered and painted with the whirling and freezing torrents.

Before noon we reached the rim rock of the canyon. We nosed up to the great double wooden doors that protect the north end of Ptarmigan Tunnel. The gate opened easily. Inside it was dark, quiet, and warm, but the daylight at the southern portal welcomed us, and Eagle, without hesitation, plunged into the darkness, and we soon stuck our noses out into the Many Glacier sunshine!

We eased on down into Many Glacier Valley, put the string into the corral, and filled the hay mangers. The next day, Elmer and Don would pull off the horseshoes and drive the horses on down to Noffsinger's Duck Lake Ranch for the winter.

The Fladmarks and the Barnums drove back to park headquarters. They had been splendid companions, constantly reminding me by their example that nobility and humility often go hand-in-hand, and that the true gentleman or lady is born with this easy grace. They were treasured friends. I had different priorities. I wanted to learn the country. Inger drove over from park headquarters. We moved into a small cabin for a few days. I kept Eagle and selected a more nimble, reliable horse for Inger, and we had a wonderful week as special tourists.

The kids were well taken care of — we telephoned them every night at Belton. It was a beautiful Indian Summer. The coyotes and their puppies saluted us and each other daily, the cold sun brightened the shorter days, and the pesky mosquitoes were frozen in for the winter. We studied the mountain geography in detail.

We visited Elizabeth Pass, the fire lookout, and Granite Park Chalet, the seasonally-closed mountain tourist camp. We rode the short trail along Swift Current Lake to Josephine Lake. (We later offered special jeep transportation here for Secretary Ickes, which was the wrong thing to do. "Is the road open to the public?" he asked. The answer was "No." "Then I won't use it either," he said, and he didn't.) We saw Iceberg Lake, and went part way to Siyeh Pass. I tried pike fishing at Sherbourn Reservoir, but the howling wind always blew my lures back into the sagebrush behind me.

The Many Glacier Hotel was impressive even when closed. In season, the famous long hitchrack on the first bench behind the hotel often had thirty or forty horses tethered, ready for excursions. But as visitors climbed the steps to reach them, the first glimpse was of a long row of horses' asses silhouetted against the blue sky.

We saw no bears, but many mountain goats. These solemn relatives of the European chamois travel the mountain sides with ease, investigating and chewing anything that might have salt on it, like a saddle cinch or a sweat-stained pair of leather gloves. Saddles unprotected from them would be ruined, leaving a ranger afoot, bareback at a high mountain stop-over.

I might comment here that porcupines have this same craving for salt. They will chew up sweated axe handles or sweat-stained clothing, particularly men's shorts. They also have a proclivity to chew the front of pit toilets as men have urinated from a seated position. A porky can chew a great hole through this board, and an incautious user will not realize his predicament until he seats himself and very quietly pees through the hole and into his own shoes.

A highly nutritious bunch grass grows here in the big snow country, but because of the wind and the intense cold — it never gets *above* freezing — the dry, cold snowfall never freezes and consolidates. It is always drifting and on the move, as the wind restlessly and relentlessly boosts it along. Grazing stock, such as buffalo or horses, learn to follow the drifting snow, grazing the clumps of bunch grass as it is periodically exposed. It seems a cruel way to winterfeed saddle horses, but experience has shown that it is highly successful. Unless there is a chinook. A chinook is simply one or two days of warm wind or rain. It is pleasant as it persists, but as soon as barometric pressures adjust and it turns cold again, the wet snow instantly freezes and creates an ice coating over everything. Days pass before the ice releases its grip and the dry snow starts to move again. A chinook is very destructive for wildlife and grazing horses.

During my four years at Glacier the park concessions, of course, were strictly on a wartime maintenance basis. A few accommodations were available, but travel was mighty light. The Glacier Park Hotel Company, owned by the Great Northern Railroad, maintained tourist rooms and modified meal service at key points. Gasoline was available, but only critically needed repairs were performed. The company lost money, but they protected their franchise, and after the war they readily reopened.

The same was true of the Glacier National Park Transportation Company, owned by Howard Hayes, a national park concessioner who had started his business in Yellowstone twenty years earlier. The Blackfeet Indians had named Howard an honorary member of the tribe with the title of Many Sorrel Horses, in honor of the fleet of red White Motor Company 1916 and 1936 model busses he operated for tourists. His vehicles were older after the war; he had sold some, but the others were still usable, and his operation continued. In 1979 these sturdy "Sorrel Horses" continued to serve the same purpose.

The Glacier National Park Boat Company also curtailed service, but maintained its boats and docks. Arthur Burch, the owner, was ready to continue when the war ended.

Wartime was a disaster for the Glacier National Park Saddle Horse Company, however. With nearly one thousand miles of park trails and about twelve hundred horses, Glacier was famed as a trail park. In the six-year period between the establishment of the park in 1910 and the creation of the National Park Service in 1916, the saddle horse business had become lucrative and highly competitive. Several of the East Glacier saddlehorse liveries would send romantically-attired cowboys to Chicago to ride the Great Northern passenger trains west to Glacier. The colorful costumes, tales of adventure, and a handy guitar would entrance the tourists. They often arrived at Glacier Park Station committed to tours with these roving salesmen.

But there was vigorous competition which was harmful to good public service. A rival company's guide might follow departing groups to stampede their horses at night. The first night on Mount Henry was often favored for such fun and games. Then the Park Service established the Glacier National Park Saddle Horse Company. It was awarded an exclusive franchise for all operations originating in the park and using the park trails. William Noffsinger and his son George became the operators, which not unexpectedly resulted in antagonism among the other companies, but it resulted in improved service. This company was operating in 1942 when I arrived.

The year 1941 had been a fairly good one, but because of the war, 1942 was a total loss, and the prognosis was not favorable. Noffsinger wanted to liquidate, and the Park Service agreed. Superintendent Don Libbey and I drove to Duck Lake, Noffsinger's winter home near Babb, and after some discussion and consultation with lawyers, we all witnessed the agreement that "deferred" the operations of the Glacier National Park Saddle Horse Company.

It was a sad event. In spite of our hopes, we knew that there was no probability of ever renewing such an operation. The store of cookstoves, tents, tables, chairs, and kitchen equipment at the high mountain camps was worth practically nothing. Noffsinger's twelve hundred head of horses were getting older each year.

But a saddlehorse concession always has people interested in running it. They never have quite enough money to buy it, equip it, and hire the help, but it still is inviting. The post-war successors to Noffsinger fragmented the spread into small concessions at separate locations. This was the best the park could come up with. So 1942 had marked the end of an era — a bold, colorful, and human era, but its time had passed. I regretted it.

The war years changed the way we looked at concessions. It also changed the way we looked at forest fire. The quantum leap that opened the door to recognizing natural fires as a necessary part of the natural resource management process had not yet occurred, but we mechanized a lot of the standard way of doing things and increased our efficiency. Calculators became a fire fighting tool!

I knew the techniques of forest fire management, of course. Fire lookouts were the equivalent of the old Casey Jones speeder I had used nearly twenty years earlier along the Alaska Railroad. It had been a portable fire lookout! Now the foresters and statisticians were studying the effect of fire discovery-time and initial fire-control time.

We had sixteen fire lookouts in Glacier when I arrived in 1942. They were not all primary lookouts; some of them might be staffed only under special conditions of danger. The calculators now said that we could speed discovery and first-control time by converting to airplane patrols. I was the Glacier National Park officer chosen to travel to Missoula to arrange a cooperative agreement with the Forest Service. We implemented this in 1945. (Missoula was becoming the center for fire control in the northern Rockies.)

We abolished thirteen of our fire lookouts at one time, substituting air patrol from points in the northern Rocky Mountains. The Glacier flights might originate at a new base at West Yellowstone, Montana. Or the planes could fly in from Missoula or Spokane. Distances telescoped dramatically. A plane with trained observers would cover a fire hazard about an hour after a lightning fire storm swept the country. This time advantage often could be helpful in fire discovery.

Initial attack would ordinarily be by smoke jumpers — tough fire control men, trained in Missoula at a special facility, paid for in part by our thirteen former fire lookout salaries. The jumpers might fly with the reconnaissance flight and jump a fire as it was discovered.

Abandoning our fire lookouts was a fearsome step. Disaster was freely prophesied. However, all the statistics supported it. So did experience. In mid-July 1945, a small fire storm left active smokes at Lincoln Pass and on Mount St. Nicholas. The Lincoln Pass fire was jumped immediately. Two jumpers with equipment were on the recon plane. They walked into Lake McDonald that evening — mission accomplished!

The Mount St. Nicholas jumpers took a little longer, but three jumpers hit the fire early in the afternoon, put a safe line around it, and late that evening hiked into a fire campsite on Upper Nyack Creek. In traditional fashion, we had started a hiking crew of fire fighters up Nyack Creek enroute to Mount St. Nicholas — a tough place to reach. With a short pack string, they had hiked all day and bivouaced for the night, planning a pre-dawn start the next morning, but the fire was already under control. They returned instead to Nyack Ranger Station.

This was a convincing demonstration of the effectiveness of the plan. A thirty-minute major fire storm the morning of Saturday, August 15, gave us confirmation of its dependability. This was a strong and violent lightning and dry wind storm. We had fifty strikes in thirty minutes. One hit in heavy fuel just below the lookout on Curly Bear Mountain, and in ten minutes a fire was roaring out of control in blow-down dead timber.

We watched the other forty-nine strikes carefully. Two of them turned into fires, but they were soon controlled. The one at Curly Bear was different. We used the whole coordinated plan. The fire burned uncontrolled the first day. The neighboring National Forests were busy with fires of their own, but they were able to send a plane with six jumpers from Spokane. We sent in men from our road and trail crews. We set up a major fire camp at St. Mary. We had to depend on our own small initial strike force with smoke jumper leadership to keep the fire from spreading laterally while we plotted for full control during the night and early morning.

We flew in a special crew of Red Hat Indian firefighters from the southwest. They were a day late, but handled the mop-up admirably.

This was the kind of emergency for which we had justified our Civilian Public Service (conscientious objectors) two hundred-man camp. Because of the primacy of forest fire control in Glacier, this extra labor force was an added security. But by August 15 there had been a series of regional lightning storms with several fires in the adjacent Flathead National Forest. We had had no fires in Glacier. The Forest Service needed help. This had been another reason for our CPS Camp — we could support our neighbors in their emergencies. We had taken a calculated risk and had sent our crews to work in National Forests outside the park, so the emergency found us in a jam. We recalled our crews immediately, but they had just finished sixteen hours of active fire line duty, and they needed rest. They would be available a day later. We sought other alternatives.

I gambled on a phone call to Cut Bank. Dan Whetstine, the newspaper editor, had been highly critical of Glacier fire control on previous eastside fires. I called and explained the emergency. I asked if there were any way he could help. He was astounded. But what could he do? Five minutes later he called me back and explained that while he kept his complete liberty to blast us if he felt that we did it wrong, he would help in this time of manpower shortage.

So he blew the town fire siren. This was a Civil Defense procedure for all citizens to assemble at the town fire house. Many of them did so. Dan announced our dilemma. He had arranged for a school bus. Who would go? He assembled a bus load of men who drove the sixty miles to St. Mary and were quickly signed up.

Their segment at the front was an active one. Vigorous construction and vigilant patrol were needed. They did well. Most of them had fought fire before. By noon on Sunday our line was completed and holding, and the Cut Bank crew was headed home. I blessed Dan Whetstine. He had done what he could in a typically American frontier fashion. I spent our entire phone allotment of twenty-five dollars on these two conversations with Dan.

The Air Force at Great Falls sent us one hundred men. They were untrained, but great fire fighters as long as any flame was showing! One of the airmen fell over a rock pile and somehow got a nasty gash in his penis. The radioman had difficulty communicating with the Great Falls air base on the nature of the injury. I had to presume that the Great Falls operator was just having fun with it, but every fire station in the Northern Rockies was aware that airman Jones needed helicopter transportation to return to base to have stitches taken in his cock.

We threw everything we had into that first night of fire line construction. By 10:00 a.m. the next morning (the start of the next "burning period") we had a lot of smoke, but it was all inside the fire line. The Red Hat Indian crew took over the mop-up, and we disbanded our rapidly-assembled fire organization.

Our initial fire reports of an estimated 2,500 acres proved to be almost 2,000 acres high. The fire was only about 250 acres — including, as we were jocularly reminded, the traditional 2,000 acres of smoke which was often added to early reports to justify high FFF (fighting forest fires) costs. But the smoke jumper crew had become a nucleus of trained professionals. These men headed off the fire at crucial points, quickly trained new workers, served as crew leaders, and soon returned to their base having helped the Glacier organization in the critical first twenty-four hours. The build-up and support plan worked!

Glacier National Park is the American unit of Waterton-Glacier International Peace Park. It was a great idea in international cooperation in conservation. (I later tried to use some of the same principles with a proposed international park at Big Bend National Park, but without success. Mexico's "northern frontier" country is beautiful, but the nation was unprepared both economically and politically for such a bold step.) In 1932, following legislative declarations by both the Canadian Parliament and the United States Congress, a Presidential Proclamation gave the park the title "The Waterton-Glacier International Peace Park." The Rotary Clubs of America and of Canada were active participants in this recognition. In late July each year the Rotarians meet, alternately in Glacier or in Waterton, to rededicate themselves to the tradition of an unarmed and peaceful boundary.

The Canadian unit of the park is all within the province of Alberta. In 1933 British Columbia had taken little action in conserving the adjoining portions of the mountains. Beautiful Kintla Lake in the United States; a continuation of the magnificent North Fork of the Flathead River; and the lovely Akamina Brook and Cameron Pass in Canada offered great opportunity for extended conservation. The British Columbia authorities were not interested in this remote wild land. In 1942, forest fires could be extinguished only if the cost were under twenty-five dollars! (Now the entire region is under scrutiny for commercial resort development based on the British Columbia resources. I wish it could have been reserved half a century ago!)

Glacier was heavily loaded with privately owned land. All were valid holdings taken up within the Flathead National Forest before

1910 when the park was established, but records of the total acreage and valid maps were needed, and I chose the development of a land record program as my special task. There were about 5,000 acres of private land scattered among about 300 individual owners, concentrated in a few choice locations such as Apgar, upper Lake McDonald, and the North Fork of the Flathead River. When I first looked at the park records, I found eight big file drawers stuffed with file folders, land records, correspondence, tax records, and the like. It soon became evident that at least three different individuals had previously embarked on similar programs, so that a lot of the records were duplicated.

I worked on the "official" base of these records in the Flathead County Clerk and the Assessor's offices for four years on a one-day-a-week basis. I was able to eliminate duplications, identify tax delinquencies, current addresses, and records of tax assessments. I joined the Kallispell Kiwanis Club, and since Kiwanis met every Thursday, I could attend by making this my land records day. I slimmed the file down to only three file drawers, but we still had the same gross acreage of private land, nearly 5,000 acres. There was an increasing number (over 350) of land owners, however, as lots were being divided and then further subdivided. We quite properly were concerned. We were losing control over logging, and over the locating of motels and stores. We had problems with schools, and taxes, and a great fracas over liquor permits. To protect the park, we needed to acquire these lands, or at least control them in harmony with the Congressionally-established preservation goals. And land values were going up.

We already were acquiring small parcels of land by trading fire-killed timber for land at the juncture of the North Fork and the Middle Fork of the Flathead Rivers, an area we called "Jill Poke." A huge fire had raged through there in the 1920s, and the partially marshy, tangled residue of dead and living trees, vines, weeds, flowers, and beginning regrowth was all but impenetrable. Most of the cedar trees there were dead, but still standing and merchantable, and there were a lot of them in the forest jungle. They did not decay and were of interest to "gyppo" loggers who used hand tools to sort out and cut fence posts, grape stakes, and firewood. They paid for the material by trading us land titles.

This messy country had had a valid survey and most of it was privately owned in ten- or twenty-acre tracts. The going price was ten dollars an acre. In fact, Flathead County had title to most of it on tax delinquencies, and they priced such land for sale at five dollars per acre outside Glacier National Park and ten dollars per acre inside the park. They gave a ten percent discount for cash. A gyppo logger could buy a tract and then sell it to the park. The park would pay for it through a cutting permit on government land. We got the cedar wood. The park got the land title. The swamp tangle got cleaned up a bit.

This long-standing procedure had both policy and legal clearance — new terms to me, but important ones. We were nibbling away at the private land block, but we had difficulty with land titles. Many ownerships were based on titles from sale to meet tax delinquencies. This didn't bother anybody, but a government lawyer prescribed that since the original owner might reclaim the land we must "clear" title by a court decree eliminating all such adverse possibilities. But this required the services of an attorney and was an expensive procedure.

We requested authority to "incorporate" the Glacier Natural History Association and let them serve as our left hand in clearing land titles. We would need at least $5,000 for incorporation — a lot of money on our scale, but I went to work on it. First, we had to agree that any residual or "surplus" funds would revert to the Association. We could not envision any such success! Then Morris Cook, an attorney from the Regional Office of the National Park Service in Omaha, offered to do the legal preparation. This saved $150.

I had just been assigned to the Chicago Office on a short detail, and I had written articles for various encyclopedias such as Colliers and Funk and Wagnalls. These were written in the name of Director Newton Drury, and he, of course, could not accept payment checks, but he could legally donate them — another $100. This would pay the incorporation fee. Herb Evison, our Chief Editor, wrote a ghost article for a farm journal and donated his $150. I put the bit on a rowdy kind of informal, brown-bag, lunching group in the Chicago office, and at one dollar each, I had another thirty dollars. I challenged the Glacier staff — superintendent and all — for five dollars each — another fifty dollars. Then, an old Glacier friend, Mrs. Maude

Oastler, ended our immediate worry with a $3,000 gift, and Doc Ruhle, our former park naturalist, added another $1,000. We had done it!

Meanwhile, in settling the estate of Otis Alderson, a Belton resident, Jack and I had bid for ten lots in the Lake McDonald tract at ten dollars each with a 10 percent cash deposit. Herb Evison helped us out again by getting the Izaak Walton League, the powerful conservation organization, to lend its support. Then the newly incorporated Glacier organization took over. A local attorney, Dan Korn (who was also the Flathead County Attorney), was persuaded to handle the "clear title" action for $100 — a great bargain. The Flathead County Commissioner accepted our bid of five dollars an acre on 400 acres of tax delinquent land in this same swamp. All of a sudden we were in the land business!

My heritage to the land program was threefold: First, a clear record and good working maps. Second, the "incorporation," so that the Glacier Natural History Association could be an "in-transit" land owner and pass a clear title. And third, we made the beginnings of acquisition in a previously moribund situation!

However, the park still contained extensive private holdings which could be purchased only when the owner wished to sell. Sooner or later land would be for sale on a willing buyer-seller basis. The park now had the tools to use. Meanwhile, we were neighbors and we must all get along. An inholding owner had a "right" to subdivide or cut trees, and while I might try to talk him out of it, I would honor his "rights" as long as he owned them. This was often galling and erosive to park values, but we got along, and we made some progress in land acquisitions.

Our Glacier CCC Camp program came to a halt in 1944. It just fizzled out with all of the other national priorities for money and men. It should have ended with a whoop, for it was one of the really great governmental endeavors. It not only had great park and conservation impact, it also had a character impact on the participants. Expected to work and earn their way, they were satisfied with the pittance wage which met the value scale of that time, and it gave a real sense of belonging and contributing. I was proud to have had a part in it.

It was supplanted in a way by the Civilian Public Service group —

the conscientious objectors. We had an Amish camp — some of the 200 corpsmen were actually from Morgantown, Pennsylvania, Inger and I had known them when we were at Hopewell Village. They were hard and frugal workers. They tore down old buildings and even saved kegs full of crooked nails and would take time to straighten them if possible. Many of them were skilled craftsmen, and at Glacier one of their great contributions was the construction, one-by-one, of storm sash for every building in the park. Beginning with the rough lumber, they would cut, plane, mortise, stain, and glaze — we ended with greatly-lowered fuel bills.

They were of many diverse skills. I realized this one winter night when our CPS night watchman fell and broke his arm as he stumbled over a snowcovered woodpile. I recognized him — he was our Ph.D. in music, inept in all physical tasks, hence the night watchman job. But in his spare time he gave music lessons to school kids and made other contributions to community enrichment. His personal amusement was to read orchestral music scores night after night!

Colonel Hershey of the national CPS leadership explained the governing philosophy for me one night as he broke his inspection routine for a social evening at our house: "In the United States, the draft is universal — everyone in that age group is included, but the United States Congress recognizes that there is a small minority — let's say two tenths of one percent — who seek the right to be different. They claim conscientious objection to war, and this is honored. However, as this is applied to 21 million people of draft age, the two tenths of one percent becomes in itself a large figure of over 400,000. Can we now similarly recognize the rights of each two tenths of one percent to be still further different?"

"The answer, of course, is no," Colonel Hershey stated, and this answered many of my questions.

CHAPTER XIII

OF FIRE, MULES, AND MORALE

GLACIER SURPRISES CONTINUED. During hunting season Ernest Hutch-
inson, the Walton District Ranger, would occasionally hitch rides down
from Marias Pass on the big Great Northern diesel helper locomotives
which helped boost fully-loaded trains from the west up the mountain
to the summit. The huge locomotives would immediately cruise back
to their home base at Essex, near Walton Ranger Station.

Once I had the fortunate opportunity to ride along. It was during
elk season, and Hutch and I stood up in the cab by that big windshield,
straining our eyeballs, watching the north, or park, side of the right-of-
way. We were looking for man tracks in the snow; anyone in this area
would be a malefactor. Tracks must be investigated. Hutch had his
skiis, and if there were reason to investigate, the engineer would stop
and let Hutch off to start his patrol promptly, while I would ride on
down to Walton and get backup help for him. But there was no trespass evident that morning. This was the hard edge of the wilderness,
a great place to make a ranger patrol.

A park superintendent soon learns that after a major emergency
such as a forest fire it is often possible to replace equipment worn out
or damaged in fire fighting without regard for regular budget limits.
An emergency is not budgeted in advance. It is still an "emergency"
until you get yourself back into condition to respond to the next one.
You draw directly on the U.S. Treasury for such catastrophic repairs
and replacements.

The Glacier Curley Bear Mountain fire was such an emergency.
In August, 1945, our Park Service mule string had just about had it.
The mules were too old — adequate that year, but probably not for
another. We needed a new pack train. Such a string was available
through the Forest Service Remount Station in Missoula. It was listed
in their supply catalog — eight mules, four and five years old, sound
and gentle, between 800 and 900 pounds, shod, broken to halter lead
and to pack.

[195]

The string was available, we bought it, and the mules were delivered in a huge truck. They knew how to use a hay manger and grain feed box, and were in excellent condition and spirits. They were suitably haltered and tied, but very unfriendly, wary, and suspicious. They were not mean, just scared. We called this behavior "being wormy," although "squirmy" was probably a better description. We left halters on them for a few days just to avoid problems in catching them.

After about ten days our packer, Jack Krober, hauled the mules to the Packer's Roost corral on the McDonald Creek side of a transmountain trail. Emergency supplies were to be packed into the Swift Current Pass fire lookout and to the Granite Park maintenance base. Would I like to go along? I would see the Upper McDonald Creek Valley; and another pair of hands and my 200 pounds on the end of a lash rope could be handy!

When I reached Packer's Roost at 8:00 A.M., Jack had the mules fed and securely tied to trees and corral posts. He had begun saddling. Each mule was a separate adventure. They were still fearful and wary, opposed to the whole thing, and quick to strike, bite, kick, buck, run away — anything but cooperate. However, a mule is a sagacious critter — it can soon figure out its alternatives and select the one that gives it the least trouble. It will crouch beside a hitching post, almost on tiptoe; tense, quivering, ears alert — and freeze there, immobile, while the packer introduces a curry comb and brush and adjusts the saddle pad. The mule flinches when the saddle is swung across, and possibly explodes as you reach under for the cinch, but you just put it back and start over and over until it is accepted. At this point I often could provide a diversion by walking up to a mule's head and stroking its taut and bowed neck.

Tighten the cinch (or cinches — we were not using double-rigged saddles — the rear cinch could often be another point of contention) and the mule is saddled. Check that it is tied securely. Repeat eight times. We are using Decker saddles so that each side of each pack is separately placed on a manta and then securely wrapped and tied. One at a time, the mantied packs of about eighty pounds are lifted into place and secured to the saddles. This is another potential explosion point, as the first pack must be precariously balanced until the second one can be lifted into place and secured. The packs are lifted, balanced, and adjusted, top packs added, another manta over this, and a diamond hitch to wrap up the whole load. Mule Number One is packed and left tied to its corral post. Each subsequent mule is loaded and then successively tied behind the first in a head-to-tail chain.

Finally, the mule string was together. If Jack could hold on to the lead mule, the others would follow. They could and would snort, kick, hold back, try to rear, back up, fart, and charge ahead, but they basically remained in a unit. Jack's spurs jingled as he checked his own saddle horse, stepped aboard, and chirped cheerfully, "Okay, mules, let's go!" The lead mule really didn't want to be Number One — a position it would later fight to defend — but finally they all charged abreast down to the creek, were yanked into place, and started up the trail. In just a few minutes we were surprisingly in an orderly, single-file line.

I had gone on ahead, but this was not our day. Someway we soon brushed down a hornets' nest. It was trampled by mule Number Three, hornets erupted, and all order vanished. The mules were bucking and kicking and tangling up among the short second-growth trees. The hornets were industriously stinging everything in sight. In a great demonstration of mule management, Jack dropped the lead rope, rode up beside me, and pulled us around the first bend so that we were completely out of sight and out of reach of the hornets.

Jack sat on a rock and rolled a cigarette carefully and then quietly smoked it down to a nubbin. In fact, he built and smoked another one. Within ten minutes the hornets were pretty well wiped out, the commotion subsided, and the lunging and threshing stopped. Only occasionally would there be a renewed surging and crashing to indicate that an active hornet was still about.

I demonstrated my own ignorance. "Jack, how are you going to get that straightened out?" His simple response was, "It won't take long, but if I go down there now, they will think that someway I got them into the hornets. If I wait a bit, I'll be the guy who came along and got it straightened out." And he was right. This was good solid mule — or people — psychology. I have used the example many times.

Glacier, 1946. The Going-to-the-Sun Highway had been an engineer's dream for decades — beginning in the 1920s — as a great way to make the park usable for people. There was give and take. I am certain that Steve Mather must have sided with the proponents, as I suspect I also would have. From Marias Pass to Canada — and one hundred miles north of that border — the Continental Divide was an impenetrable barrier to east-west travel. Wilderness? Great, indeed! There was a lot of it. How could people use any of it?

My own conclusions were that the Going-to-the-Sun Highway's great value was as a safety valve. It released pent-up pressures of those who wanted to at least look through a window to the wilderness. You could quickly be in the fringes of wild America. You could explore a short path at Logan Pass and try it on for size. You could scan the cliffs for the tell-tale white "snow banks" which turned out to be mountain goats when you got the glasses on them. You could park at Packer's Roost and go up McDonald Creek if you wished. Or you could park at Logan Pass and follow the Garden Wall toward Swift Current Pass and Granite Park. Hidden Lake beckoned you. Mountain tundra could be beneath your feet. West was the Pacific and China. East was the Mississippi and the Atlantic. Northeast was the Hudson Bay watershed. Probably you did not want more than a taste of wilderness — but if you did, here was the gateway from the exciting Transmountain Highway!

There were many other Glacier happenings which might be included in this compendium. Burton K. Wheeler was a U.S. Senator, a kind of a homestead-squatter politician. Title to his Upper Lake McDonald land had been finally legitimized by Congress in the early 1940s after his thirty years of residence on an expired Forest Service special use site permit. I had the task of appraising the lots in Apgar that were owned by Mrs. Lulu Wheeler. These we offered in exchange for the site at the head of Lake McDonald on which they had constructed a magnificent new home. The political signs were clear — the transaction came with no problem.

The Wheelers were really very lovely people. They had political acumen and courage to support the unpopular side of great issues. They shared my feelings of respect and identity with the mountain environment, and reared their children in accordance with these beliefs. I liked them. He was hilarious and revealing reminiscing about his summer as a book agent along the Mississippi River in Iowa, and his meeting with Farmer White's daughter, Lulu. He was a human sort of a guy.

Glacier had a 1937, twelve-cylinder seven-passenger Lincoln sedan with full armor plate protection for its original owner, J. Edgar Hoover. Hoover's assistant, Clyde Tolson, was the brother of the National Park Service Assistant Director, Hilory Tolson. I presume this may have been part of the machinery of acquisition. Our park mechanic, Harold Mahoney, drove the car out from Washington. It could pass anything on the road except a gasoline station. We used it for a moving "committee room" for several years.

One day on Logan Pass I was approached by a park visitor wanting to ask a question of a ranger in a full uniform and hat. Seated in the Lincoln, parked with the motor running, I cranked my front window down, revealing the two-inch safety glass inside the four-inch armor-plated door. He forgot his question as he touched the glass cautiously.

"Is Mr. Hoover letting you drive his car today, ranger?" he quavered. My easiest answer was just "Yes" as I drove away.

Another remarkable Glacier character whose political and environmental interests persisted for many years was Judge Charles Pray. He was a lawyer from Fort Benton, elected Congressman for Montana in 1910. He served several terms and was then appointed to the bench of the United States District Court. When he was nearing the age of ninety, he retired from the bench, and since he always claimed paternal support for Glacier National Park, it seemed appropriate to have him as the featured speaker at the retirement party for Superintendent Jack Emmertt in 1958 at Kalispell. All their Glacier friends were in attendance. I was honored by invitation to be the Master of Ceremonies for this gala event.

Of particular impact was Judge Pray's hilarious revelation of the political role he played in that first Glacier legislation. He made a great jest out of it, stressing his own "freshman" status, his ignorance of congressional protocol, and his zeal to serve Montana well, which he could do most effectively by getting Glacier National Park authorized. His meetings with other members of Congress were simple: "I'm Charles Pray. I am the new Congressman from Montana. I have a bill on which I need your support. Do you have a bill?" This grass roots tactic attracted a lot of attention, including that of the Congressional leadership, which attempted to stifle his direct solicitation, but someway his positive, homespun, practical approach paid off, and on May 11, 1910, Glacier National Park was established.

In the next session of Congress he was rebuked by the leadership. "You got your park, but you didn't get any money. How do you intend to run it?" Pray's response was familiar: "I'll get the money the same way I got the park!" which he did, and rejoiced in the simplicity of the American political system ever after.

Our neighbors along the east side of the park were the Blackfeet Indians. Their reservation is actually larger than the park. Like all beginners, I had to learn that the true designation is "Blackfeet." Even if there is only one Indian, he is a Blackfeet. In fact, the only place the word "Blackfoot" is properly used is in the name of the town of Idaho which was perhaps christened by an English major or an engineer, but not by an ethnologist!

They were exciting people to be around. Like other great Indian people I have known, a Blackfeet might be a substantial and outgoing citizen, but on occasion he could look right through you while focused on something about a mile behind you. They were great individuals, solid in their tribal social patterns, greatly appreciative of the utility and the beauty of their natural world. Skin teepees must be decorative and comfortable. A saddle and bridle must be elegant. They were responsive to both nature and beauty, and at the same time could be insensitive. Their lack of housekeeping at beautiful reservation camp sites was often explained simply with the comment that an Indian seldom saw a reason to clean up the out-of-doors. Rain, snow, wind, and dust would arrange it.

However, Francis X. (for Xavier) Guardipee, one of our famous Glacier rangers, was different. A full-blood Blackfeet, he was a communicative Indian and a great interpreter of the Indian way of life. He was prominent in Boy Scouts of America councils. At a scouters meeting in Great Falls, dressed as a proper Blackfeet chief, he reviewed the life way of his people as he had known it in his youth and as it could contribute to youth programs of today. I listened proudly as he illustrated the harmony of life as an Indian knew it.

He and his charming Flathead wife Alma and their son Gunnar were special treasures. We loved them for who they were and for what they stood for. Frank and Alma were devout Catholics, and upon Frank's death the funeral mass was held at the Browning Church of the Little Flower. There was a large attendance, with representatives from all neighboring Indian tribes, and a contingent of National Park rangers in dress uniform. Frank was deservedly popular and respected. Bob Frausen, St. Mary District Ranger, reported that following the graveside rites the mourners were loath to leave. They chatted freely about Frank Guardipee and the moral leadership he displayed in all aspects of living.

An elderly Blackfeet woman reminisced about Frank Guardipee as an Indian boy, as a student at the Carlisle Indian School, and as an eager and proud park ranger. "I will sing a song for Frank," she said. "I will sing the Victory Song!" And she did, a fitting and moving tribute to a powerful friend. Others shared similar memories, and it was a warm and moving occasion.

Kootenai Brown was another Indian folk hero. His legendary career antedated my time, so all I know is tales of his endurance and strength, of his tamed grizzly bears, pack saddle buffalo, and the like.

Ben Miller and Elmer Ness were rangers I knew and respected for their drive and will in surviving winter catastrophes. Ben fell through the ice on the Flathead River below Nyack, and even though encased in ice, raced the two miles to his cabin and survived.

Elmer Ness, a solid and substantial Scandinavian ranger, was stationed at Belly River one winter. He left on a round-trip ski patrol to St. Mary, but a chinook melted the snow down rapidly. The following freeze iced the snow, his skis slid out from under him, and he rolled down a long, icy hill, bouncing off several rocks and breaking his hip. Even with his broken hip he began to crawl, half-crouched and reaching ahead with his hands, back to the Belly River Ranger Station. That day, that night, another full day, and into the next night he crawled through the snow in near-zero temperatures, ever-fearful that his trail might be picked up by a hunting wolf pack.

By a last supreme effort, Elmer hoisted himself onto the ranger station porch, frightening his wife Margaret badly. With a loaded rifle, she challenged the barely-animate brute on her front porch, only finally to recognize Elmer. She was able to drag him into the cabin, telephone park headquarters of his injury, and then begin thawing, feeding, and curing the courageous fellow, who for another twenty years was a mainstay of the Glacier ranger force. But that was the end of one-man patrols. By my time, two- or three-man patrols were the recognized procedure.

Glacier wildlife stories were usually about elk or moose, or about cony or marmots or birds. Bears were not the problem they were at Yosemite or Sequoia, but our Glacier bears were usually grizzlies, and everybody took them seriously. There were no major bear injuries or incidents during our time at Glacier. In later years the problem became very serious. There were a number of fatalities, most of them caused by failure to give grizzlies the proper respect. A grizzly bear is always unpredictable. It is also mainly a carnivore and it survives by hunting. Man can be a proper prey for the grizzly just as he is for polar bears. This is frightening when you think it through, but I have not heard of any rangers directly attacked by grizzly bears, even though most rangers had much more exposure to bears than the tourists do.

Someway we seem to have had more dependable measures of self protection.

(A few years ago Ranger Tom Milligan of Yellowstone had an encounter which appears to reverse some of the previous observations about bears. Tom and his young bride Charlene had gone fishing on the Bechler River about two miles above the ranger station on his day off. With fly rods rigged and ready, Charlene was leading the way along the trail when she suddenly, unknowingly, walked between a mother grizzly bear and her twin cubs. Charlene's first awareness of this was her discovery of Mother Bear reared up in front of her, jaws agape and threatening. Charlene's alarmed reaction was to reach around with the fishing rod and shove the tip down the bear's throat as far as she could, meanwhile screaming loudly at Mother Bear. It was a temporary stand-off, but Tom, an all-conference tackle on the University of Idaho Southern Branch football team, came bursting through the brush and in the best athletic style threw a hard rolling block on Mother Bear. He bounced about five feet without budging the bear and she just dropped to all fours and turned her attention on Tom. She actually took the top of his head in her mouth, and Tom was sure that he had had it, but apparently the cubs came back into view and Mother dashed away after them. So grizzlies are usually even-tempered as the reports indicate; they are always mad. But on occasion they can ignore an easy meal or a tremendous opportunity.

Our Yellowstone Chief Ranger, Nels Murdock, hurrahed Tom a bit about the scientific report he should write for the wildlife journals. "Tell me, Tom, did the bear's breath smell bad? Did she have a lot of B.O.? How did her fur feel? Was it silky and soft? Did she tear your jacket with her teeth or her claws?"

Tom simply replied, "I don't know. All I know is that she could have killed me if she wanted to and she didn't. I am lucky!" I think authorities all agree. Grizzly bears are unpredictable.)

There are other wildlife angles to consider beside bears. But in Glacier and Yellowstone wildlife was a way of life — it was everywhere, and we lived with it intimately.

Another winter trip in the park could give glimpses of a solitary moose browsing near Lake McDonald. Beaver dams were often seen, the conical beaver houses well frozen in with the lake surface. I knew that the beaver had cut branches and anchored them in the lake bottom for food. The skill of a beaver in sinking a branch so that it stayed down ready for winter forage was a specialized skill. If by chance I jiggled one of these branches loose, it would float to the surface and I could in no way get it back onto the stream bottom.

The chicaree, a little noisy red squirrel, was a constant companion. So was the pine marten, although we seldom saw it. A flying squirrel frequently shared our bird feeder shelf. By chance one of these lustrous and soft creatures sailed in through our bedroom window one night, sending Inger into a tizzy of evasive action before I could get it back to the open window. Its enormously round eyes were appealing, and it showed no interest in biting her attractive toes.

One morning Superintendent Jack Emmertt had an emergency telephone call from the Regional Office in Omaha. "Get Garrison on tomorrow's train to Omaha without fail. We have an emergency meeting he must attend."

Six of us from field stations, all with ranger jobs or backgrounds, were confidentially informed about the newly-discovered Japanese paper balloon fire bombs. One had been recovered blowing across an open prairie in Wisconsin. It hung up on a barbed wire fence and the discovery alerted the military. This was something new. It could tie in with a news flash heard the previous Sunday evening on Walter Winchell's dynamic broadcast. At a Sunday School picnic in southern Oregon, some explosive device had killed at least one person. There were other explosives on it, but other than that one newscast, we never heard another word.

Actually, this represented a unique bit of restraint on the part of the U.S. news service. Military intelligence calculated that a whole fleet of these balloon bombs had been released from a Japanese island and the prevailing winds were bringing them to America. By imposing a complete blackout on news of the arrival of the devices, it would hopefully discourage the Japanese from sending more of them.

Our little meeting was given a view of one of the machines. A paper balloon about six feet tall had been filled with helium; suspended beneath this was a wagon tire ring of metal with about twenty bags of various loads hung on it. A barometer was set for the elevation of the trade winds (about 20,000 feet) which were whistling our way steadily. If the balloon leaked gas and began to drop, the barometer would explode a small charge in one of the pendant bags and drop about twenty pounds of sand. This would lighten the balloon and it would return to the 20,000-foot altitude. There were only a few of these ballast loads — theoretically, after the ballast loads were gone it would be timely for the balloon to descend on shore in the United States or Canada and start exploding the other bundles of anti-personnel bombs. Literally, there were thousands of these things in the air. They would create real havoc in cities! We had to admire the ingenuity of the device, but we were hopeful that some action could be taken to stop them; for if such machines began dropping phosphorus "leaves," or calling cards, in July or August they could literally burn the whole forest of the West Coast.

The Japanese timing was wrong. Spring was not a good time for fire bombs. The forests were wet. The anti-personnel bombs could strike viciously in isolated locations, but the haphazard, wind-blown distribution almost guaranteed that most of them would land in open country instead of cities.

Later we heard that an American scientist, who knew Japanese
marine life, identified the island from which the bombs were launched
simply by the small marine shells found in the sand ballast which had
been recovered. With this information, American bombers gave serious attention to blasting the preparation sites.

Obviously, I was to alert our key people — rangers and road foremen — without creating general alarm. Late in April, the Belton
school — all of our community kids — wanted to have a picnic at
Avalanche Creek Campground and could not be persuaded to select a
closer and more open picnic site where we could conduct a thorough
preliminary check. We did the best we could without handcuffing the
kids! We had rangers there in abundance, and with great relief we
got the youngsters home that afternoon.

Later we found one of these lethal devices deposited in a canyon
above Many Glacier. The charges were all exploded. It had landed
in a snow bank.

The Garrisons were on the move again in the fall of 1945. Our
total number of major moves would finally run to twelve, prompting
an Omaha friend to comment in disgust that I was just like a tree
planted in a bushel basket. I could be picked up and moved around,
but must be careful not to let my roots escape and tie me down. This
observation was humorous on the surface, but did not recognize the
extent to which we entered community living wherever we were. Cultural, educational, social, vocational, and community conservation programs — we were always involved. Our debt to our host community
was always repaid by this kind of personal contribution. It became increasingly difficult for Inger as the cultural programs in which she participated demanded more and more continuing commitment of personal time. She drew from the local cultural resources, she taught
ceramics classes (at Georgetown, Big Bend, Yellowstone, and Omaha),
she was a volunteer worker at the Jocelyn Museum in Omaha, and she
participated in arts and crafts events in arranging or judging or ex-
hibiting. She accepted silently when I broke it all up periodically by
career promotions and moves.

For Inger and myself all this was part of our enjoyable and rewarding growth-career pattern. We liked Glacier, but we also were adventurers. And, Ray Vincent, the regular Assistant Superintendent,

was returning to Glacier from military furlough. Fortunately for me this coincided with a turnaround at Grand Canyon National Park, where Assistant Superintendent John Davis was moving to the Southwestern Regional Office in Santa Fe. The Grand Canyon job was suggested to me as an inviting new kind of briar patch. The salary and the job title were the same. I would have to learn a new kind of geography and a different scenic resource. "The Grand Canyon? Let's go!"

CHAPTER XIV

AT THE GRAND CANYON

WAS I BECOMING A LOCKED-IN, professional, assistant superintendent? It was a dead end proposition in many ways. To do my job well simply strengthened the ties that bound me to it. I could not expect to become the Superintendent at Grand Canyon. I would have to move to a smaller park as a beginning superintendent. Yet I knew of no other way to work than to become indispensable so that my boss — whoever he was — looked good.

I honestly believe that being a good Number Two man is often far more difficult than being a satisfactory Number One. The catch to it as Number Two is that you often temporarily become Number One. Your decisions must be made on the basis of your judgment of the action Number One would take if he were there. So you might momentarily enjoy the luxury of responding for yourself, but you then stop, take a deep breath, and ask yourself about Number One's probable reactions. Is it the same as your preliminary thoughts? If not, what other factors might need more consideration? Had the boss talked to you about this one? If you decided it his way could you then support it logically without ducking responsibility, and just saying that it was his decision? Or could you accept a reversal?

I recognized immediately that my new Superintendent, Harold Child "Doc" Bryant, was a creative and solid guy to work with. He had a practical mind. He was one of the first Ph.D. s in the biological sciences to become interested in utilizing the National Parks for educating the public about the natural world. He had seen the parks as the equivalent of a third school system. His work on bird cataloging was perpetual. He had been a research scientist with the California Fish and Game Department and was affiliated with the University of California at Berkeley. With another biologist, Dr. Loye Miller of U.C.L.A., he developed an interpretive nature program at Lake Tahoe's Fallen Leaf Lodge. National Park Service Director Mather had then invited them to establish a similar program in Yosemite. It was so successful that Doc was invited to create a nature interpretation program for all the National Parks. He was doing that while I stumbled through my first years as a ranger at Sequoia and Yosemite. By 1932 park interpretation had become a normal part of park management and a welcome expectation of park visitors. In 1941 Doc was named Superintendent of Grand Canyon National Park, since the interesting jobs and the higher salaries were in the field positions at that time. In 1946 I became his Assistant Superintendent. It was a most rewarding situation — the man, the place, and the program.

Doc's operational plan called for me to do more than just "assist" the superintendent. I was put in charge of park operations. I supervised park maintenance, park protection through the rangers, and the office staff. Doc, in turn, was the supervisor of research and the park interpretive program with the creative and inspirational Louis Schellbach as park naturalist.

Doc also handled public relations, and his list of national and international professional and political friends was immense. As the Number Two man I met most of these great people as they came by. Grand Canyon was an exciting place to work.

"Doc" — Harold Bryant's preferred title — stayed deeply involved in national programs, particularly at the Yavapai Station where the Grand Canyon's story was told triumphantly. It took advantage of exacting studies of the visible panorama, emphasizing the key features to illustrate the chronology of our world. An outstanding committee of scientists had developed the theme and selected as illustrations examples from the canyon walls before us. Simply, the program related the dimension of time, the probable sequence of geologic events, and the reality of land and water and life in the present. All this as the untamed Colorado River carried an average of one million tons of silt a day past us through the canyon towards the sea. A lecture at 2:00 P.M. was a major feature of the daily calendar of events. It was an "illustrated" lecture, as the narration focused on various geological points.

On Louis's days off or during other absences, Doc and I filled in. I was third in priority, but it was a proud moment for me when the opportunity came. I simply repeated the regular message. The audience always responded to the quality of the event by applause which was rewarding to me, but I realized that I was only the mouthpiece for the minds and the knowledge which had made the program possible. It was beautiful interpretation.

But as "manager" I was often disheartened by another response. The audience was starry-eyed with appreciation of the glory of nature around them; they were momentarily blinded with good emotions. Yet they would leave a confetti-strewn building and rim walk. Packages of matches, film boxes and wrappers, cigarette butts, and paper handkerchiefs were discarded blindly and with unhappy results. The immediate foreground below the parapet along the rim was always messy. "Kleenex" was the new national flower. It festooned every bush unless we picked it up regularly, and below the rim this was time-consuming and dangerous.

Louis and I talked about it often. Would a mundane reminder to the audience be effective or would it destroy the spell we had woven? How could this successful interpretive program convey to visitors the necessity of good outdoor manners? I am still working on that one.

This was in 1946, immediately following World War II. Much of vacation-minded America must have had its cars packed, ready for a fast start to visit National Parks the moment the peace treaty with Japan was signed. Doc and I were trying to continue the traditional ranger contact with visitors, which had been the Service hallmark. Ranger patrols and roadside information services were helpful, but time-consuming, and resulted in long days. The operational details seemed to escalate at the same time. Sophisticated maintenance equipment created new tasks and standards. New stresses on law enforcement for urban-oriented visitors and minorities were endless. Budget and finance controls proliferated. A manager not only controlled ongoing programs, he also needed political skills to anticipate and propose new services. He would experiment, evaluate, write reports, and implement the tested programs.

Attention to distinguished guests was top priority, and often this meant that reports were late. The Grand Canyon had been one of the "Seven Wonders of the World" a century earlier, and pictures of its grandeur were in all international scientific and travel literature. As an illustration of geology and scenic revelation, Americans, as well as many people from other lands, wanted to see the Grand Canyon. And this was our job — to preserve it and at the same time use it. Again and again I was reminded that you couldn't wear it out by looking at it!

Visitors would travel incredible distances to get there. The early travel industry in America gladly arranged for this. There were tours and tourists long before the railroad construction. The railroad towns coupled with extensions of tours by W. W. Bass and John Hance, and were the real beginnings of a park "tourism." Services included hotels, river trips, Indian Country trips, inner canyon trips, and mule trips. In 1903 the famous Santa Fe Railroad tour trains began daily service to the South Rim, with long lines of sleeping cars which unloaded their tourists into more lines of waiting buses. But by 1925 hotels and camps were serving more automobile tourists, called "sagebrushers," than train passengers.

Then air trips became popular. In 1946, these were a combination of air and bus journeys, for the nearest commercial airfield was in Flagstaff. The "Rain Tank" Grand Canyon airport came after 1970.

Famous international visitors were often accompanied by U.S. Department of State officials. Visitors were now less concerned with geology than they were with the political science of National Parks in America, or the lives of our neighboring Navajo or Hopi Indians, or our innovative management of sewage water. In the 1920s Harry Hommon, a National Park Service engineer, developed a successful filtering, aeration, and chlorination plant which reclaimed our sewage into an effluent for "industrial" uses. The actual need was for great quantities of water to recharge several steam locomotives daily. The reclaimed water could be used for this, and any extra used for lawn irrigation or for watering greenhouses. (It could not be used for drinking water.) The fame of this plant and our parallel water systems brought planners and political leaders from arid lands worldwide to inspect it. But meanwhile there were no more steam locomotives.

The Shah of Iran was one of these visitors in 1949. There was a full bus load of press and public relations people with him. Today we call them "the Media." I was the official greeter, since Doc was away on a scientific journey. As we toured Grand Canyon Village we passed the Grand Canyon school. We had grades 1–6 at that time. I was chairman of the school board. I asked the Shah if he would visit our school. We arranged it for the next morning.

He appeared in a beautiful white robe and turban with the royal insignia in gold — a dazzling sight. He was a charming and handsome young man who was not only a ruler, but a famous skier and athlete.

Unfortunately our school kids were not really prepared for the Shah. He spotted a map case and soon unfurled a large map of the Middle East and asked our youngsters to show him where Iran might be. It was a complete disaster. The kids sat there with eyes popped wide open — "Just look at that sword!" — and their mouths closed. They had stage fright, but the Shah spoke briefly of his homeland, the deserts just like we had, the oases and camels which we did not. He talked of their great horses, about the people and their tribes and their languages. He did it beautifully, concluding with an invitation to visit Iran some day. They could visit an Iranian school and they could ask the Iranian children where the United States was!

Prince Faisal of Saudi Arabia was another similarly important and inquiring visitor. He and his party were guests in our home for tea, both to see our home and to meet a number of our local community leaders. They drank tea. All our Moslem guests rigidly eschewed all forms of alcohol. Faisal, at that time, was the Interior Minister, with a voracious appetite for information about Hopi and Navajo tribes, their school systems, their governance, their religious and cultural practices, their crops, and their water management.

He was a tall, slender, handsome, and self-assured fellow. Among his own party he was a jocular and teasing leader, speaking freely of himself, and deprecatingly of his "big nose" (not evident to me), a hilarious in-house joke for them! Was this an ethno-quip?

The Khan of Kalat was a Grand Canyon visitor. He was the leader of the Pakistan principality north of Karachi and was a permanent delegate to the United Nations. As often happened, Doc's many scientific interests had taken him away. The Khan was accompanied by a secretary — a very capable thirty-year-old Moslem fellow from Kalat. He was a graduate student at the University of Chicago, working towards a Doctorate on Asiatic Religions. Both he and the Khan spoke excellent English, so there was no need for a State Department assistant. Among his other duties, the secretary was head of the Moslem foreign missionary movement to the United States. He was well-supplied with literature on such topics as "How Mohammed Freed The Women" which pamphlet, unfortunately, I did not preserve.

The Grand Canyon journey with these two was provocative. They were questing: Why did we have National Parks? How did the Fred Harvey Company get their contract? What was the religious significance of the Hopi Kachinas? Where did turquoise come from? Our journey to the Indian Country was lively!

They spoke freely and frankly of themselves and their country. Kalat was only thirty miles long and inhabited by one million people. They had very limited roads — a total of about fifty miles. Similarly, they had very few automobiles, the Khan's two Cadillacs being the most noticeable. They were free to practice polygamy, but the Khan had only one wife and eleven children. He did not "need" a second wife. His children were in school in Great Britain, where school discipline was more to his liking.

They were equally inquisitive about our living and family mores. They drank tea or lemonade. They mainly ate boiled eggs, rice, and broiled fish. They did not trust American fried food. There was too much hanky panky about American cooks and their use of pig fat, but they stopped at our home and met Inger and our youngsters.

My phone rang at 9:00 A.M. the next morning. "His Highness desires that you and Mrs. Garrison join him for dinner this evening at the Bright Angel Lodge at 7:00 P.M."

We accepted, and thereby started an unusual chain of events. The secretary did not accompany us on our tour of the Grand Canyon Village and the water reclamation plant. He stayed with the Fred Harvey maître d' and Tony, the Greek chef. A special limousine was sent to Williams, Arizona, sixty miles distant, and returned with six live, fat hens. These were dispatched with Islamic rituals. Tony, who had French training, received detailed recipes and menu instructions. At 7:00 P.M. we sat down to a preliminary lemonade and then the chicken-rice-curry feast.

Actually, these two gentlemen for some weeks had been existing on a diet of eggs, rice, broiled fish, or various salads. The curry with its ritualistic preparation was a most welcome event. We attacked an incredible mound of it on an oversize platter. Inger and I each had a piece of chicken. Our hosts had two pieces. Then we had a small green salad with olive oil dressing and then more chicken-rice curry. Our hosts had more pieces of chicken. We sat, we talked, we drank tea, we learned more of the religion of Kalat. We saw family photographs. Our hosts ate more curry. We dawdled with a slice of melon. We drank more tea. Occasionally our hosts would have more curry. They practically demolished the mountain of curry! We parted lethargically and most amicably.

My uncle, John Firth, had been a Baptist missionary for thirty years in Assam, India. He was a teacher — telling the Moslem and Hindu people about Christianity. I thought it ironic that I was now meeting with the Moslem Foreign Mission leader to the United States. "Turn about," I thought. They had been gracious to Uncle John. I was delighted to be gracious to their leaders. It was no problem at all. They were both charming people. It was one more grand prerequisite to being a park ranger.

The Santa Fe Railroad held all the main concession contracts on the South Rim of the Grand Canyon. These were for the hotel rooms, restaurants, laundry, and mule rides into the Canyon. Fred Harvey and Company was the operating agent for the Santa Fe Railroad all along their line and in Grand Canyon. The Grand Canyon concessioners — part of my responsibility — were all family establishments at that time. Fred Harvey Company was the main operator on the South Rim, and we dealt often and directly with members of the Harvey third generation. In fact, Byron Harvey and I had been Stanford classmates, although we had not met there. The Harvey name had a personal meaning for Byron, Daggett, and Stewart, as it had had for Frederick, their grandfather. It was rewarding to deal face-to-face with individual owners who shared feelings of responsibility for the Fred Harvey name. It represented good quality of public service.

Verkamps' store was under second-generation management. Jack Verkamp and his sister, Peggy, were managers, although Catherine, the founding mother, was still a part of the romance of the store's pioneer beginnings. They, too, had pride in ownership and in quality public service.

Emery Kolb was the third concessioner. He ran a photographic studio, and had recorded the history of Grand Canyon through scenic

photographs, decades of mule party photographs, and his motion pictures of the 1911-12 float through the Canyon in the old dories. (We
now call them "hard boats," to distinguish them from the more recent
air-tank rubber boats.) Kolb had a magnificent collection of Grand
Canyon art. He had a great eye for color and had had the perception
to recognize and collect the paintings of Gunnar Widforss and other
early artists.

Frankly, from where I sat in review of the rate structure and the
scope of services offered, I felt very comfortable. In return for exclusive business privileges, the concessioners accepted government control
over individual prices. I made price comparisons for similar services
and merchandise in adjacent communities, and I knew a family could
always get a reasonable meal at the park cafeteria. Many times meals
were provided "at cost" by the concessioners. They would make up the
difference on other items. Souvenirs and curios were always given a
100 to 200 percent markup in the park. This was traditional in the
trade.

Babbitt Brothers Trading Company operated a general store. They
had a chain of trading posts in Williams, Flagstaff, and Winslow, Arizona. At Grand Canyon they sold groceries and camper supplies. We
let the business level in other communities establish their Canyon
markup of 10 percent, permitted because of the isolation.

On the North Rim, the Utah Parks Company, a subsidiary of the
Union Pacific Railroad (which also bussed tourists in from the railroad
at Cedar City, Utah) had the concession contract, and provided com-
prehensive tourist services at the Grand Canyon Lodge and cabin
camp. In our negotiations with them I represented the public through
the National Park Service. The company was represented by Pat
Rogers, who was the pioneering manager of several Union Pacific
Railroad hotel facilities. Pat's hallmark of quality service persisted
through his generation and the successors whom he trained. Pat was
a sharp operator, and the railroad had a sweetheart contract. Operational losses were cumulative year-after-year, ready to be charged back
in high priority whenever the Company returned a profit. They did
not do so during my term of seven years.

I have a personal memento of the Utah Parks Company through
a permanent kink in my right index finger. I broke a knuckle as I dug

Charcoal hearth and collier's hut, Hopewell. At hearths like this one, a dozen Hopewell colliers annually converted 5,000 cords of wood into charcoal. *Richard Frear, photographer. National Park Service. Chapters 10–11.*

The superintendent's house at Hopewell, 1942. *George A. Grant, photographer. National Park Service. Chapters 10–11.*

Ruins of the old furnace at Hopewell, 1942. *George A. Grant, photographer. National Park Service. Chapters 10–11.*

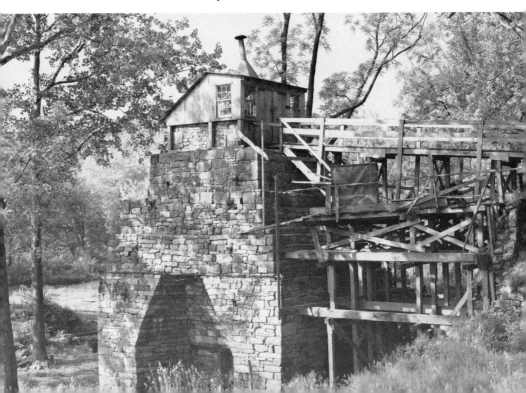

The Iron Master's house from the French Creek bridge, Hopewell, 1942.
George A. Grant, photographer. National Park Service. Chapters 10–11.

Many Glacier Hotel on Swiftcurrent Lake, Glacier, 1932.
George A. Grant, photographer. National Park Service. Chapters 12–13.

Ice cave on Boulder Pass, Glacier, 1932. *George A. Grant, photographer.
National Park Service. Chapters 12–13.*

Going-to-the-Sun Mountain and the Logan Pass highway and tunnel east of the summit, Glacier, September 15, 1940. *George A. Grant, photographer. National Park Service. Chapters 12–13.*

The old cabin at Bowman Lake, Glacier, September 20, 1940. *George A. Grant, photographer. National Park Service. Chapters 12–13.*

Forest fire on Shoshone Point, South Rim, Grand Canyon, May 5, 1947.
Author and Superintendent Harold "Doc" Bryant on truck.
J. M. Eden, photographer. Grand Canyon National Park. Chapter 14.

A visiting group from Brazil at Mohave Point, Grand Canyon, October 12, 1952.
Vice Admiral Renato A. Guillobel, Minister of Marine, Brazil, middle;
Rear Admiral Whitehead of the U.S. Naval Mission to Brazil, second from left;
author third from left. *Steve Leding, photographer. Chapter 14.*

Easter sunrise service at Grand Canyon, April 9, 1939. *National Park Service.*
Chapter 14.

Overlooking the Rio Grande near Boquillas, Big Bend, June 1955.
Sierra del Carmens of Mexico in background. *Glen Burgess, photographer.*
National Park Service. Chapter 15.

Century plant (agave) and "window" in Chisos Mountains Basin, Big Bend, June 1955. *Glen Burgess, photographer. National Park Service. Chapter 15.*

Opening the south entrance to Yellowstone, Spring, 1957. *Chapter 17.*

Temporary superintendent's office after the August 1959 earthquake, Yellowstone. *Jack E. Boucher, photographer. National Park Service. Chapters 17–18.*

Transporting tourists on dusty Yellowstone roads before 1915.
National Park Service. Chapters 17–18.

Soldiers drilling near the Bachelor Officers' Quarters, Fort Yellowstone,
from W. A. Hall album. *National Park Service. Chapters 17–18.*

Superintendent's residence, Yellowstone. *National Park Service. Chapters 17–18.*

Grant Village dedication, Yellowstone, June 23, 1963. National Park Service Director Conrad "Connie" Wirth, General U. S. Grant III, and author. *William S. Keller, photographer. National Park Service. Chapters 17–18.*

Author at right and Howard Baker, Director, Midwest Region,
in Old Faithful Geyser Basin, during meeting to discuss winter use
of Yellowstone, 1961. *Chapters 17–18.*

Yellowstone, 1963. *Chapters 17–18.*

Fire Island National Seashore groundbreaking.
Left to right: Senator Jacob Javits, Lester Wolff, Otis G. Pike, Gordon U. Noreau, James R. Grover, Secretary of the Interior Stewart Udall, Charles R. Dominy, and H. Lee Dennison. Author at center lecturn. *Chapter 19.*

Regional Directors meeting in Washington, D.C., May 1968. National Park Service Director George Hartzog, Jr., in center, author at left, rear. *Cecil W. Stoughton, photographer. National Park Service. Chapter 19.*

Secretary of the Interior Walter Hickel's visit to Independence National Historic
Park, Philadelphia, April 1970. Secretary Hickel in center, author at left.
Cecil W. Stoughton, photographer. U.S. Department of the Interior. Chapter 19.

Mrs. Elizabeth White, author and teacher, and author at Albright Training Academy, Grand Canyon, 1972. *Chapter 19.*

a hot grounder out of the dirt in front of second base in the annual *National Park Service vs. Utah Parks Company* baseball game in 1950. The batter was the dynamic Pat Rogers. The NPS lost, but it was close — and friendly competition and cooperation were the hallmarks of most of our operations.

We had one humorous problem in the Fred Harvey barrooms on the South Rim. I was supposed to check the quantity, quality, and price of mixed drinks at all barrooms. My expense account was the difficulty. Actually, I paid for a few, looked at the back bar to learn the quality of liquor served, and checked the size of the jigger. It was hilarious, but Doc was a teetotaler and he refused to okay a travel voucher showing the purchase of an alcoholic drink with government funds. So my verification of bar rates was a vicarious operation. Fortunately, friends helped me.

The perversities of the Fred Harvey mules were the subject of a little booklet that *Arizona Highways* and I put out — "Grand Canyon's Long-Eared Taxi!"

Cornelius — (Shorty) — Yarberry, a Fred Harvey muleskinner, was priceless. He came hobbling out of the stable one afternoon, obviously lamed and in great pain. "Shorty, did you have an accident?" was the inane inquiry. His salty reply left no doubts, "Hell No. She done it a' purpose."

The National Park Service had pack mules, too. In fact, in 1946 we were in the market for replacement mules. (We lacked the convenient services of the Forest Service Remount Station and the emergency funds we had used at Glacier.) I noticed in a news item in the Phoenix *Daily Republic* that Fort Bliss in El Paso, Texas, was giving up their mule string operations. The pack master had retired and the mules were to be "disposed of."

Doc and I talked it over with Hub Chase, our dynamic maintenance foreman. Then I called the Quartermaster's office at Fort Bliss. "Yes, the mules are surplus. They are available for other federal agencies." In fact, the officer was hopeful an agency like the National Park Service would claim the mules and save them from the usual surplus sale. (The euphemism for this kind of abattoir was "the glue factory" in those days. This has been replaced by the "dog food" syndrome.

Either way it was abhorrent to the officer.) He hoped we would call him back.

I called Tom Boles, the popular Superintendent of Carlsbad Cavern National Park, near El Paso and Fort Bliss. "Yes, Tex Worley is available to go down to Fort Bliss to inspect the mules if you will pay his expenses."

I called Tex — a well-known and dependable old Yellowstone ranger and packer. He was delighted. He called me from Fort Bliss. The mules were big ones. They were old, averaging ten years. There were a few decrepit ones which could be culled out. He selected fourteen of the best ones, and with a government bill of lading, got them in a railroad car, and they were soon at Grand Canyon.

They were big, 1,200 pounds each, huge by comparison with the Fred Harvey saddle mules or the Montana-type 900- to 1,000-pound critters, but they were great pack animals. They could carry anything you could get onto the saddle, but were not good riding animals.

I rode one of them on a North Rim trail exploration one summer. "Iron-jawed" is the correct description. He would occasionally start to gallop away. If my reins didn't break first, I could lean back and haul his mouth open and finally get his head turned sideways so that we went in a circle. I suppose he thought he was running away until I got his attention.

Riding one mule to catch another mule is a futile job. A mule will gladly chase another critter — horse, cow, or mule — but having overtaken it is quite content to follow docilely behind it. To get a running mule to head off another one defies all reason. But our mule string was temporarily adequate. In a few years we too began weeding them out.

The war had ended, but things did not return to "normal." We stubbornly persisted in trying to meet our old standards for park preservation and public service, but the money wouldn't go around and personnel ceilings were restrictive.

I saw it daily at Grand Canyon: not enough parking, not enough maintenance, erosion of resources like the Grand Canyon rim and its trees by too many feet. We suffered from traffic jams, sanitation demands, inadequate camp space, too few hotel rooms. After a day of frustration, a quick visit to the Canyon rim could slow me down. The

Canyon sets its own standards of quality. It demands "The Best." We continued to try to do it. We ignored forty-hour weeks.

There were many bright realities. The Easter Sunrise Service with Howard Pyle was a delight. I always worked with the park telephone man, Joe Gaustad, since we had to install a temporary telephone line between the road and the South Rim for the broadcast. Joe would string a temporary telephone connection out to the rim after Howard Pyle had made his site selection. Two or three weekends in advance of Easter Sunday I would drive to Valle Airport and meet Barry Goldwater and Howard Pyle. Barry was another Stanford student of my era and subsequently a merchant, Arizona Governor, and United States Senator. Howard Pyle was the featured Minister for the Sunrise Service. He was an Arizona radio and television news commentator and later State Governor. He was deeply religious, highly perceptive, and very articulate.

Barry flew his own plane and I provided ground transportation for them. In the dark pre-dawn hours on Easter Sunday, Howard and I would drive out along the rim road and in a solitary vigil Howard would trudge out to the rim and await the first rays of the sun above the dark line of Buckskin Mountain to the east. Does the sun rise or does the earth drop away from it to reveal its glory? It does not matter. For Howard, the turning of the earth would bring into silhouette the highest points along the North Rim and illuminate the world beyond us. It would slowly creep back across to us as we waited for the final burst of glory.

On my radio set I would pick up the beginning of the broadcast: "This is Howard Pyle on the Rim of the Grand Canyon this Easter Morning!" Inspiration touched Howard on these holy journeys. He was a deeply sensitive and communicative fellow.

We had had a Saturday afternoon rehearsal so the cameramen could get pictures, but it was difficult to convince them to do it. I had frequent conflicts with network technicians who would come to the Canyon a few hours before the broadcast and demand power hookups, telephone hookups, photographic points. We did what we could, but we kept foremost in mind that this was a Holy Day Memorial Service. The live audience was in the Temple right out on the rim and the cold with us. For that brief hour we worshiped also.

One irate cameraman commented loudly that it was easy to see why I was just a lackey at Grand Canyon, since I obviously had no sensitivity to the magic of *Life Magazine* or the National Broadcasting Company as an "open sesame" for whacking down a few trees to improve the light, or moving a group of worshipers so he could rearrange telephone wires. I invited a recalcitrant *Life* photographer to meet Doc Bryant. Doc was a positive, rock-ribbed Congregationalist who had scant use for such Philistines, anyway. The chastened cameraman gave us no more trouble. His writer, Bob Cahn, turned out to be a very great friend and celebrated author.

A serendipity experience was a short flight with Barry Goldwater to the breaks of the North Rim to show me a "window" he had discovered in the jumbled formations east of Hayden Butte. Barry is a fine photographer and explorer. He discovered this window from his plane and wanted to share the experience with someone from the park. Tourist flights by helicopter and plane still go over the park, but they are in quieter machines now. There was a time when large Army planes were not allowed under a 5,000-foot ceiling over the park, because they frightened the mules on the trails and the wild animals. The reverberations of engine noise were compounded by the narrow canyons.

The Havasupai Indians and their enchanted valley were our neighbors in the Canyon. A number of them worked for us in the park. Elmer Watahomagie was one of the "reliables." He was a mechanic's helper, and along with all his tribal companions left us on the Fourth of July each summer to go to the pow-wow in Flagstaff. Elmer would always come into my office about July 1 or intercept me in the work yard. "Mr. Garrison, I go to pow-wow in Flagstaff. I be back about July 8." This was all, but Elmer had told me of his plans. It was okay. The others all went; only Elmer kept the job in mind, and I was greatful.

I visited the Havasupai Indian Reservation fifty miles west of Grand Canyon Village. The Indians' vicissitudes in boundary adjustments about 1890 and pressures from greedy miners were unbelievable, but it is a beautiful oasis (although in 1950 a lot of it was untilled simply because of uncertainties about the Indian laws of inheritance). I enjoyed knowing "the People," visiting and being a helpful friend to all possible. Father Francisco Garcés had visited the Havasupais in 1776, and according to his description their land was much the same then as when I saw it in 1950.

Havasupai Creek was a magnificent, rushing, milky stream of heavily mineralized water. It was closed to fishing at the time Inger and I were there with a spring jaunt of the Sierra Club. It was a very orderly outfit, and we all enjoyed visiting Indian homes, the school, the hospital, and Rev. Jim Crook who was the Resident Lay Pastor for the Episcopalian faith.

I noticed one of the Sierra Clubbers carrying a fly rod case, and much to my surprise I soon found him with the rod assembled, fly fishing the turbulent waters. What he expected to catch I have no idea. It was just a great place to go fishing!

I addressed him, "What are you doing with that fishing pole?"

It was obvious what he was doing. It was also obvious that he knew the tribe had decreed there would be no fishing, but he looked up as if greatly startled and transferred the pole to his right hand and held it upright behind his back. The pole was three feet taller than he was and projected high above his head.

"What fishing pole?" he asked simply.

I had to laugh. I had not expected to be a law enforcement officer with this group in this location, but I had my ranger hat on.

"All right," I said, "The Indians are watching me to see what I'll do. Just fold it up and put it away, but it sure looks like good fishing!" It wasn't and it was not humorous to him either but it was obvious that if I had wanted to overlook it he was agreeable. No further trouble.

I had packaged our camp outfit and mailed it to myself so we had no pack loads to carry. We ate or gave away all our extra groceries. We enjoyed the beautiful Mooney Falls and the great travertine draperies that have grown around it. We purchased a few of their beautifully-made small baskets; they are still greatly treasured.

Elmer Watahomagie's father was one of the hereditary chiefs of the Havasupai tribe. He was over eighty years old and died while we were at Grand Canyon. He was to be buried traditionally in a secret place on the Great Thumb near the reservation. Their traditional cave burial sites had been vandalized some years earlier. The tribe had selected a secret small and rocky canyon on the route to the Great

Thumb. I was invited to the ceremony — a great honor. In delivering the invitation, Elmer stressed that I should bring a pickup truck and that he would be my guide to the secret place. I should meet the Saturday morning train at seven o'clock at the Grand Canyon Station.

I made sure I had a new and reliable pickup. Elmer and I loaded the burial box for the funeral rites. We drove west out past Rowe Well, the Lauzon Ranch, the Metzger place, and on beyond Pasture Wash. Near here in an open field with several pickups the Chief's body was resting on a door supported on two sawhorses made of logs. The Chief was dressed in buckskin and his body was partially covered with a blanket. Three Hualapai Indian women were with the Watahomagie family as professional mourners. Their wailing and keening was constant, in fact had been since his death two days previously. This wordless and piercing dirge was carried by one mourner and then picked up by another in variable key and volume. It went on and on and on as long as we were together. I drove over by the body and the Chief's sons lifted him into the burial casket. The daughters and other female relatives brought out his dress clothes — a dark suit on a hanger, a white shirt fresh from the laundry in its glassine envelope, a necktie, a handkerchief, a new pair of shoes, socks, underwear, and a pair of dark glasses. When the Chief reached the Happy Hunting Ground or the Valhalla which serves his people, the people greeting him would know that he was a chief because he was so well-dressed.

More Indians arrived and the casket was loaded and surrounded with boxes of food, Navajo rugs, and turquoise jewelry. The wailing had stopped. The world seemed empty without this salute. It was depressing, but it was real. A chief had died.

There were two other white men present. The Reverend James Asa White was a part-time priest to the Havasupai. The other was John Bradley, the corral boss for the Fred Harvey Company. He had come to fulfill a promise made many years before that he would place a silver-mounted bridle in the casket for the Chief's funeral. Simply and humbly, John paid this debt.

Guided by Elmer, I drove the pickup cross country for about two miles. The back of the pickup was loaded with Indian men to keep the casket upright. Slowly, we led a cortege of battered pickups and Indians on horseback. A small assemblage awaited us at the burial grounds. The grave was ready. The wailing began again briefly. Other Indians gathered around to view the Chief. More supplies were contributed. The casket was unloaded into a rope sling waiting on cross logs above the open grave.

Rev. White gave a brief ritual prayer. Jim Crooks, the Havasupai priest, gave a message and led a prayer in Havasupai. He led vigorously in the hymn, "Shall We Gather at the River?" The rituals were over. Elmer came to me. "You go now," he said. "Do you need a ride home?" I asked. "No, I have a ride." He waved me away past the grandson Victor Pearl Watahomagie, born December 7, 1941, who was leading the Chief's fully-saddled horse to the ceremonial site. As I drove slowly away, following John Bradley in his Fred Harvey pick-up and Dr. White riding with a young Indian, I heard a single rifle shot behind me. I assumed that this was the sacrifice of the horse to complete the burial equipment and the ceremony.

I never attempted to relocate the secret burying ground. It was none of my business. I suggested to Elmer, however, that they really should re-dig the grave and lower the burial box well below ground surface. The turquoise and the Navajo rugs alone that went into that box were a great treasure. I hope that they have protected them for the Chief. He needs them!

Grand Canyon was rich in lore of colorful people. At the Bright Angel Creek confluence I rowed one of Norm Nevill's "hard" boats around the circle of the big eddy. There were others of these "odd-ball river rats," like "Dock" Marston. Doc Hudson was hipped on running the river with motor boats. Georgie White began experimenting with big doughnut rafts. Jim Riggs in a hard boat went through the Canyon with oars in two twenty-four-hour days. Bert Loper, an old river man from Salt Lake City, disappeared on a last "solo" run between Lee's Ferry and Phantom Ranch. He was in his early 80s. His empty boat was recovered later. (When we moved away in 1952, the roster of successful river float passengers was just one hundred. Today it is over 10,000 a year, and Inger and I finally made the float trip in 1974.) Old-timers like John Hance and W. W. Bass became important subjects for historians. Jimmy Owens, the North Rim lion hunter, Texas cowboy, and guide for Teddy Roosevelt during a Wyoming hunting trip, was a fascinating citizen. His historic tree-mounted advertisement of his services on the North Rim simply offered "Lions caught to Order; Rates Reasonable."

I wrote "Hard Rock Shorty," a column of tall stories, for *Desert* magazine. The Garrison's made many weekend vacation trips — what a great vacation land it was! We began Inger's work in ceramics. This was something we could do together. I would be the janitor, mix the clay, and sweep the floor. She would learn the art of ceramics and how to use a kiln. It was an inexpensive hobby.

A look back at my Grand Canyon years brings mixed emotions. In career growth I had made my first move by going from Yosemite to Hopewell Village in 1939, and then to Washington. This was a real break for an ambitious young ranger. Then the war disrupted events and while I went ahead from this new plateau (I spent eleven years as an assistant superintendent at Glacier and at Grand Canyon) national events kept advancements bottled tightly. "So, Garrison, just put your head down and do your job. Do a good job! You wanted to be a ranger — what a glorious new kind of ranger this is!"

At Grand Canyon we had excellent staff, good neighbors, and many community involvements. I was active enough in non-political affairs — schools, Rotary Club, wildlife groups — that I was known both within the National Park Service and in the larger external Arizona community.

In counselling young rangers I always stressed the expectations that a ranger must live with. If he had an in-park job, the agency policies often limited the life pattern. For example, household pets were forbidden. Glacier and Grand Canyon were isolated living places. Most men liked the situation but some wives found it oppressive. Such unfortunate situations did not usually last long. Either they soon joined in sharing the special environment privileges, or they found other locations. These could often be found in the National Park Service at different locations. But my emphasis to the young people was that each of them carried a responsibility to participate within the community.

A ranger is secure in his job, but at Grand Canyon we had a village of one thousand people with all of the community amenities. We shared schools, the church, the stores, the professional and social groupings, the entertainment common to most small communities. I felt that I must pay my way for this part of community living by membership and participation. There were twenty-five local organizations, each with regular monthly meetings, committees and task forces, and social evenings. As Assistant Superintendent I was eventually on many of these community action groups — but not all at the same time! It took seven years to get around to it.

Did we need twenty-five groups? That was not for me to decide. Some of the members of each group thought we did and worked at it. So, as Assistant Superintendent and Chairman of the Community Council, I established a meeting schedule and a social calendar for our Community Hall. Each group was assigned non-competitive time for its money-raising events.

The major thrust, of course, was with church programs. We were aware of the needs of the Protestant Community Church, the Roman Catholics, the Mormons, the Seventh-Day Adventists, the Missouri Synod of the Lutheran Church, the Episcopalians, and the Southern Baptists. Some preferred home meetings, others needed an assigned time and place, and all desired listing in the Community Council Calendar. Then we left them alone — no problems. As a personal duty, I was the Chairman of the Board of Stewards for the Protestant Community Church.

The Rotary Club, the Boy and Girl Scouts, the Cubs and the Brownies, the P.T.A., the School Board, the Sportsman's Club (known irreverently as "The God and Run Club"), the Masons, the Red Cross, the Federal Employees Unions, the Community Council — it was a busy seven years and I loved it. I paid my dues.

Inger was similarly occupied with youth programs as our own youngsters went ahead through Girl Scouts and Boy Scouts. When she was Treasurer of the Girl Scout Committee, she inadvertently used our personal check book to finance their annual camping trip. They went to Mount Charleston, near Las Vegas, Nevada that year. I was suddenly overdrawn at the bank — Inger was still in Nevada with the car, I was isolated on the North Rim, the bank was in Williams, Arizona. Lars was getting ready to enroll at Wasatch Academy in Mount Pleasant, Utah, and I was trying to finance his enrollment and allowance by telephone with checks that bounced.

Inger began to develop her great artistic skills, particularly in ceramics. We bought a kiln, found an instructor, and set up a workshop in our garage. Also, we often visited neighboring Indian tribes and learned about their culture, artistic interests, and skills. Inger got to know many of them well, particularly the Hopi. This was a dividend of our broad acquaintance with the northern Arizona land.

Superintendent Bryant and I shared assignments to the North Rim for two or three weeks each summer. Our North Rim quarters were only partially furnished, so that slowly we built up a small supply of living conveniences which we left there year after year. At Hopewell we had purchased a bread box at a Pennsylvania farm house auction. I believe it was part of a "lot" which included some hand drill bits. The lot cost me a nickel. The bits went to the Hopewell black-smith shop. The bread box was a convenient packing shield for small and precious dishes, like a Delft cup and saucer. So we moved it along with us and finally took it to the North Rim, just as Jack Gray, our warehouseman, was making an official inventory of government prop-erty in the house. It was a big bread box and I was amused at Jack's quick evaluation: "One bread box, tin, japanned, $5.00."

When we returned to the South Rim we left the bread box in the kitchen and North Rim ranger Art Brown saw it. It was in the fall and he was having the annual invasion of field mice. The bread box would be a great place to store over-wintering food supplies like the cereals. I agreed by telephone. Art moved it across the road and we both for-got it. But the inventory did not forget about it. As I checked out my 14 million dollars worth of physical property, I was short one bread box — value $5.00. The ranger cabin had one but Garrison didn't. My last official act on the day I finally moved out of Grand Canyon was to approve a Board of Survey report transferring the damned bread box from my inventory to the ranger cabin! It was my last immersion in this kind of cleansing bath. I should have known better. It was one of those management lessons you learn but then never get to use the new wisdom.

A personal tragedy strengthened our home ties at Grand Canyon National Park. Erik, our Yosemite-born son, was now an active thir-teen years old. He was loving and loved, an excellent student and eager for new adventures in living, particularly Boy Scout programs. Begin-ning on his twelfth birthday he soon mastered the First Class Scouting skills and began to work on the Star Scout level of Merit Badges.

Skiing was one of his options and he loved it, especially Saturday trips to the Bill Williams Mountain Ski area near Williams, Arizona. One Saturday morning in mid-January, 1952, the ski tow rope was ice-clad. Because of the ice, Erik used a fold of his sweater to cushion his grip. The spiral twisting of the tow rope trapped him so that he could not let go. He was pulled through the safety gate which did not operate and was killed instantly in the bull wheel.

I was in a car with three other National Park Service people enroute to Washington, D.C. By chance, we called the Petersburg (Virginia) National Battlefield office that evening for information and found that the National Park Service had blanketed all the Virginia parks seeking me and hoping that we would touch base somewhere. Inger had to bear the brunt of this tragedy alone until I could return the next day after a hairy night flight. But the Grand Canyon cemetery is the one permanent land tie that we have. Inger's ties to Norway and to Alaska were history, as were mine to Iowa or Nebraska. We had been transients touring through California, Pennsylvania, Washington, D.C., Montana, and now Arizona. So the Grand Canyon cemetery is a meaningful base point, always in our hearts as a bit of homeland. The Boy Scouts have memorial grave stones and one of these appropriately and silently reports that the spirit of Erik Lemuel Garrison, a First Class Scout, is forever in the sunshine within the great ponderosa pine forest of the South Rim. We remember his courage, his love, his expectations for me and for Inger.

We tried to spend more time with Lars and Karen — difficult for Lars because he had left home at age fourteen to go to boarding school. He was now in college in Flagstaff. Later that year we took Karen with us on a trip to a National Park Service Superintendents' Conference in Glacier — a harbinger of things to come. Six months later I was offered, and accepted, the Superintendency of Big Bend National Park in Texas. Omar Khayyam has said it well: "The moving finger writes and having writ moves on."

CHAPTER XV

THE BIG BEND

Enroute to Big Bend we stopped at Santa Fe to consult with Regional Director Minor R. Tillotson. "Tilly" had been my Regional Director at Hopewell Village. Prior to that he had been at Grand Canyon as Park Engineer and later as Superintendent. He had supervised the construction of the Kaibab Trail on the South Rim to the Colorado River crossing at Phantom Ranch. Congressman Louis Crampton of Michigan had worked out the legislation and appropriation. Coconino County had traded its 1890 "toll road" franchise on the Bright Angel Trail for the new Kaibab Trail, a bridge crossing at the river, and funding for a new approach road to the Grand Canyon from the National Old Trails Highway—U.S. 66—to the South Rim.

Tilly was a very competent administrator, although he seemed more naturally at home in the Southwest than he had in Virginia. I had worked with him at Grand Canyon; he wanted me to pick up the lore and the political background of Big Bend before I was immersed in the daily decision making. So I received an informative introduction that had been lacking at Hopewell. "You know me and I know you," he emphasized. "I want you at Big Bend. Give special attention to public relations problems. Just do what comes naturally — drive in to Alpine occasionally and telephone me. We don't want any secrets from each other."

My predecessor, Dr. Ross Maxwell, was a great research geologist. He had done the preliminary evaluations on the park. Moving to the University of Texas, he had been a natural candidate to be the first park superintendent. He had been an eager and enthusiastic administrator. Great things were planned, but the grandiose dreams of highway changes, boundary adjustments, a visitors' center and park interpretation, and blossoming of user economics collided with the reality of the federal budget. There was never enough money to carry out these dreams.

[227]

The optimistic Superintendent submits his programs to the Regional Office. The Regional Director works under a financial ceiling. He must reduce the program to fit the money, and although Tilly might be generous, there is another control called "the program of the President." So the budget is cut. It is submitted to Washington, and the Interior Department cuts more, comparing the needs of the "empty" Big Bend with the pressures from Senators from Wyoming and California — Yellowstone and Yosemite — where visitors already need services. Hopefully, the Alpine Chamber of Commerce has been in touch with the Texas Congressional delegation about the park needs. Local Congressman "Slick" Rutherford is the key man and, of course, the Senatorial side of political influence is great, but money bills start in the House. Slick is not very potent. And, of course, the park superintendent cannot tell the Congressman his true needs. He can only support what has survived in the President's budget. Old hands in Congress and knowledgeable bureaucrats learn how to work within this crazy patchwork. But it is slow starting!

Meanwhile, the Superintendent has become overcommitted to his public supporters. I have seen it many times. It has happened to me. Suddenly the budget approach is a pile of bitter ashes. Everything gets deferred. It is embarrassing. But I knew the rationale of living with this and with the neighbors. Ross had gone through the real rough-and-tumble beginnings of park establishment.

I often wished that Ross had not been so optimistic about the number of park visitors in the beginning years. In 1952 he had reported 90,000 people. I was too naive — I used it as the base for my own projections. The park concessioner cautioned me that it was too high, so we installed a traffic counter at the entrance at Persimmon Gap. In 1953 actual visitation was just over 29,000 people. That was generous considering the number of working ore trucks. Should I just report the 29,000 and go on from there? It would invalidate a lot of local and regional statistics and question the validity of all our reporting on many subjects. We finally decided to reduce reported travel by one-third in 1954 and to take another look at it in 1955. Three years later travel was above 90,000 real visitors.

The local communities of Alpine (ninety miles distant) and Marathon (sixty-five miles) were loaded with advisors and well-wishers. I picked up a lot of informal historical background just by listening. Every friend and every dissident tried his proposals on me. This was only normal, and I expected it.

"Charlie" loved to shoot eagles from a small airplane — probably a very difficult skill to acquire, but I simply informed him that although the superintendents had changed, the policy had not. "Don't shoot our eagles!" A neighboring rancher discussed the problem of mountain lions and his sheep herds. "No problem," I told him. "If a lion kills your sheep and takes refuge in the park, send us the message immediately and we will join you in the hunt with your dogs." This never happened. A mail-order merchant from El Paso threatened to garnish Jose's wages for a delinquent bill. This phony claim was dropped, and employee morale was raised, when I helped Jose. He had a cancelled check and a receipt.

I became an honorary member of the Alpine Rotary Club; the Chamber of Commerce group were hearty supporters; I was invited to local Sul Ross university events and to regional and state affairs such as the West Texas Chamber of Commerce and the Texas-Mexico Good Neighbor Commission.

Inger established her own cultural outpost in our garage with her ceramic kiln and equipment, and with a bridge club circuit joining others in the eighty mile drive to Marathon once a week. It seemed to be fun. In two years there was only one day that the "creek came up" and the bridge players could not get home.

Our first journey from El Paso to Van Horn, Marfa, Alpine, and Marathon was eventful. The endless blue sky dome with drifting wisps of white clouds, the great vistas, the occasional herds of antelope, the clumps of mesquite, juniper, and oak, and the dry brown grass-covered hills, were the same as those in Arizona. We loaded up with $100 worth of groceries in Alpine, went on through Marathon, and turned south — just as far south as you could go in the United States except in east Texas and Florida. The first large highway sign cautioned us that no gasoline was available for the next eighty miles.

Marathon was a railroad siding community. It was one of our major supply points, but it had a particular allure for me. I was told that it was named about 1860 by a retired sea captain because it reminded him of the Plains of Marathon in Greece. The legend named

him Lemuel Shepherd. Later reports indicate his first name was probably Albion, but I had been intrigued by the name Lemuel, my own
first name — a Biblical King of great wisdom, a book of proverbs in
Isaiah — for other than for my father I seldom heard the name. And
even my father had diluted events for me by my second name of
Alonzo. There were not many of us.

The Marathon Lemuel (or Albion) was a meticulous housekeeper
and had insomnia. He would reportedly arise at 3 A.M. and, after a
cup of tea, go out to the chicken house and light the lantern, meanwhile telling the hens, "I can't sleep and you shan't either!" It was
great legend, but hardly suggestive of west Texas.

There are many great place names along the route into the park.
The Appalachian Fold is a series of scalloped hills rimmed with white
rock, the western-most outcrop of an eastern Appalachian rock stra-
tum. Six Mile Tank is a windmill and water tank. El Puerto del
Camelos is the short pass near Persimmon Gap through which Lieu-
tenant William Echols brought his experimental camel and mule expedition in 1860. Santiago is a flat-topped mountain, the land on top
reportedly having been subdivided and sold at one time. The Rosillos
may mean simply something like "The Rosy Colored Mountains," although it also may be derived from *roscillos*, or dew.

A decade later, when I was appointed Superintendent of Yellow-
stone, the oldest National Park in the world, I was asked to address the
Bozeman, Montana Rotary Club as my initial community meeting. In
his introduction, Jack Ellis Haynes, the capable proprietor of the
Haynes Picture Shops, mentioned that I had been *Superintendent* of
Big Bend — the newest National Park.

The question was later asked, "Is it true that the state of Texas
wanted a National Park so badly that it bought one and gave it to the
United States?"

This is so plausible that it deserves a comment. *Pro forma*, it is
what happened. But the park itself, the natural resources, had a long
history of evaluation and recommendation, so that in 1944, when
Texas Canyons State Park became Big Bend National Park, the transition had been carefully planned. The Texas legislature appropriated
the money, the State Park Commission bought it, and now, almost a
decade later, I became acquainted with it as the second superintendent.

First, and most startling, of course, is that it is a park of recycled land. Parks of pristine wildlands were traditional — it took a considerable amount of flexibility to accept a used one! But it fit the scene. It was the beginning of a new dimension. I had begun my career as a forest fire fighter in Alaska. I had graduated to a commitment to nature and the sanctity of wild lands. I absorbed the reality of O'Shaughnessey Dam at Hetch Hetchy as the price civilization exacted for protection of the whole block of Yosemite back country. I found historic lands compatible with this same dream of love — love of land, love of nature, love of people. Now I was enthused with the drama of a love of natural process. We had not done right by this land, but we could give it another chance and it would bloom again in the sense that it would fulfill its appropriate role in the series of microcosms of which our world is made. I felt the excitement of my high school years and the discovery of the unity of nature. Here we were giving this flow of vitality a chance.

We were at the nadir of a historic cycle, of nature's vaunted process of self-healing and regrowth — what a beautiful laboratory Big Bend was! I was the alchemist, and it was as if all my previous experience was meant for this moment.

Big Bend is a land of strong beauty — often savage and always imposing. It is magnificent. The bold mountains rear abruptly against the endless blue sky with traceries of white clouds. The "Long Look" never fades. The enticing view to the horizon ends in a haze of gray or blue or brown as the sky eats up the land. The land disappears but the sky is still there, the forever edge of the world that is always inviting.

Big Bend is a land of many contrasts, and each component is a positive statement. Mount Emery is almost 8,000 feet in elevation. Straw House or Stillwell Crossing at the mouth of Santa Elena Canyon is about 1,700 feet. Mount Emery carries a remnant Canadian life zone vegetation. The Rio Grande River is either tropical or subtropical. The animal populations are usually Mexican species. Any bears left in the mountain recesses are probably Mexican black bears. One species of deer is the Sierra del Carmen whitetail. The ground squirrel is a Mexican species. Javelina are often found; a mother coyote conducting a singing lesson for puppies on the slopes of Burro Mesa is unforgettable; a too-friendly mountain lion is another problem.

Yes, this is a land of contrasts. And it took us two years to become acquainted. This was the information I presented at Bozeman. I'm sure the Rotarian was disappointed, except that as a new Yellowstone superintendent I was pleased to report that National Park standards were still honored.

Let's explore Big Bend more closely. The land had been used and reused. In 1953 we were ending a ten-year drouth period. Two-hundred-year-old oak trees had died. Past overgrazing was evident. Beautiful Green Gulch had had one year of recovery from the 2,000 sheep "Waddy" Burnham was reported to have held there.

Tornillo Creek also showed signs of this abuse. It had been beaten down fifty years earlier. Hundreds of tons of Mexican flour spar ore had been hauled from a U.S. Customs Station tramway near Boquillas Canyons to Marathon, a distance of 120 miles. There had been hundreds of horses, mules, or burros hitched to freight wagons. They had all lived off the native vegetation, devastating a strip about five miles wide. This was now recovering very slowly. It just needed time, faith in nature's cycles, tolerance, and some grass seed and rain. We had these to offer after the drouth broke.

In spite of these special insults to the land, the general beauty of the Big Bend country is impressive. The Canadian life zone atop Mount Emery is not imaginary. There are ponderosa pine in sheltered habitats, Douglas fir, white fir, and even quaking aspen. Arizona cypress grows near Boot Spring (named for the towering rock cowboy boot at this location). On the shoulder of the big mountain, Juniper Flat, transitional zone plants appear: the drooping juniper, which always seems sadly flaccid as if dying of thirst, and the madrone, locally called "the naked Indian."

This transition continues to the Rio Grande, through a vegetative wonderland of giant daggers, yucca, lechuguilla, allthorn, candelilla, pineapple, nicotinia, sotol, agave, resurrection plant, leather brush or devil's blood, ocotillo, river cane, cholla of many varieties, and other cactus which bloom brilliantly in season.

It is not a barren land. Pat Miller, the Persimmon Gap ranger, and I spent two hours one morning inventorying a walk through the shrubs near his station to determine if we could establish a short nature trail. In less than a quarter of a mile we identified nearly one hundred plant species.

There are over 350 bird species on the official lists. The peregrine falcon, probably a Mexican variety, soars above the South Rim where the rare Colima warbler nests. The American cuckoo, or road runner, also called paisano, is a most unusual character. Mocking birds and cardinals are cheerful companions. The varieties of smaller birds — finches, sparrows, wrens, larks — are impressive. Bird watchers are eager visitors to any source of water, like K-Bar, Sam Nails' windmill, or the Rio Grande. We kept a water pan filled near our dining room window so that we had daily bird visitors. At the Johnston Ranch, near the southernmost point of the Big Bend, a river gauger calibrated a square pan which he filled regularly. The total evaporation was 130 inches a year in a land with an average annual rainfall of about 2 inches but a soil temperature as high as 120 degrees.

The international park concept was intriguing. I had served in the Waterton-Glacier International Peace Park in Montana. Canada and the United States had jointly decreed this designation. Local international Rotary Clubs were influential and active. There were good roads. But Mexico was not ready for this level of cooperation. It was inviting, but it would require a lot of political maneuvering, such as allocation of funds from other projects, a supporting citizens' group (which was not available), and a great change in priorities of road construction.

Mexico is a proud nation. A Fronterisa National Park must be truly representative of Mexico and not just another border community as an American tourist attraction. Mexican people must use it and be proud of it. This was not possible at that time.

But the charm remains. In Big Bend the great recumbent Chief Alsate, broods quietly atop Pulliam Bluff over the array of surrounding attractions — Casa Grande Mountain, Lost Mine Peak, Carter Peak, Ward Mountain, Toll Mountain, Mount Emery, Saddle Mountain, Panther Pass, The Window, The Basin, Government Springs, Green Gulch, and Juniper Flat. It is a startling display of scenery.

Traditionally, the Mexican paisanos were small farmers. The word literally means "countryman." (It also titles the ubiquitous road runner, or chaparall cock, the American cuckoo.) The native farmers

were everywhere, even before this land had become independent of
Mexico. In sandy washes and below occasional springs the farmers
often kept a few goats, a few chickens, and a burro, raised corn, beans,
melons, peppers, and often a few flowers. Gilberto Luna's jacal near
Castalon is a residual example. This decrepit, low structure of adobe
and cottonwood poles was Gilberto's home for decades. He survived
eleven wives, sired thirty children, and was in his late nineties when he
finally moved in with his grandchildren in Fort Stockton. A broken-
wheeled wagon rests beside the building. A rusting cultivator lies under
the wagon. An optimistic visitor has tacked a horseshoe above the door.

This farmstead was immediately above a rock dike which crossed
a branch of Blue Creek and created a sandy flat across the valley. This
shut-in dike trapped underground water from the infrequent rains.
Deep plantings reached down into the sand for this moisture. Similarly, a deep sand pocket might seep enough water into a pit to provide drinking water. It was very primitive, but this sandy expanse,
strewn with a loose rock cover, was the key to survival.

We had a suggestion of the extent of the farm populations from
ruins of old adobes, melted into the ground from which they had been
fashioned. An undated church ruin two miles below Gilberto's home
revealed occasional mounds of earth and rock marked by crude and
anonymous, but obviously human, graves.

Large ranches had been superimposed across many of the smaller
farms. But most of the big ranch operations had found the sparse vegetation inadequate for cattle. There were only occasional natural springs
or constructed water tanks. Natives did not speak of the number of
"cows per section" that the range would support; it was usually the
number of "sections per cow," often four or five. Where ranchers
adopted range management practices and made water improvements,
they could make it. Some of them still survive.

But much of the land continued in small farms, or the Texas
equivalent of "homesteads," such as the Hot Springs development of
the J. O. Langford spread at the mouth of Tornillo Creek. Langford
tried to develop a spa, but he also depended on some grazing and farming, and the dry cycles forced him out. "Homesteading" simply meant
buying the land from the state of Texas. There was no federal public
domain. Texas entered the Union by treaty, after it had wrested free-

dom from Mexico; so any "left over" land was owned by the state. It had been homesteaded by optimistic farmers through a bidding process in the 1920s. "Clear a few acres, run a few cows, pray for rain!" Some of them did well for a while with a succession of several wet years, but drouth eventually wiped them out. Then, in the Big Bend, the state had purchased many of these small holdings for the park in 1943.

With 127 miles of common boundary with Mexico along the Rio Grande, we obviously had many Mexican contacts. For a "friendly" and undefended boundary, the United States had established a powerful force of police. The usual Immigration and Border Patrol rules applied to border crossings, but our three park rangers near the river were the action force. While on park patrol, they would make notes and report any problems to the Border Patrol and the U.S. Customs. There were no permanent patrol stations on our side; roving patrols would come through the park occasionally. We found a few wetbacks, who would travel many miles north to possible farm employment.

There were only three major Mexican communities south of the Rio Grande: San Vicente, Boquillas, and Santa Elena. I made a point of fording the river at these places to become acquainted with the Mexican officers. The problems of dope smuggling had not developed at that time. In fact there was a comfortable informality about much of the interchange. Maggie Smith, who operated the Hot Springs store, Jess Gilmer, who was farming at San Vicente, and Bob Cartledge at Castalon served as contact points for mail pickup and delivery. The Mexicans occasionally made individual "wet back" trips to the U.S. trading posts for groceries. We understood that the same freedom of basic exchange guided the La Jitas operation just west of the park along the river, although park personnel were seldom there. The stores sold canned goods, flour, cheese, onions, lard, candy, some fruit, shoes, kerosene and gasoline, nails, shovels and picks, and doubled as post offices.

We were ever mindful of the protocol of dealing with the sovereign government of a neighboring nation. By 1953, memories of the 1916 Pancho Villa raids into the United States had faded from memory of most people, but history and legends kept the stories alive. The Mexican revolutionaries had invaded the Big Bend at Glen Springs and at

McKinney Springs. Four people had been killed at Glen Springs. There were other raids, most notably at Deming, New Mexico. But at the Big Bend the relics of adobe ruins and titillating tales kept us aware of the pioneer border heritage.

A quarantine had been established by the Department of Agriculture along the entire international boundary in response to an outbreak of aftosa — foot and mouth disease — in Mexican cattle. Horseback patrol stations were established within the park at Castalon and Hot Springs or San Vicente. Every day a horseback patrolman would ride the boundary looking for cloven hoof prints. Trespass horses were fairly common — these were the park rangers' responsibility — but trespass cattle were doomed. They were shot, an incident report completed, and patrol resumed. We had few such incidents during my time in Big Bend. Earlier patrols, particularly into Mexico with authority to round up, pay for, and shoot border cattle, had produced international tensions. The Aftosa Patrol was not considered a friendly group by the Mexican farmers along the Rio Grande. There had not been any incidents for several years, although we felt that Ross Maxwell could have been a shooting target at one time. So we had a "river rider" border patrol.

A different situation was Texans' insistence that their police officers must have the authority and the right to carry their guns. This was no real problem, although every Texas law enforcement officer from city cop, game warden, and deputy sheriff, on up to highway patrolman and Texas Ranger made a visible point of displaying his firearm whenever he was in the park. This was especially noticeable at Big Bend, where these authorities operated in conjunction with park rangers in uniform, and who were nearly always without guns or gun belts.

The Mexican side of the river also had special police arrangements. *The Policia Federal de Candelilla* was a roving patrol of Mexican police officers with the task of preventing *exportation* of candelillia wax to the United States. The candelillia wax plant is a leafless cluster of gray or green pencil-size stems two or three feet high, with a chitinous rind covered by a thin, waxy coating which prevents plant transpiration naturally. If the wax can be removed and collected it is an excellent preservative, similar to cosmoline, and also great for polishes, waxes, and bubble gum. The wax is removed by digging the plant up and boiling it in a vat with water and a dollop of sulphuric acid, which separates the wax as a surface scum. This process was well known, and a thriving industry developed wherever the plant grew along the border — except in Big Bend National Park.

The Mexican dilemma was that a Mexican *cartel de candelillia* by law provided the acid and then collected and exported the wax. The principle market was the United States. The cartel payment rate to the wax makers at that time was about three pesos — twenty-five cents — per kilogram. Wax making was home-style industry in Mexico, and United States custom regulations did not prohibit importation. It just must be reported.

The American border wax buyers would pay as much as fifty cents a pound for it — a direct invitation for smugglers to get going, and they did. The Mexican acid supply someway did not produce as much wax as expected. So the Policia Federal de Candelillia patroled their side of the border searching for contraband wax which was being smuggled out of Mexico into the free port of the United States.

Every border trading post operator was also a wax buyer. It was reported that in Mexico, near Castelon, an unguarded government warehouse full of wax was empty when customers called for it. This contraband probably came into the United States right through the park, but nobody knew anything. Bribes were reported, special favors of food and equipment were mentioned. An unarmed and uninvolved park ranger was wise to be like the Chinese monkey that does not hear, see, or say anything.

It was hard to be impersonal, however, when Maggie Smith, the storekeeper at San Vicente, informed me one morning that one of the most industrious river pirates (the Mexicans also stole the wax from each other along the Mexican side of the border) had just bought two *trienta-trienta* (30-30) rifle shells and had carefully written the names of Chief Ranger George Sholly and me on them. This was a great joke! Fortunately, the bullets were never delivered. But it tickled Maggie. (She had been a trader at several of the stores over a period of thirty years. She was as hard as nails, but when she saw a Mexican in real need her heart always softened.)

Big Bend was part of our pioneer American heritage — our neighbors were friendly, outgoing, independent, and helpful. A neighboring rancher confessed that he didn't "like the National Park one damn bit!" It interfered with his cattle grazing and he had had to put up fences. He intended to make our operations as difficult as he could. But Inger played bridge with his wife, I helped him plan a mule deer hunt on the North Kaibab in Arizona, and he found that his natural friendliness conflicted with his opposition. He didn't really like that either, "not one damn bit!" But "Why didn't the National Park Service get another superintendent, somebody I can dislike?" We helped him locate his boundary line on the north side of the park, clean up some abandoned ranch wire, and build a better boundary fence. He mumbled about the need to do all this, but finally agreed that it was a lot better than trespass grazing conflicts. He didn't like those either, "not one damn bit!"

By courtesy of the U.S. Border Patrol we had a base station on its nationwide radio network. Each morning at 7:00 A.M. and each evening at 4:00 P.M. the Marfa station would call us and transmit any emergency messages for Big Bend. "Emergencies" were defined rather loosely, but it was a very helpful communication aid for a new park. There were occasional technical problems, particularly the phenomenon called "skip." We might miss communications with Marfa, but Alpine, El Paso, or Pensacola, Florida could read us perfectly.

Soon after our arrival an early morning communication from Alpine, 120 miles distant, carried an invitation for me to join Mr. Hugh White, President of the Alpine Chamber of Commerce, on a visit to San Antonio for a meeting of the West Texas Chamber. I was not completely unpacked, so I responded that I could not attend and Chief Ranger George Sholly could go in my place. In a few minutes there was another communication stating that a group from Alpine would visit Big Bend that day to welcome us to the Big Bend Country.

They drove into park headquarters at Panther Junction in the early afternoon. I had met Hugh briefly on our grocery stop in Alpine earlier in the week. He had written most cordially congratulating me on my appointment. With him were two professional photographers, the Brewster County Judge, several businessmen, and the newspaper and radio station owners from Alpine. It was a cordial and warm group. Their mission was simply to bring greetings, a welcome, a pledge of support and cooperation, and warm friendship. It was a "heart-to-heart" communication, for I sensed their sincerity and warmth. Inger and I responded in kind. What a gesture! It was the first of many similar outpourings.

Over a private cup of coffee Hugh White added comments on Texas culture for my guidance. When the West Texas Chamber of Commerce invited the new superintendent of Big Bend, they wanted the superintendent and not a substitute. If I could not go, this was acceptable. They would arrange another opportunity. As the Number One man they wanted to meet me in person! A *segundo* might be acceptable in other places in America, or even in West Texas after I got acquainted, but they asked me to reconsider — to ask for a rain check on the invitation, or rearrange my own priorities and attend with them. It would be an honor for them to introduce me!

This advice from an old campaigner such as Hugh White (who became a treasured friend) was presented graciously and humbly. I grasped his concept immediately and was ashamed that I had missed the implications. I had not known the ground rules and the power structure. I had been an assistant for so long that I had not adjusted to my new "front window" image. I did not forget it again! Honor to the superintendent was simply honor to the park. I must build this image. I traveled with Hugh White to San Antonio. It was a successful trip. The friends I made were helpful. Big Bend National Park was a vigorous part of the west Texas scene, and we kept it that way!

We had many sightings of mountain lions in the park. A lazy one spent many sunny hours on top of a huge rock next to the motel cabin office in the Basin. "Shorty" Chambers, a park equipment operator and mechanic, had a Buick roadster with a spotlight. Shorty was courting Leona Smith, the cook at the Basin Motel dining room, and she did not get off duty until 9:00 P.M. Shorty's big roadster would be waiting and they would drive the park roads at night, watching for the telltale reflections of animal eyes in the car headlights. For many months our file of lion sightings was principally from Shorty. I am certain they were all valid — in fact I saw two lions myself. But when Shorty and Leona were married the frequency of midnight lion sightings took a big drop.

A small plane landed in the road near Panther Junction one morning. It turned out to be my good friend, Senor Jesus Maria Ramon, a Mexican politician and senator from Ciudad Acuna, who was interested in Big Bend National Park as a guideline for his thinking about the possible Mexican companion park. We tied the plane down and went on a tour of the park. I noticed that as I met Jesus, he was carrying a small, black revolver. He quickly locked it into his brief case, where it stayed. We forded the river for a brief visit to Boquillas. We called at the police office, the school, and the bar — *la tienda*. I noticed that as soon as we left American soil and drove into the river ford, Jesus had his gun back again. In our park it once more disappeared. As he climbed into the plane to return to Cd Acuna, the gun was back in sight. I thought Jesus handled his personal security arrangements quite adroitly.

I arranged a float trip through Boquillas Canyon with Chief Ranger George Sholly and his wife, Reece, Inger and myself, and the president of Sul Ross University in Alpine, Dr. Bryan Wildenthal, and his wife. Our trip to Marufa Vega was serene and delightful. With our shallow-draft pontoons and a strong up-canyon wind, we had to paddle vigorously most of the way. We were tired that night, and canebrake sleeping was restful and quiet.

About noon the second day we discovered a great pile of candelilla wax on the park side of the river bank. It was as big as a house. Three burros indicated that this was the site of an active wax camp. The "weed," as the Mexicans called it, was mostly collected in the park, we presumed, although some of it might have been gathered in Mexico. Stacking it in the park protected it from any investigation by the Mexican candelilla police. A split fifty-gallon steel drum was mounted on the rocks, ready to begin cooking the wax out. A fifty-gallon drum of sulphuric acid was above the camp on a rocky promontory. It had obviously been rafted up the river to this location, ready to go. Tools, clothing, and small caches of food were scattered around. A pot of beans was bubbling briskly over a small, open campfire. A mongrel dog barked at us vigorously, but then gave it up and ran across the river into another canebrake. He obviously responded to low-voiced commands from one of the workers in the canebrake. Then a vigorous commotion indicated that the observer had abandoned the campsite and started running down the river through the cane. He kept on going and the dog kept on following, barking occasionally to salute his hidden master.

The campsite was left to us. Sholly, who had been reared in Lordsburg, New Mexico, and was very understanding of the Mexican people, carefully gathered up the food and the personal belongings around the campsite and laid them safely to one side. We would destroy the camp and burn the "weed," but we would not retaliate in any way against the workers. One of the wax buyers had organized and financed the raid on the park. Destruction of the acid, the drum, the tools, and the weed pile would make it an expensive venture. We never knew who had set it up. We never asked. Somebody got hurt financially. The other buyers got a chuckle out of it. Future wax-making teams were never again of this dimension. It was a small hit-and-run game from then on. The wax makers ran for cover immediately once we suspected they were in the park. Even a passing small airplane on a sight-seeing tour was enough to send them to cover.

Our guests, the Wildenthals, were obviously jittery, but good sports. My own blood pressure was also up. Our bullets through the walls of the acid drum trickled the acid into a pit in a sandy, dry wash. I accidently stepped in the acid-loaded sand and then on the gunwale of the boat. Then I sat in it! Shortly, we regrouped as my pants began to fall apart, the only casualty.

The place names of the Big Bend region have a beauty and significance of their own. On the river below the park and above Reagen Canyon stands Sierra El Burro — a single great butte famed in early Mexican tales as a wilderness outpost. Pico Etereo was just what the name suggested — the Ethereal Peak. El Jardin, or the Garden, was a lush portion of the Sierra del Carmen in Mexico. Sierra Fronteriza was the higher extension of the southern Sierra del Carmen. A great square butte in the Sierra del Carmen profile was Schott Tower, possibly named for its similarity to an eastern American tower built to facilitate the pouring or casting of lead into bullets or buckshot. It may also have been the name of a German geologist or an American surveyor — I heard it both ways. Within Boquillas Canyon the winding river at one point revealed three adjacent buttes, Los Tres Hermanos, skylined in silent beauty. On the west side of the Chisos, the double-pointed butte above Castalon Peak was obviously the Mule Ears. North of this was another twin peak, Las Corezones, the Two Hearts, also known as the Mule Ears. This was often vulgarized to "la tetas de Juana," similarly to the Three Tetons of Wyoming. Juana or Juanita must indeed have been a female of Amazonian build, suckling màchismo hombres!

The first year I was in Big Bend the developed areas at Panther Junction and the Basin were furnished electric power on a fairly regular basis from large electric generators. These were noisy, smelly, and given to break down on Friday afternoons at 5:30 P.M., just after the park mechanic had left for the weekend. Candles, flashlights, and lanterns were normal household furnishings. But electric power was brought to the park in 1954. We had a "turn on the lights!" party, which was a great success. We could converse with the Marfa or Alpine Border Patrol Stations, regardless of the time of day! We could use electric pumps at our gasoline service station. We gladly abandoned the hand-cranking ones. But the morning after the party everything was silent. Our three-phase power setup had broken down. We could not operate the short wave radio to get the Border Patrol to make a call for us. We would have to send a car to Marathon to alert our power sources that we were in trouble — an outage, we called it. But we needed to fill a gasoline tank to make the drive to Marathon, and, of course, the new gasoline pump was silent also! Like a group of youthful raiders, we found short gasoline hoses and empty cans, and siphoned gas from several cars so that one car could make the town to report that we had an outage. Our glory had been short-lived! Rueful Red was the new color describing our faces that day!

Our work crews were wonderful. Unfortunately, we had bowed to national custom so that ours was the standard eight-to-five work day, and we had abandoned the tradition of the afternoon siesta in spite of the midday sun. But our crews gave it all they had. Our men possessed many different skills, so we could take a small allotment of money, and by joint and concentrated endeavor paint a house, repair a road, or build a bridge. (I recalled this in later years at Yellowstone — to repair a road would require a grader, a bulldozer, two trucks and loads of sand, an oil truck, men and their hand tools, and an account number so that the cost accounting was accurate. It would cost $800 just to get the crew together in the utility yard on Monday morning. At Big Bend we could all pitch in. With $800 in equipment rental, materials, and wages, we might finish the entire project by 4:20 P.M. the first afternoon.)

The men were nearly all of Mexican ancestry, gentle, shy, respectful, industrious, courteous, and honest. It was rewarding to get to know them. Some of them had moved their families into the park where old ranch houses were available close to their work. The women were well-groomed and genteel with soft voices. Their housekeeping was immaculate. Even the yards would usually be swept clean. The children were soft, smiling, round, and curious. On these outposts, their lonely existence was accepted as a normal life style.

During the winter of 1953 Art Minish, our maintenance foreman, submitted a proposal for "Lito" Garcia, one of our trusted temporary employees from Alpine, to become a permanent employee. We started Lito's file through the paperwork. The old form 57, "Application for Federal Employment," was designed to expose undesirables by asking about membership in un-American organizations, as if such members would simply confess to it. It also asked, "Have you ever been arrested?"

I admit with some humor now that since I was seventeen years old I have had to respond affirmatively to this inquiry. For over fifty years my application record has faithfully reported that in 1921 at age seventeen I had indeed been "haled," or hauled, into court and tried on a charge of assault and battery following a neighborhood dispute over the use of irrigation water. The charges were dismissed. But Lito did not possess my righteousness or faith, so instead of acknowledging his sins, he chose to deny them, and answered the question with a simple negative — "No."

This soon proved to be an improper whopper, for in a very short time we received Lito's records from the United States Civil Service Commission. He was now in deep trouble. Lito had been jailed for being drunk and disorderly at some time in every local community in three counties! These were verified records of arrest, trial, sentence, and jail release — Lito had indeed painted the towns!

But the Commission generously offered us an alternative. Lito had not been in trouble recently. After we had investigated the matter we might go ahead and hire him if we wished, but we must get a report of penance, and we must counsel with him. His offense was not in being "D&D," but in telling lies about it on a sworn application for federal employment — no less. "Shame on you, Lito!"

Now we had it in perspective. Art checked it out: Lito had indeed been a weekend lush until about a year ago, when there had been a marital rearrangement, he had made special reports to the priest, and had become truly a changed man.

However, the Commission stated that I must counsel with him, and Lito was working down at K-Bar digging a ditch. We were rearranging the drainage from a small water seep to provide permanent bird watering facilities. Birds and birdwatchers loved the tangled thicket. Lito climbed over the rocks and came over to me standing in the shade of a big mesquite tree. He took off his hat as he always did when he spoke to me. I was El Patron, the Big Shot! But there was always a twinkle in his eye. He knew something. He trusted me.

"Yass, Mr. Garrison. You wanted to see mee?"

"Yes, Lito. I want to talk to you. We sent in your application for the year-around job. One of the questions asked if you had been arrested." I showed him the Civil Service Commission letter. "You said that you had never been arrested."

"Yass, Mr. Garrison. That's right."

So I brought out the bundle of police records and under the shade of the mesquite tree near the tules around K-Bar Spring, we conducted our personnel counselling. But first I had to verify the records.

"Lito, this record shows that you have been in jail in Alpine, Marathon, Marfa, Redford, Presidio, Fort Davis, . . . and all of these other places for being drunk and disorderly."

"Yass, that's right Mr. Garrison. That's right. I was drunk and disorderly." He pronounced it dronk.

"But you have never been arrested?" I was incredulous. There was something I did not understand.

"Yass. That's right Mr. Garrison."

"But Lito, if you have never been arrested, how did you get in jail?"

He hesitated. He had never connected being arrested with being put in jail. You got arrested only when you stole something or stabbed somebody. A light dawned in his eyes. To Lito, I just didn't under-stand the way it worked. It must work differently in my world than it did in his.

He elucidated for me quite simply.

"Oh, I get dronk; I get in jail. Just like anybody."

My report was favorable. I had counselled with Lito; he had also counselled with me. We both had indeed been sober and reliable citi-zens — "Just like anybody!"

CHAPTER XVI

PARK PLANNERS

SOON AFTER WE MOVED TO BIG BEND IN 1953 I attended a staff meeting at the Regional Office in Santa Fe. Regional Director Tillotson discussed the support function his office offered a superintendent in running a park.

"Quite often," Tilly observed, "a park superintendent doesn't know what he really wants to do or should do and asks the Region for instructions. Lon and Doc Bryant seldom did this at Grand Canyon. They made suggestions. Lon is doing the same thing at Big Bend. Here is one: 'We want to establish a trail crossing at Terlingua Creek at the mouth of the Santa Elena Canyon. We will need $800.00.' He says 'we' want to do this so I assume he has had staff advice. He must know how he can get it done.

"The easy decision for this office is just to tell Big Bend to go ahead. We agree with the idea and we can allot the money. We wish more superintendents would make up their own minds!"

Tilly was perceptive in this comment. It was a deliberate pattern I followed. Doc and I had worked it out at Grand Canyon. "Tell the Region what you think should be done and if you have done your homework they will help you do it. Let the park staff be part of the decision making. It is a great boost to park morale and a compliment to the Regional Office."

I was reminded of the time I was asked about how I learned "good judgment," as if I was a successful practitioner of this delicate art. My final defense was pragmatic. I had learned about "good judgment" by using "bad judgment." Most of my management techniques came from this same crucible.

National Park Service Director Connie Wirth loomed more largely on my horizon. As an Assistant Director in 1940 he had been most helpful to me at Hopewell in courageously financing the purchase of the measured drawings of the Hopewell twenty-two-foot water wheel

[247]

and its blowing tubs from the Franklin Institute. They had cost $600! Then he had met one evening with community leaders to share future plans and urban expectations — quite an education for a Yosemite ranger!

In 1954 Connie was the Director and a continuing, constructive leader. He was exploring management techniques for more effective ways to capture and channel the talents of his support staff. I went to Washington to meet with a team of field officials to review two ideas.

We first looked at National Park staff growth. The Service was getting increases in manpower which seldom went out to the firing line where park visitors met National Park rangers. The new staff people were intercepted by the empire builders in either WASO (the Washington Office) or in the ROs (the Regional Offices). Superintendents needed help on the real face-to-face functions of preservation, protection, and interpretation. (Twenty-five years later, arguments continue about this maladjustment. It is an inherent conflict between staff and line functions.) This was my first real exposure to office politics.

The second concept was to consider the superintendent of a park as Captain of the Ship. He needed authority to make many policy interpretations and to adjust his program in light of the political realities he met. He could be reversed only by the Regional Director — not by a professional advisory or technical staff. This idea was revolutionary, and has survived. I was a Captain!

Sadly, I recall that our team recommended establishing more Regional Offices! "— Garrison, you have lost your mind! You didn't think that way last week!" Could the new ROs come from shrinkage at the WASO level? "Unlikely, but let's set some staffing quotas. Let's improve recruiting and training. Let's speed up policy guidelines for the Captain. Let's work on communications. Let's–let's–let's–" Well, almost any way would be an improvement. Victory to the bureaucrats! I now was one. The transition was defeatist but instructive. The National Park Service was consistently good to me but it had some weak spots.

Connie must have been disappointed. He announced that he would not share with us any abrasive responses he might receive from the Interior Department on his report. They were getting efficiency-minded also! If he were turned down it would not be in public. Our committee members would have to recognize their ideas if they survived. If not, the ideas and the committee would just disappear. I guess Connie did not think much of us either! But it was a great exercise for me in meeting other superintendents, some WASO and RO leaders, department officials, and the competent clerical staff who created logical sentences out of our belabored rhetoric. I was disappointed, too. In retrospect, I knew I should have been more suspicious and aggressive, but it was my first major meeting and I was bemused by some of the great names involved. The status quo prevailed, and the good ship Big Bend National Park, and her captain, Lemuel Alonzo Garrison, would continue their lonely way down there in Texas! The course was approved and in the wheel house with me.

The towns of Marathon and Alpine were the embarkation points for Big Bend visitors, and each community was proud of this distinction. Publicity and development by necessity included both travel routes. If we repaired and publicized the trail to Boquillas Canyon at the south terminus of the Marathon entrance, we should match this with equal attention to Castalon and the Santa Elena Canyon and campground on the Alpine entrance. This seemed picayunish but it was important for the Superintendent to remember. The Congressman did!

Big Bend was an ideal size for a one-leader coordination of all affairs. I could grasp the geographic reach, the physical dimensions of elevation, rainfall, vegetation, wildlife, and climate. I could respond appropriately to Senator Lyndon B. Johnson, Congressman Sam Rayburn, local Congressman "Slick" Rutherford, or Governor Alan Shivers. I could work with the Brewster County officials, such as the reliable and cooperative County Judge, Felix McGaughey. We enjoyed the Mexican-American citizens and the friendly Texas ranchers. The Alpine Chamber of Commerce businessmen, Hugh White, Paul Forchheimer, and Johnny Newell, met us joyously and constructively. In El Paso, Woody Wilson, the Executive Secretary of the Chamber of Commerce, was a great supporter and friend. (I recognized that "Woody" was probably an affectionate diminutive of Woodrow, a good Democratic name! I was getting politically-minded.) Park facilities for better visitor services were needed, but I felt up to the challenge. It was a satisfying job.

Then Bob Pulliam called on me one afternoon. Bob was from an old Brewster County family; Pulliam Bluff at the northwest side of the Basin is a well-known landmark. The crest of the bluff shapes naturally into the great reclining figure of Alsate, the legendary Indian chief. But this was not a social call. Bob had been the owner of the Mariscal mine down in the deepest part of the park near the Rio Grande. Park acquisition of the property included a commitment that he could recover all mining machinery or materials on site. This had been arranged several years previously but it had not been carried out at once.

Now Bob sought to recover a 200-gallon fuel tank which had been left underground at the mine. No problem — except that the tank was missing. It had been dug up. In fact, Bob Pulliam's suggestion was the National Park Service crews had taken it and it was part of our gasoline supply operation at Panther Junction. This installation was before my time. Bob politely asked to have his oil tank returned.

Did we have it? Or had it been "liberated" by a Mexican miner or a neighboring rancher? I called Art Minish, our vigorous maintenance foreman. He talked with two of the workmen. Nobody wanted to be quoted. I finally pinned Art down. "Is our blankety-blank gasoline tank really the Mariscal mine blankety-blank tank? Don't give me any crap. I can't deal honestly with Bob Pulliam unless I know where we stand."

It was. But I could not find fault with the construction crew that had lifted this apparently abandoned tank and used it. It saved about $100 on the headquarters construction costs, and the mine was miles beyond Glen Springs on the Rio Grande River road. Mariscal Mountain was desolate and forbidding, pockmarked with mine shafts and prospect holes. Much of the mining equipment had really vanished, probably into Mexico. "Finders, keepers" was a rule of the primitive games along the fronterisa! You could keep it if you were big enough. But what were the legalities? I did not want to claim it and then be forced to give it up. I was law-abiding and it appeared that we were losers.

I offered Bob a new tank delivered in Alpine. He gladly accepted. Had we been bluffed? Frankly, I did not care. Honesty and fair dealing with our neighbors were more important than any loss of face or minimal expense. A clear conscience is a comfortable frame-of-mind!

Assistant National Director Tom Allen spent two days with us. Tom was an old Rocky Mountain National Park ranger and superintendent. He was an early forestry graduate and had successively been a ranger at Rocky Mountain, Zion, Bryce Canyon, Hawaii, and Sequoia, and then Regional Director in Omaha, Richmond, and Santa Fe. His steady advancement with the Service was an exciting model of the potential for a ranger career. Tom always believed that he was a ranger, just like I did. His philosophies of park protection and helpfulness to park visitors fit mine. We identified with the same reasons for being in the outfit.

Tom was traveling with the Chief of Personnel from Washington, Hugh M. Miller. Hugh had been a long-time participant in National Park affairs in the Southwest, principally as Administrative Officer with the old Southwestern National Monuments at Casa Grande National Monument in Coolidge, Arizona. He managed the paperwork for about twenty National Monuments, each with a separate program and budget, so his signature was needed on dozens of documents. He was an extremely able park manager, so it is ironic that his signature soon degenerated into a flowing, inky undulation which became his famous trademark. He might sit before a revolving drum of paper and produce a mile of the signature squiggle which read like it was pronounced *MMmmmmmmmmmmmmmmm*. If he was just Hugh Miller he used fifteen squiggles — *MMmmmmmmmmmmmmmmm*. But if he was formally Hugh M. Miller that day, it took seventeen — *MMmmmmmmmmmmmmmmmmm*. These extra loops were an important identification in some way — mainly, I surmised, as a topic for good-natured banter.

Tom and Hugh were powerful leaders and both part of the legendry of the National Park Service. They explored with me a dream which came from many evenings of discussion by park rangers in ranger patrol or snowshoe cabins, or from "Taurian sessions," as the term developed in the Southwest. Mather and Albright had created a great management unity from the varieties of organization in the first parks, but they had a few pieces left over. One of these came from the term originated by Horace Albright. "The rangers are the eyes and ears of the park superintendent."

"If the rangers are so important," ran the ranger discussions, "why isn't the superintendent just called the Chief Ranger? And, why isn't there a Chief Ranger in Washington?"

Of course, the park superintendent title had become so entrenched, honored, and vigorously defended that it would be unthinkable to change it. It was the most distinguished of all temporal job titles in my mind. I was one. Tom and Hugh had been imprinted with the same belief.

Even Albright had said that he did not need a WASO Chief Ranger. He was the ranger representative! He was a good one, particularly after he and Frank J. Taylor authored the guideline publication, *Oh, Ranger!*

But it remained an exciting field for discussion. Probably Albright's successors could have used a counselor and a public spokesman in traditional ranger affairs. Certainly, the Regional Office seemed incomplete without a Chief Ranger to be the "eyes and ears" on resource programs for the Regional Director. There were many challenges — pressures to open the parks to hunting, woodcutting, mining, grazing, railroad construction, irrigation dams, pipe lines and power lines, roads, sightseeing elevators, artificial lighting, commercial marketing of resources (like cactus), and urban recreation. These are just some that I met and knew about. I was like Horace — as a later Regional Director I might well act as my own Chief Ranger. But when it happened I did not have the time. I could have used an articulate Chief Ranger who could intervene at the political level and communicate with conservation groups and politicians. Others were doing these kinds of jobs. The title would have been important. Travel to parks was increasing rapidly. We needed the politicians. They did not want to make stupid decisions, but sometimes they failed to understand our purpose and our strengths.

Parks were good politics with the travel industry and the conservationists. The same parks were anathema to the traditional American exploiter. I suspected that we could have survived with fewer bruises if we had really kept the Chief Ranger banner flying high, just as Mather and Albright had done in their courageous battles to develop belief in the worthiness of ideals of beauty and inspiration. Step on a few toes, if necessary. The results were worth it.

This, of course, had been part of my own dream. Then it developed that Tom and Hugh were more than nostalgic. They were laying the groundwork to create a Chief Ranger job. Would I like to be considered? Heavens! Was I a logical candidate? I guess I was — a ranger identity, a record of successful management, too old for a Navy commission, still on the upbeat in the Service. I almost swallowed my pipe! *No!* "Go try somebody else!" I had chores to do in Texas. In fairness to the friends who had made commitments in community affairs, I simply could not abandon the job. Would I look at it a year from now? This would be agreeable.

This was a time for introspection. Did I really want this new job? Or did I just want to be asked? Did I want to leave Big Bend at all? I knew that I must at some time. Was I content at this level of responsibility, or did I want to advance further? Where to? I did not know. How about being superintendent of a big park some day? Like Yosemite. That was as far as my expectations might take me. But I was not ready. Where could I best advance my ideals of park purpose? Beyond the enjoyment of the day-by-day job? When my questing reached that point, I would be lost. I would have to go. (I later observed the effect of this enticement on others. Exposure to a "possible" job offer in some other direction would excite competitive behavior, and the poor guy was lost. He convinced himself that an immediate move was preferable to growth where he was.)

In the meantime I was proud of being Superintendent of Big Bend National Park. It matched my ideal image of a park ranger, and was a new dimension of the same challenge. I did not hold my job by a popularity contest within the community, but I might lose it that way some time. It helped to have the support of the park employees. I must be faithful to the purposes of the park and protect the resources which made Big Bend a "special" enclave. I must speak out about park purposes. It was easy.

I was not a native Texan, but I was a kind of natural one, and this had become another geographic love affair. We identified with people, the culture, and the vistas across the colorful, brutal landscape. It is a beautiful land and we revisit as often as we can. We revel in the response of nature to our beginnings of preservation and healing techniques, such as the soil and moisture work and revegetation efforts along Tornillo Creek; or the regrowth of candelilla wax plants. These are warm memories that a harsh land impressed on adventurous spirits!

Tom Allen faithfully sent me informative notes. The Chief Ranger job idea was undergoing some changes. Many of the proposed duties were in conflict with other staff responsibilities. The title would be Chief of Conservation and Protection.

I accepted, and we moved in January 1955. I had been Superintendent of Big Bend for two years, one month, and thirteen days. It left an indelible imprint.

More and more, Inger's career growth in arts and crafts, particularly in ceramics and sculpture, were shared parts of my own life. She added a specialty in American Indian cultures. We lived with Native Americans on many assignments. We treasured these friendships. Inger pursued and expanded on them. Beginning with the Tlingit Indians in Juneau, she had known them as friends and neighbors. Many were her schoolmates, and Indian youngsters were also classmates of our children. From Grand Canyon she had shared her ceramic work with Hopi women, and she had studied Indian silver and Navajo weaving. We became personal friends of many of them.

The urban life of Washington, D.C., and later of Philadelphia, might seem like a difficult transition compared to the primitive pioneer life style of pioneer Alaska and the parks, but the adaptable and outgoing Norwegian gal moved right with it. She was the helpful mother of two active young adults. She was culturally attuned to the seas, the mountains, the wildlife of my job, and also to the folk programs of our neighbors. Happily, Washington became for her a great new learning opportunity. I traveled with her to her meetings as she had with me. It all fit together, including my new role as a color-blind patron of the arts which she had discovered around us.

Her ceramic kickwheel, her study of the chemistry of glazes and the techniques of hand building, her awareness of color harmonics, of bold patterns of design texture and shape, and of contemporary design thinking — all are part of her gain from this special Washington experience.

I began to move into my new tasks. Tom Allen and I had identified segments of the National Park programs to which I must be alert and aggressive with my own participation. I was a Branch Chief, one rank below the Division Chiefs and the Assistant Directors. My office was on the front corridor, adjacent to Assistant Director Allen. This was good status, I learned. We had a connecting door so that we could communicate without going out into the hallway. I was advised that some of the secretaries were instructed to snoop on hallway traffic and report to their chiefs, so I seldom used the hallway to go in to talk to Tom. Also, about this time a Washington Cabinet-level official had a public dispute with one of his aides whom he could not fire because of his political clout. So the Cabinet officer just whipped out a screwdriver, took the connecting door knob off, and left the offender incommunicado. Tom and I had no such problems.

However, a gossipy secretary could be a great communicator about local affairs. We had one in our front hallway. Her door was always open, and her self-appointed duty seemed to be to counsel the park ranger so he knew where his hazards lay!

I wore a business suit and necktie to work. I built my own telephone list of important numbers. I was on the telephone intercom with the upper level staff. I was almost immediately, yet briefly, "Acting" Assistant Director for Tom, an exalting experience. I began procedures to select a secretary. The feel of power and importance was beginning.

One morning Connie called a special meeting of selected staff people and addressed himself to the park budget and the park visitor situation in honest recognition that many of the parks were being "loved to death." What could we do about it? He recognized that depending on routine budgeting and planning procedures was not going to be enough. The parks would be destroyed by overuse and financial starvation unless the situation improved. Bernard de Voto and other writers were urging that the parks be closed simply because we could not care for them adequately. Could the NPS go on the attack? We had nothing to lose that was not already endangered. "Let's try to fight our way out of this bag!" Connie had a campaign planned.

First, we would ask each park superintendent to give us a program listing everything needed to put "his" park facilities into immediate condition for managing the current visitor load, while protecting the park itself. Next, the superintendent would project ahead ten years and establish a program for handling the load at that time.

Then the Washington office would put them all together — in effect, dream up a contemporary National Park Service. We would end up with a statement on legislation, funding, and boundary changes that would be needed. It would encompass such items as more sophisticated maintenance at higher standards, and recognize accelerated costs and broader advance planning. It would make a statement on land use, with regard to such concepts as wilderness, recreation demands, and coordination of NPS plans with other federal agencies and with other levels of government. It would review not only park standards, but also manpower standards, campgrounds, sanitation, roads, concessioner roles, housing for employees, recruiting and training, public affairs, and political support. The National Park Service had a head start in its permanent planning staff and in the traditional park preservation policies and management philosophies. The new approach sounded wild, but exciting and innovative as long as we did it ourselves and clung to the honored goals of the enabling legislation.

Congress would be a part of the planning endeavor, for the only way this job could succeed was by using the full democratic process. We would keep it all public, share it with the local people, the newspapers, the conservation groups, the political forces, the housewives and the women's clubs, and the schools at all levels. Congressional support was essential from the beginning. We would let public interest and local publicity create the demand to make it happen.

I never knew how Connie managed to sell this great dream and bold adventure to the Interior Department. I just know that someway he did. When I left his office that morning we were on our way. The working task force had been created with Bill Carnes, the Assistant Chief of the Branch of Plans and Design, in charge of planning. Several staff men were assigned to the job full time and immediately relieved of their regular duties so the new program could go ahead. Refinements were added from time to time. It was then 1956, so we named it Mission 66, reminding us of the ten years time frame to get it done, and the fiftieth anniversary of the Park Service in 1966.

I was named Chairman of the steering committee, which consisted of the Assistant Directors and the Branch Chiefs who were not on the working staff — a prestigious outfit! I was to solicit ideas and keep them all informed of progress, concepts, needs, responses, and immediate plans. It was a great arrangement. I worked in detail with the planning staff. My committee members were often so busy with their own affairs that keeping them briefed on Mission 66 — or just M66, as it was soon christened — was difficult. But M66 was a go-ahead outfit. We couldn't wait. Bill Carnes immediately set up a special task force to develop a formula for estimating 1966 park visitation. Bob Coates, an economist and ex-ranger, was in charge. We were on the way very quickly!

My plans as Chief of Conservation and Protection were partially shelved. Tom Allen concurred that my major task must be to help keep M66 afloat. Reactions were mixed. The program had been launched by two Mission 66 memorandums, but most park superintendents didn't really believe it. Eivind Scoyen, the beloved and courageous Superintendent of Sequoia National Park, had derided previous thinking when he had developed his "105-year priority list" of needed work in 1955. He had figured it should take just 105 years to catch up with deficiencies recognized that year, given the then-current rate of appropriations. Eivind — born in Yellowstone of Norwegian parents — was a respected and outspoken leader. He was selected as Associate Director of the Park Service in January 1956, and his first major communication to the park superintendents, that Mission 66 was for real, was most helpful.

Mission 66 proposed to wipe out the accumulated deficiencies, to project a ten-year plan, and to protect the parks as we presumed Mather and Albright would have done. This may have been wishful thinking, but in retrospect I believe that only an heroic program such as M66 could have preserved the National Park system somewhat in the form we had known it. Connie put it all on the line at one time.

Fortuitously, much of the initial planning needed for Mission 66 was already in place. Beginning on December 7, 1941, when all major construction and development ceased in the parks, Connie had had the wisdom to move ahead with a "Plans-on-the-Shelf" program. This was now full of goodies! The National Park Service professional architects, landscape architects, and engineers were ready for Mission 66.

National Park visitors in 1956 totaled about 45 million. What would it be in 1966? This kind of projecting had been pitched to Bob Coates and the M66 task force. The base data was reviewed from many angles. What were the indices that should be applied? The projected number of new telephones? Projected bank deposits? The number of new automobiles? Actually, the rising curve of park travel coincided beautifully with the number of new automobiles, but would this continue? A number of cities were developing community swimming pools. This was a new factor which might not affect park travel directly, but it created a new focus of family interest which kept youth involved in home activities instead of encouraging travel.

Our preliminary figures modestly estimated that by 1966 our 45 million park visitors would increase to 80 million. This horrified the conservation groups. Eighty million visitors! "The parks can't handle them. The parks will be destroyed," they said. But the parks survived.

During the Mission 66 research period, Frank Kowski, then a forester in the Washington office of the National Park Service, related to us the travel statistics of 1934–35, when there was a special Pacific Northwest Exposition in Portland, Oregon. (This was a regional fair, and since the travelling public made vacation plans early, people coming from the south, east, and north would often make a great circle, from Salt Lake City to the Tetons, Yellowstone, Glacier, Mt. Rainier, the Olympics, Fort Vancouver, and Crater Lake. They would include the fair in this itinerary, and fill two-and-a-half weeks. The entire region benefited from the exposition travel.) Kowski had been a Yellowstone ranger at that time, and the entire ranger force had handled a phenomenal half-million visitors to the park without disaster. The rangers met that fall to recapitulate events and note especially successful procedures that might be used in the future. The conclusion was reached that it had been a great experience, highly successful, and that they were fortunate to have taken part in it. There was no need to worry, however, for they assumed that that travel level probably would never be reached again. But the next year Yellowstone drew another 500,000 visitors, plus an additional 75,000.

Dr. Marion Clawson of "Resources for the Future," a blue-ribbon committee which advised President Eisenhower on the short- and long-range use of the country's resources, now reviewed our preliminary

Mission 66 data and stated that our projections were far below probable travel. The parks should reach our alarming 80 million level late in 1962 or early 1963, he predicted. He felt that by 1966 the figure would be 120 million. (It was, and even today Yellowstone continues to serve nearly two million visitors a year. These figures say nothing about the quality of the visitor experience amid the incessant flow of summer traffic. We had to get visitors on the roads, flowing easily through the "travel tubes" that we had created, diverted as needed at intersections through multiple lanes and modern signs, sidetracked occasionally for scenic views or a roadside moose. But we got the job done with more celerity and provided more enjoyment for visitors than I would have believed possible.)

This whole program became a highly articulated and accelerated study. Eventually every park superintendent sent in proposals for "his" park. The M66 staff reviewed each one in detail. The evident concern for park preservation as the major goal of National Park management was startling. We had imprinted the whole outfit effectively! It was occasionally desirable to recommend more public use services, but the mix that Connie gambled on was successful.

We realized that travel was not going to be reduced. The family car was becoming the principle means of transportation. Concern for wilderness was stronger than anticipated. Appropriate development of facilities such as roads or trails actually could be viewed as a conservation and protection measure, as it tended to channel and restrict use. For example, the boardwalks in Yellowstone's geyser basins protected both the geysers and the people. The so-called "moral ditches" in Yosemite Valley not only prevented evening roadside parking by youthful lovers, they also channeled driving and protected the forest floor from wandering motorists.

The details of Mission 66 are Connie's story. My story is simply as I was involved as chairman of the steering committee. Mission 66 working staff director Bill Carnes and I toured the Regional Offices and met with regional groups, particularly the design sections. As "missionaries," we carried "the word" successfully.

While travelling I took time to review the status of park ranger affairs. We were seeking professional status both in ranger functions and salaries. What was happening in cooperative forest fire programs?

Were we adequate in people management? Did the National Park Service need special wilderness legislation, or was our enabling mandate adequate? The National Parks were wilderness by original legislative intent. Most of us thought that we did not need new specialized legislation. But the conservation groups did not trust the strength of this designation. We got the wilderness legislation in 1964, anyway, and it is faithfully heeded. I cannot see that it has made any great difference in management of the *natural* parks, as we were managing them according to wilderness precepts already. I felt the Wilderness Bill was redundant as it related to National Parks.

Off-trail inquiries found their way to my desk. A citizen of New Jersey wanted to visit Custer Battlefield in Montana and spend a moonlight night on the scene of this historic tragedy. He was a descendent of one of Custer's troopers — his ancestor had married and sired a family before joining the cavalry. Now the romantically-inclined descendent wanted to relive that fatal night under the stars — he did not want to camp or to sleep at all. Bugle calls, military commands, restless and stamping horses, the creak of leather, the jingle of saddle bits, the ululation of frenetic Indian ceremonies across the valley, the barking of Indian dogs, the smell of wood smoke, all would be his companions that night under the glittering stars. He was a human yearning for remembrance. But there was no campground at Custer Battlefield. Could he be given permission to walk out onto the bivouac grounds with a sleeping bag and live this memory?

Of course he could — he really did not even need to ask. But he had started by writing the President, who bucked it to the Secretary, who bucked it to the Director, who bucked it to me, the Chief Ranger. I bucked it to the Regional Director in Omaha with a copy to the Superintendent, Captain Edward Luce, a great Custer authority, with my response of encouragement. I think this one came out all right. I felt like the Chief Ranger about it!

We started on a long, continuing discussion of ranger duties. A forest ranger was, first of all, a forester. He grew trees and harvested them. The protective-custodial tasks of the park ranger were different than those of the forest ranger, who was classified as a professional in the scientific field of forestry, and received a higher salary. The uniqueness of the park ranger's job lay in its variety of duties — forest protection, forest fire control, resource management, wildlife management and observations, many interpretive services, information duty, and public safety and service. Most of the special and important parts of the ranger jobs were either fragmented bits of other professional skills or lesser grade duties (according to the Civil Service Commission classifiers). So instead of beginning at P-1 (step 1 of the Forest Service professional series, at $2,000) we began at CPC 5 (crafts, protective, custodial, at $1,860).

While park rangers enjoyed their mixture of responsibilities, over the years we had watched all of the higher-salaried specialists splinter off and assigned to other agencies — the foresters, the biologists, the interpreters or park naturalists, the historians, the geologists, and so on. Public service (Tom Allen's greatly favored role of helpfulness to park vistors), according to the classification book, was simply information duty, a stereotyped kind of ticket office routine. But this description ignored the background rangers needed. Their sensitivity reduced the abrasiveness of visitors' experiences and achieved helpful custodianship. No wonder the National Park Service needed a Chief Ranger! Could I salvage some of the guts of the position?

We later abandoned this professional quest and worked to achieve ranger recognition in the CAF (Clerical, Administrative, Fiscal) series of jobs, or positions. The rangers became managers! We were able to achieve better salary levels. We even hired a few professional foresters, and by using hyphenated titles, created a variety of "quasi-rangers." This process went on long after my departure from the scene, and successfully culminated in the capable hands of my successor, John Davis.

Mission 66 added enrichment to the whole National Park program. In retrospect, we must recognize that with the public awareness and political reality of the late 1950s, the National Parks (in fact, all conservation programs) were in financial difficulty. These were bleak years for the old Biological Survey, as it struggled into the age of the Fish and Wildlife Service. The Forest Service was heavily involved in state and private forestry programs. These were indeed creative directions for these agencies to take. And the National Park Service now had Mission 66. We were moving more toward "people services" as a proper role for our land management programs.

The Interior Department endorsed Mission 66. The program was welcomed as a great meeting between the American public and their government — meaning the Republican Party. The National Parks were pleasant representatives of the government, as compared with the routines of the Postal Department or the problems of the Internal Revenue Service! "Hail to the National Parks! Hail to the Republican Party. We will do right by you park people!" And they did. Roger Ernst, the Assistant Secretary of the Interior from Phoenix; Douglas McKay, the Secretary of the Interior from Oregon; Ben Jensen, the great Congressman from Iowa; John Saylor, the Johnstown, Pennsylvania giant of conservation leadership. All were solid backers.

Connie's broad approach proved successful. Congressman Mike Kirwan of Ohio, the ranking minority member of the House Interior Committee, decided that the funding proposed by the Republicans was inadequate, and proposed to double the immediate level of money for the National Park Service. The conversations about this were at a higher level than the Mission 66 steering committee, but it was heartening to consider Connie's response to the question, "If you had fourteen million dollars, could you spend it?" He thought he could. He needed twenty!

Herbert Kahler, the Chief Historian of the National Park Service, had become friendly with conservationist Bradley Patterson, the assistant secretary of the Cabinet. Secretary of the Cabinet Max Rabb and Brad arranged a presentation of the M66 proposals to the Cabinet and President Eisenhower. As the President's illness rearranged events, suddenly the Department of the Interior got the word: "get it together!" Timing was critical. We were to have nineteen minutes. Suddenly this was cut to seven minutes. Then it was back to fifteen minutes, and we went on from there. Secretary of the Interior McKay was the keynoter, of course, but the principle presentation was by Connie Worth. (He was a great leader and idea man — one of the best in one-to-one or free discussions — but a poor reader. He received much preliminary practice on this one. I never again saw a manuscript as carefully edited, re-edited, revised, intoned for sequences and word meanings, scrutinized, and edited for illustrative materials.)

Brad Patterson arranged for a preliminary dry run. We had selected material from the 3,000 best kodaslides the park staffs could send us;

we included current motion picture briefs showing crowds of people, line-ups of cars, and visitors fishing, mountain climbing, hiking, camping, and looking at scenery — even waiting in line at a privy; with easel charts we highlighted key aspects of leisure time, recreation economics, and demography. Connie's support consisted of Bill Carnes, the working staff leader; Howard Stegner, a great interpreter and writer; and myself, responsible for the "quicky" punch lines on the chart easel. We anticipated every catastrophe imaginable. Armed with spare bulbs and asbestos mittens, Howard and Bill Carnes could pop hot bulbs in and out of the projectors in seconds.

Then Brad gave us a tour of the environs. The President was out of town. The Cabinet room held a long table with high-backed square chairs, each with a silver name plate for the incumbent Cabinet secretary. The Secretary of the Interior's chair was conveniently located in the middle of the table, directly across from the chair marked "The President of the United States." I timidly touched this one — it moved! The others were looking elsewhere. I sat in it for a moment. Nothing exploded, but my heart went bumpety-bump!

An adjacent hallway was lined with oil paintings, each made by a Cabinet officer during his incumbency. In the Oval Office hung an unfinished painting we recognized as Longs Peak from Wonder Lake in Rocky Mountain National Park west of Denver. This lovely painting bore the bold initials "DDE," the guy we were giving the slide show for!

Bill and I were instantly on the telephone. Eddie Alberts, the Park Naturalist at Rocky Mountain National Park, was supportive. "Yes. We have a superlative slide of Longs Peak from Wonder Lake. I can drive to Denver and air mail it special delivery to you today. What's the deal?"

Without fanfare, the third slide of our presentation had a message for one member of our audience. The fourth was of a fly fisherman at Trick Falls in Glacier National Park — a beautiful photographic point. Great pictures, both of them.

The presentation was a career highlight for me. Mission 66 had the finest political credentials. I was impressed by the precise formality of timing as the Cabinet session got under way. The row of chairs behind the Cabinet seats filled rapidly. One of the staff was my old friend, former Governor of Arizona Howard Pyle, now a special White House aide for state relationships. Suddenly the room was quiet. "The Man" had arrived. At the President's request, Secretary of Agriculture Ezra Taft Benson presented a brief invocation. This call on the Lord was a normal part of the governance of the United States of America, and I was impressed. The agenda was on schedule. The National Park Service's approach to the problem of protecting the parks and funding their programs was expeditiously presented.

The President knew about National Parks. He had his home at Gettysburg. He vacationed in Rocky Mountain National Park. I had met him briefly at Grand Canyon. He made a brief comment to the Cabinet about the importance of parks in building patriotism. I do not know who raised the question about financing, but someone suggested that since we anticipated 80 million visitors a year, and this was a ten-year program, a charge of one dollar per person would balance out at the 800 million dollars we anticipated would be needed. The President said "No! The parks need not be self-supporting!" They had greater values. Ike turned to Secretary McKay. "Doug, why haven't we done something about this before?" The reply was straightforward and political. They hadn't gotten around to it. Actually, the Department had not recognized it as a political bonanza. "Let's get on with the job!" was the final word from the President.

We took it from there. We waited until the conclusion of the Cabinet meeting for a rerun for what Brad called the Junior Cabinet— the Undersecretaries and their staffs. This kept the departments alert and informed much more effectively than simple written reports. "Let's get on with the job!" We did.

Immediate action began through the budget programs of the Interior Department. But it was deliberate and slow, "by the numbers," and with true glacial speed! But it worked. M66 became the major operating program for the National Parks . The working staff of M66 was reduced as the paper work was translated into policy and budget procedures. The steering committee became simply an M66 advisory committee. I functioned part-time with this for two years.

Meanwhile, the superintendency of Yellowstone National Park opened. Would I like this? Or would I sooner fit into the WASO hierarchy? Connie left the option open for me. I was a field man by nature and by training. Yellowstone was the supreme experience — the first, the greatest, the most beloved and admired of the parks. The world was mine! But I must deserve such an appointment. Hard work and chance timing had brought it to me. Now the Park Service had a new day — Mission 66. Could I make it work at Yellowstone?

CHAPTER XVII

THE YELLOWSTONE DISCOVERY

LEAVING WASHINGTON, D.C., FOR YELLOWSTONE NATIONAL PARK
was quite a celebration for us. In the Uncle Remus tradition, I was
being tossed into the greatest briar patch in all creation! I had worn
out my Mission 66 welcome with the steering committee. The program was a success. My duties as Chief of Conservation and Chief
Ranger were assumed by John Davis, who did beautifully with the job
I had started before being intercepted by Mission 66.

Before I left Washington, Director Connie Wirth quizzed me
closely. The implication was that by moving out of Washington I was
probably relinquishing a lead into the line of succession for Connie's
job as Director. But there was no heir-apparent. I was a field man at
heart. I was only four years younger than Connie, and he was doing
an excellent job. It had been exciting working with him. I hoped he
would stay around for a long time. However, being part of the headquarters power structure or even near it has a powerful magnetic
attraction. It was tempting to consider continuing to be a part of it,
but not impelling. I remembered that twenty-seven years earlier,
Horace Albright, as Superintendent of Yellowstone (with the additional title of Field Director), had become Director of the National
Park Service. He was twenty-nine years old at the time. If Connie
began making noises about leaving I would look at it again, but probably a successful superintendent of Yellowstone would have as good a
competitive position as one of the Washington hierarchy. I'd take my
chances.

Our Yellowstone arrival was very casual. We came up U.S. Highway 89 from Idaho Falls, Idaho, to West Yellowstone, Montana, and
the West Entrance Station late one cold afternoon just before Thanksgiving Day in 1956. There were six inches of softly-fallen snow on the
ground, but the road was passable. I got my tire chains out with the

help of Bill Appling, one of the West Entrance rangers, and found that I had not forgotten how to mount them. We smoothed the snow behind the rear wheels and spread out the chains right side up and right end to. I backed the car on to them, and we crawled under and flipped each chain over its tire, fumbled the fasteners into place, and then yanked and hauled on the chains and rocked the car to get the slack out before latching them closed. Rubber band tighteners were an innovation since my Yosemite years.

I telephoned ahead to park headquarters at Mammoth Hot Springs, fifty miles away. Bill unlocked the gate and we drifted with the wind through the snow into the gray early dusk — a great way to begin this new job. The moving car easily brushed the fluffy snow from the roadbed and we glided quietly and smoothly along between the occasional roadside reflector buttons. The directional signs were all in order but plastered with clinging snow. About ten miles east of "West," a tiny red reflection beside the Madison River revealed a great hump of snow with horns — a lone bull buffalo, his tail end into the wind, unconcerned about the snow, one red eye turned toward us indifferently as we ghosted past him.

At Madison Junction we kept to the left. The road sign was only partially visible. Several miles later we could smell sulphur. Fog and steam vapor mingled with the swirling snow. We were passing a "thermal feature," probably Beryl Spring, and a glimpse of a snowy sign assured us that it was.

Norris and Norris Junction — reminders of the second Yellowstone superintendent, Philetus W. Norris — were just points along the road. But suddenly beside us the blurred whorls of snow had a wraith-like substance. We paused as a small band of ten elk materialized and then vanished across the road ahead of us. Later I identified this point as Brickyard Hill. It all was an unreal wonderland, but at an elevation of 7,484 feet and in a November blizzard, it was wise to remember that our security blanket was the warm haven of the car with its heater set at "High performance."

An hour later the Golden Gate roadside sign vanished behind us and lights through the storm framed Mammoth Hot Springs-Old Fort Yellowstone with the parade ground and cluster of buildings of our civilization outpost. We were home again!

The Hamiltons greeted us. Warren was the seasonal ranger in Sequoia in 1932 who had suddenly been offered and accepted a move to Grand Canyon. This had left the mid-summer seasonal ranger vacancy for which I was selected, and marked the beginning of my own National Park Service career. Warren was now Assistant Superintendent at Yellowstone, keeping the park protection job and the administrative work in readiness for the new superintendent. It was a productive combination and a great beginning for me.

The "rotation" policy for administrative jobs in the National Park Service meant that I was moving into a ready-made environment of park duties, community and political status, and social life. I knew something of life on a pioneer army post from my exposure to Chilkoot Barracks in Haines, Alaska. Now I was looking at the same arrangement of buildings, roads, functions, and communications.

We were moving back into American history in the huge, eight-bedroom Commanding Officer's home with its gracious amenities. Fort Yellowstone had great relevance to the local history. The park had been created in 1872, four years before the Battle of the Little Bighorn. In 1877, a party of Yellowstone tourists were captured by the Nez Percé Indians during Chief Joseph's attempt to lead his people to Canada. (Their travois trail ruts are still seen near Tower Falls.)

With the passing of the buffalo the possibility of Indian contact faded, but awareness of this fact had little influence on subsequent Congresses. Hence, the military stayed in Yellowstone for thirty years, and its presence contributed greatly to the protection of the park.

At Mammoth Hot Springs in the Territory of Montana and Wyoming, the Army had in 1888 clustered facilities for park administration. The parade grounds, the barracks, and the homes and offices for two troops of the Fifth and then the Seventh Cavalry had been built over the years. The fort was the major point of identity for the park concessioners, and a political and social focus for the three surrounding territorial governments. An enclave of residences developed, with a hospital, church, school, the post exchange, and recreational space. There was a community center, a post office, jail, storehouses, barns, restaurants, and hotels that served everyone.

Thus, when the United States Congress cut off the park funding in 1889 and an agreement was made with the War Department to administer the park, it seemed a completely logical arrangement. The Army could administer the park while Fort Yellowstone would be a regional defense bastion.

Quarters Number One, the superintendent's residence, was built in 1909, a gracious and attractive three-story, cut stone building with a red tile roof. We had a slight surplus of eight bedrooms. The five fireplaces had served as the original heating system until replaced with the central steam heat from the nearby Bachelor Officer's Quarters (now the Albright Memorial Library). The fireplaces remained operative until the 1959 earthquake cracked the flue liners in all but one of them. They had beautiful tile mantles, and using them was a "living history" experience. We lived right in the center of old Fort Yellowstone. There was ample room for entertaining official and personal guests. Garage and stable space was nearby, and I had only a three-minute walk to the office.

We even had a Yellowstone National Park cemetery, a legacy from the military. All military burials were removed when the post was decommissioned in 1918 and the cemetery was transferred to the National Park. There remained, however, a small cluster of civilian graves. Surprisingly, this became the focus of attention on one occasion during my first year of duty. We received a call from a San Francisco, California mortuary about a Mrs. (Eugene) Jeannette Clark from San Francisco, a seventy-three-year-old widow who had died. She had willed funds for her funeral expenses with the instructions that she was to be buried in the Yellowstone National Park cemetery beside her husband and their infant daughter. Both of them had died in 1905. Mr. Clark was listed in our cemetery records as the Assistant Electrical Engineer for the post. There was no record of the cause of death for either him or his daughter, but they were buried side-by-side in the Fort Yellowstone cemetery. A grave site had been reserved for the widow, who had moved to San Francisco, did not remarry, and fifty-one years later requested that she be reunited with her family in this remote haven. Fortunately, a local mortician was willing to handle the details. The cemetery had been "closed" for thirty-eight years. It was "reopened" briefly. I never knew what state permits might be required. It was a federal reserve. I signed whatever was required to clear the records, and the Clark family was together again as she had desired.

This leads to the uniqueness of Yellowstone National Park administration. The park is a true federal enclave. Yellowstone was established as a National Park in 1872, years before statehood was granted for any of the three surrounding states. Enabling statehood legislation for Wyoming, Montana, and Idaho, as passed in 1889 and 1890, specifically excluded state jurisdiction over any of the land included in Yellowstone National Park. This created three "enclaves."

For the Yellowstone superintendent, this arrangement was more than a curiosity. Congress had also authorized certain federal tax collections, such as gasoline (use and sales) taxes. State fish laws were to be enforced, and 1 percent of the park gate receipts were allotted to finance local schools at Gardiner, Cook City, and West Yellowstone, Montana.

We had no state authorities to provide registers for such routine events as births, deaths, or marriages. Care of insane people or of indigents was impossible unless we could persuade a neighboring state to let us borrow their authority. Park County, Montana, often was the generous helper. Our alternative might have been to establish our own registers, but this seemed to be an impossible arrogation of authority. Most of us at Mammoth registered our automobiles in Montana because we had access to Montana in the winter months. After our daughter Karen was married in the beautiful little Yellowstone National Park chapel, it was necessary for the bride, groom, minister, and witnesses to have a Montana ceremony performed north of the forty-fifth parallel. In the summer this could be under a juniper tree near the Gardiner River bridge. In the winter we could use the unheated, but sheltered, Gardiner Chapel (as Karen and Eldon did for their brief exchange of vows). This was the ceremony that was registered with the State of Montana.

Voting was another problem. Political jurisdiction before 1872 had been under Park County and the town of Powell, Wyoming Territory. If I wished to register for a national election I might do so in Powell. But I never tried it. We didn't have a local voting precinct. There was no demand for it. All 150 of us were effectively disenfranchised. Rather than fuss about it, most of us retained our voting residence in the state we had come from and voted by absentee ballot. It was simpler that way.

Our local grammar school (grades 1–8) held classes in the old military canteen at Mammoth. School funds came from a 1 percent "hold-back" on North Entrance gate receipts. The superintendent appointed the school board, but it occurred to me that the community might want to have an elected school board. We issued a straw ballot in the community and the overwhelming response was affirmative.

I appointed a committee. It was an experience all of us will never forget! What would be our geographic boundary for the school district? Who was a resident eligible to vote? How should we handle voter registration? How could we conduct an election? Check eligibility? Count the ballots? Who could certify teacher eligibility and curriculum scope? Our graduates must be eligible to enter other school systems and continue their education. How could we select and pay election judges and clerks?

I have watched with interest as Alaska has moved from a territorial form of government to statehood. In Yellowstone I was part of a similarly successful and fascinating experience, and having been through it I do not expect to ever need it again. I note that a May, 1981 Yellowstone newsletter includes a notice of a school board election. The machinery is still working!

A University of Arkansas law professor was intrigued by our situation, and often required his students to report on the specifics of this jurisdiction. All we could do was refer them to the legislation. We understood that a similar circumstance existed at Hot Springs National Park, where an 1833 withdrawal of land was similarly excluded from state jurisdiction.

This approach to the Yellowstone superintendency is typical of my entire career. Events moved so rapidly around me that I seldom seemed to have time to back away and decide on priorities. The immediate happenings always demanded attention.

By my career standards, Yellowstone was high on job potential, adventure, excitement, livability, reward for public service, and challenge. It was all there, including the title: Superintendent, Yellowstone National Park. The first National Park in the world. I could hardly believe it! I was just a lucky seasonal ranger!

Our daughter Karen was in school in Wasatch Academy in Mt. Pleasant, Utah; our son Lars was in Denver, just beginning his career in international energy sales. We could see them both often, as Yellowstone was a great place for them to visit. Besides, the job was a G.S. grade 15, the top of the "apolitical" heap.

Inger had actively continued in ceramics work. She had filled her Washington, D.C. days with the study of glazes, shop projects, teaching, visiting local exhibits, exploring, and cultivating friendships with regional artists. We had acquired a larger electric kiln. We bought a plan and parts for a good kick wheel from Dr. Giam Petro of Catholic University, and Inger and I assembled it in our kitchen with the help of young Johnnie Kahler, who lived next door to us at Fort Hunt. (Johnnie's father, Herb, was National Park Historian. He had been my Coordinating Superintendent while I was at Hopewell Village.) Our world was continually expanding, yet it always maintained its original size. All our friends seemed to be interested in parks and in ceramics. At least they all heard about them!

Thus our basement in Yellowstone soon became Inger's workshop. At one time it was loaded with buckets of native clay. This was mixed with coal fragments which were removed and washed, pugged, and then molded. The clay came from roadside banks in the coal mining country around Aldrich, just north of the park. Frances Senska, a ceramist at Montana State University at Bozeman, helped prepare and test fire it. We still have the first pot.

But I was Superintendent of Yellowstone, I was continually reminded, and there were many things to do. So, to work!

I approached this new job with considerable humility. It was the top field job in the world — the most visible park management position. I was custodian of the world's greatest natural curiosities, the collection of natural resources that had sparked the world-wide park conservation program in the first place. My support came from rangers, interpreters, maintenance men, and politicians I had worked with who trusted me. I would depend on similar back-up from the park staff and from the Regional office, the planners, the researchers, and designers. I could not foresee all the use and preservation challenges that might arise. But I could anticipate concern about the Yellowstone Mission 66 program. Travel was on a great upswing. What road improvements were reasonable? In what sequence should they be scheduled? It seemed that many problems would come in pairs — park protection should balance park use. The Old Faithful side of the park must not outweigh the Yellowstone Lake-Canyon side. Concessioners were needed, and similarly the campers and the day-users were important. I believed that use must not destroy the resources. We would give priority to preservation.

I was at the same time both user- and preservation-oriented. My charge was stewardship, but to reasonable degrees of utilization. My own formula was, simply, first, the greatest use of scenery (such as the Grand Canyon of the Yellowstone) was in the viewing of it; second, looking at it did not wear it out; and third, the best way to preserve it was to leave it alone. The minimum of tinkering was the best course. This simplistic philosophy was a major guideline. Similarly, the principles of the Lane policy letter of 1917 — that natural interests must govern the decision-making process — were indelibly impressed in my mind. Commercialization of park resources through such activities as mining, grazing, lumbering, and dam construction were forbidden by the preservation policies that were my goal.

It was challenging. My predecessor, Edmond Rogers, commented that every June he had had a recurrent nightmare in which he was running along a railroad track, pursued by the smoking and steaming Yellowstone Special, its whistle screaming for the right-of-way. He always awoke abruptly at the moment of annihilation. I was the new "fugitive," and suddenly we were in the summer deluge of park visitors.

At 8:00 A.M. on June 16 I drove by the huge Canyon Hotel, which had been boarded up for seven months. Huge wooden shutters were on the windows. As I watched, a Yellowstone Park Company bus drove in and a crew of twenty workers unloaded and began dismantling the barriers. Busloads of supplies, more workers, and maids followed. By 6:00 P.M. an American Express Company tour group of 300 people was housed and served dinner.

The three traditional park concessioners were a major part of my new responsibilities. From year "one" in 1872 this had been a matter of concern for the park, and most importantly for the United States Congress. If the park was for visitors to enjoy, these visitors would need roads, rooms, meals, and transportation, and for many members of Congress, parks meant business opportunities with a possible profit. At one point in the beginning, it was suggested that National Parks were a "cheap" form of land management because they utilized otherwise unprofitable lands and converted their rocky terrain and marginal forests into assets that visitors would pay to enjoy. It was felt that charging a fee for these visitors would generate enough revenue to pay for management — with a small profit included, of course.

By the time of my arrival in Yellowstone in 1956, the concessioners had been reduced in number to three, the Yellowstone Park Company being the major operator. In over a half-century of commercial tourist services (with a variety of owners, expansions, combinations, and agreements, and with changes in types of services given) the pattern had boiled down to just three companies. They had divided the services among themselves, and were all successful enterprises. There had once been camping companies with canvas-topped tent frames (which in 1955 still survived in other parks — such as Yosemite — with a more benign climate). The Wiley Way Camping Company was one. It had offered both tent platforms and primitive, but enclosed, cabins. (In fact, a block of Wiley Way cabins has survived on the North Rim of the Grand Canyon since about 1900.)

The idea of "concessioners" supported the implied but usually unexpressed concept that running a National Park really shouldn't cost anything. The land in the early parks was often "waste land," anyway. It was usually of high elevation, rough terrain, and unsuitable for farming. It probably was soil of poor quality and inaccessible for timber or grazing. Its value for traditional uses was considered low. But because it was scenic and beautiful, people were willing to travel great distances to look at it. This opened the door to beginning tourist businesses and a potential commerce in travel and visitor services. Franchise fees from contracts for marketing these services provided enough revenue to pay for the upkeep of the parks. It was all meant to be inexpensive. In fact, some of the early Congressional hearings stressed this constructive use of our scenic wastelands!

Some thought was given to the future use of this beauteous bounty by separating buildings "one-fourth mile from the features" such as Old Faithful Geyser. However, this was ineffective, for builders had already adopted one-eighth mile as the standard.

The Yellowstone Park Company, with hotels, meals, busses, saddle horses, boats, gift shops, and bars, also owned a half-interest in the service stations and garages. They employed nearly two thousand summer staff, mainly university students.

Hamilton Stores operated general merchandise outlets at nine locations. They handled an incredible inventory and volume of curios, fishing tackle, groceries, western clothing, lunch counters and soda fountains, general camper supplies, and the other half of the ownership in the service stations and garages. Their summertime staff totaled another thousand.

The story of Hank Klamer, a concessioner who operated a general store at Old Faithful, is of romantic interest. About 1920, Hank died and left the business for sale. Harry Child, the head of the competing Yellowstone Park Company, refused to buy it. He felt that it offered a plebian, low-priced kind of service, not in line with the elegance his company promoted. However, Mr. Child's secretary, C. A. (Charles) Hamilton, was interested, and rode horseback the fifty miles from Mammoth to Old Faithful to look at it and talk with Mrs. Klamer. The price agreed upon was rumored to be about $20,000. A downpayment of $5,000 was required. "Ham" was not bashful, however, and was certain that his boss might loan the money to him. This arrangement would ensure that someone familiar, rather than a newcomer, would run the store. So Hamilton again rode horseback all night to get back to Mammoth Hot Springs, confess his audacity, borrow the money, and ride another sixty miles to deposit it in a bank in Livingston, Montana before Mrs. Klamer reached town! Thus, Hamilton's Store Number One at Old Faithful contains Hamilton's office with the $5,000 check prominently displayed. It is surrounded by a wallpaper display of the first one million dollars in checks that C. A. Hamilton wrote as his enterprise began building. It was known appropriately as the Million Dollar Room! Thus, the three major park concessioners were still in charge when I arrived in November 1956; the third being the Haynes Picture Company.

The Haynes Picture Shops were founded by Frank J. Haynes, a very talented and imaginative photographer who was introduced to Yellowstone National Park in 1881. He accompanied President Chester A. Arthur on a Yellowstone expedition as official photographer. His Haynes Picture Shops soon became a part of the Yellowstone scene, although he also operated a stagecoach company into the park from the west for many years. At his death the business was continued by his son Jack Ellis Haynes, also a skilled photographer and a grand gentleman, who became a warm friend of ours.

In the 1920s it made business sense for both the YP Company and the Hamilton Stores to drop photographic services, film sales, post cards, and books from their franchise authorities. So Haynes Picture Shops emerged as the sole purveyor of these services in the park. A major contribution of the Haynes concession was the publication of the *Haynes Guide to Yellowstone Park*. This was the bible of Yellowstone history and geography from the early 1890s to 1975, a period of great interest in photography and film sales. By 1960 this arrangement was no longer sensible, however. For example, the quality of the post cards (which were sold by the hundreds of thousands) was excellent, but limiting them to one sales outlet at each of the five villages was not good public service. In this case we waited until Jack Haynes' death to alter the contract.

The pattern that had evolved was good for the modern period. Mission 66 was underway. And while services provided by the YP Company were adequate, family dissension had led to unwise leases for management contracts, and I was finally forced to advise the YP Company Board in 1963 that the quality of service was so poor that I felt their contract was in jeopardy. This created a major fracas, and unfortunately the major drive seemed to be to get me fired, instead of improving service. Fortunately, complaints by the public created both Congressional and Interior Department concern, and ultimately support for action to buy out the YP Company in 1978 — not the most desirable option for improvement, but the most politically feasible.

Mission 66's programs were just beginning, with emphasis on, first, catching up on deferred maintenance and construction; second, a new pace in providing facilities and services to serve anticipated 1966 visitor loads; third, bringing parks and people closer together through community involvement and citizen advisory commissions; and fourth, continuing park preservation. Our first major Mission 66 project at Yellowstone National Park was the creation of Canyon Village.

I sensed that community involvement with our three neighboring states had traditionally been on the basis of occasional participation in meetings to report on what we were doing in the park. We did not seek input of the neighbors in our planning; we just told them what to expect.

Politically, Yellowstone was an island not only because of its exclusive jurisdiction as specified in the state Enabling Acts; I was also informed by staff members that our park program was "none of their community business." We knew best about our park needs. We would inform our neighbors as they evolved. But I could not work this way — I planned to get Yellowstone off the island and join the communities. I could not say "rejoin," because we had never been a part of the neighboring political affairs. In the spring of 1957 we tried it. We held a Community Leaders Day — a bus tour with a few citizens who responded to our invitation. This was possible thanks to the willing cooperation of the concessioners.

At a Chamber of Commerce dinner in Livingston, Montana, we entertained Governor Simpson of Wyoming, Governor Aaronson of Montana, and a representative of Governor Smiley of Idaho (Charles Stark, the Chamber of Commerce secretary from Idaho Falls). I proposed that we have an annual birthday party for Yellowstone National Park, to be hosted in sequence by each of the governors, and since our actual legislative birthday was in March, when all park roads were snowed in, we should just select a convenient day in early June and call it a birthday party. We had ample precedent in the Canadian celebration of the Queen's birthday — any convenient date would do! This met with favor, and we began the sequence which was still in operation when I left in 1963. Livingston, Montana, the northern gateway community, eagerly participated. Cody, Wyoming, was equally responsive. We had one birthday party at Jackson, Wyoming. The Idaho Falls Chamber of Commerce was also a willing host.

Since local communication was also a problem, I made certain our park staff meetings included future planning for economic and political events. I organized a park concessioner group, and once a month, year-round, the representatives of the concessions met. This group included the park medical service, and later the telephone company and power company. We sought and accepted invitations to speak to Chambers of Commerce, travel organizations, and wildlife and fishing groups — we were always available to inform our neighbors of the park programs.

While I tried to encourage this communication, there was little input from the neighbors. In fact, there was general approbation for the park plans. Comments came mainly from fish, game, and boating groups. The Billings Chamber of Commerce arranged a "thank you" party for Yellowstone one year. It was given not by the tourism committee but by the wholesalers' committee.

The creation of Grant Village was one of the "horizon" events from the beginning. I encouraged it because we needed to replace the West Thumb complex. Hamilton's Store was new and adequate. Everything else was dilapidated. The public campground was worn out by our standards — road ruts, dust, crowded, and scant vegetation; however, campers used it and used it. Overnight cabins were forlorn and maintenance was poor. A tiny dock and marina were inadequate. Roads, campers, playing children, all were mixed up with each other around the boat areas. The abrasive gravel land surface of West Thumb lacked dignity, usability, safety, and information services. Yet it was at a major road intersection, and from the shoreline we had a great view up the lake to the Absaroka Mountains and "the Wilderness."

We had so much wilderness. It was a popular topic of planning. But there had been few access points. Grant Village would become the wilderness take-off point. Trails would lead to Heart Lake and the Witch Creek geyser basin, to upper Yellowstone Lake and Flat Mountain Arm. A short trail from Lewis Lake would provide access to Shoshone Lake and on into the Bechler River country. The interpretive theme of our visitor center would be "The Wilderness and Ways to Enjoy It." Our new marina would be a takeoff point for canoes, and include a major campground, a campfire circle, and a visitor center. This would be a great congregation point.

The park concessioners would not make commitments as to when they would begin development of Grant Village, but the NPS roads and facilities were ready. And, while the construction of the five hundred cabins, the photoshop, and concessions was indefinite in timing, the concessioners were aware of expectations and did not want to be left out. The new campground was filled the day after we opened it. But so was the old West Thumb campground. Since their opening was in mid-August, we just decided to continue using West Thumb and then close it out in the fall. The vegetative response of grass and weeds was spectacular. A year later it was difficult to believe that this had been a beat-up campground. A few dollars for maintenance care had changed all that. A lesson!

The whole thrust at that point in time was to serve more visitors. Travel was on the upswing. The roads could handle more cars with only minor work, such as turn-outs, vista clearing, and curve straightening. But the pressing need was for visitor services. We were still destroying wilderness. Grant Village was a normal outcome of this growth pattern in 1963.

CHAPTER XVIII

A CONVERSATION WITH AN OSPREY

DURING MY SECOND YEAR AS SUPERINTENDENT of Yellowstone National Park I became curious about the conspicuous osprey nest platforms on the Yellowstone Lake shoreline. Each was as big as an untidy bushel basket, so I asked ranger Wayne Replogle about them. ("Rep" supplemented his summertime ranger career with a "moonlight" job as football coach at Kansas State University. This happy combination continued until Rep's death in 1977 after forty summers on the ranger job. He had just written to give me information about boats and people on Yellowstone Lake for this manuscript. Rep was a great and beloved ranger friend.) "The osprey all moved back from the lakeshore about ten years ago," he told me. Remnants of several of the bulky tree-top nesting platforms still existed, but early photographs showed that many of the older ones were now non-existent. Some had been abandoned recently — others had been down for so long that both the nest and the tree were missing.

And, in 1958 Rep had used a traditional "vanishing species" euphemism — "the osprey had moved back." I had used the same phrase myself from time to time. It implied that there still was a wild-lands "backcountry" they could move into. But literature about wild duck nesting suggested that other territory possibly attractive to osprey was probably already full of nesting osprey. We did not know. If our Yellowstone osprey had moved back they had probably done just as the grouse, the buffalo, the passenger pigeon and the timber wolf when they moved back. They were dead. We did not want to accept this hard reality.

Of the 140 miles of Yellowstone Lake shoreline nearly thirty-five miles of the west shore were rimmed by the paved Grand Teton highway. This ran from Grant Village and West Thumb around to Lake Hotel, Fishing Bridge, and on east to Mary Bay. There were no active osprey nests along this segment. There was one out on Frank Island.

[281]

There were others on Heart Lake, Shoshone Lake, and on the upper Yellowstone River around Bridger Lake, just north of the park. A "live" nest was almost certain evidence of the absence of man. The Yellowstone osprey needed wild lands and fishing water for their food supply.

This eagle-like osprey, also called a fish hawk or a falcon, is a high-flying soaring and seeking hunter. It is a large bird, black above and white below. Its head is largely white, with a large, black cheek patch. The osprey's wing spread is four-and-one-half to six feet. It will often fly with an angle in the wing, showing a black "wrist" patch below. It will lazily and quietly circle high above a lake or a large stream until its sharp eyes pick up the incautious moves of a surface feeding fish — at Yellowstone Lake this would be a cutthroat trout. Then in a silent thunderbolt dive the osprey will hurtle down. Its aggressive plunge carries it into the water, claws extended, grasping for the trout which will have been stunned or bewildered momentarily by the abrupt attack.

This magnificent assault was famous in early park literature. It was inelegantly labelled a "stoop." The strong talons would sink deeply into a living and squirming fish. The powerful wings would beat the air and water to generate lift and air space for return with food to its waiting youngster in a treetop aerie.

I had observed an osprey distribution pattern earlier that year when I rode my horse Stormy on a wilderness journey from the Thorofare Ranger Station to the Trail Creek cabin. We were two days on the trail, travelling via Lynx Creek, Fox Park cabin, Two Ocean Plateau, Chipmunk Creek, and the South Arm of Yellowstone Lake near Peale Island. The site of the 1934 Chipmunk Creek burn was a residual of sombre and blackened trees laced with bright patches of green brush. The trail detoured around unrooted stumps. We leaped over fallen trees. Stark and silent black silhouettes stood around us as we maneuvered our way down the Chipmunk Creek trail to the lake.

A solitary floating osprey was my trail companion for several miles. It would curtsey gently to me, hover, wing ahead, drop back, and circle, calling frequently with a single shrill note — "kee! — kee! — kee!" Was it a recognition signal, or a warning? My first suspicion that this might be a domesticated falcon which had escaped to the wild was dashed. It ignored my upheld fist, which was a proper invitation for a trained hunter to land and await further orders. I had no food samples. I tried to scream back at it, but only startled Stormy. I suspect I was naive and lucky. I had no gauntlet to protect my hand, and a perching falcon would have ripped me badly.

A lone osprey in soaring flight is poise in fluid motion, demonstrating smooth grace, a natural flow, and movement in harmony with the wind and the thermals. Even the sunlight is brighter for the osprey. It belongs there. There was an occasional glint from the plumage and the white-streaked head gave a quizzical and inquisitive cast to its presence. It lulled me to inattention, suddenly drifted in as if seeking a landing on my head or shoulders, and then squalled "kee — kee!" into my ear and vanished briefly.

I had no doubt now — this osprey was escorting me through its territory. I got the word. It was "Get out!" I was an intruder. This guardian was alerting all other osprey of the region. I was convoyed all the way to Trail Creek.

In 1958 I had several Yellowstone Lake management problems on my mind. I had learned elsewhere that a solo horseback journey was often a great environmental occasion for rumination, for speculation, and for question-and-answer sessions with myself. I was trying it again. I had Stormy to talk to and also the vociferous osprey. I called it Omar.

And one of my many problems that day was Omar's kin. They were in deep trouble. We did not mean to, but we seemed to be making their habitat unsurvivable for them. We were crowding them. Osprey could not "move back" in any real sense. Neighboring territory contained the same beautiful mountains, lakes, and streams. It looked spacious and inviting, but I was not an osprey. I was learning that each species of life and, ultimately, each individual creature establishes its own territory. How much space was enough? The osprey knew. I didn't. I must depend upon the osprey to tell me, and a negative response might only be in a fatally euphemistic "move back." Osprey have little tolerance for people, noise, cars, or boats. Omar was becoming a displaced person. He screamed at me in protest one more time. On Chipmunk Creek he wasn't a displaced creature! I was the intruder.

Stormy snorted and fox-trotted along an open section of trail in his magnificent, running walk. He was the last of the Yellowstone experimental colts, bred from range mares and a Morgan stallion in the Wakefield stable. Stormy was a real beauty — big enough to easily handle my 210 pounds, a proud, light-colored bay. His normally trustworthy behavior concealed a mischievous streak. This occasionally led him to spook sideways from stumps or chipmunks in an explosive carousel which never quite unloaded me but occasionally left me with a gut wrench for weeks. Stormy had an hereditary physical defect. He was a unilateral ridgeling. His male gets had never completed descent of their testicles, so that major surgery was needed before he could be gelded. Prior to that he had been a poor herd sire, although a magnificent riding animal. A real beauty.

I discussed my problems that day with Stormy and Omar. *Silent Spring*, by Rachel Carson, had not yet alerted us to the bad news about pesticides and egg shells and nesting birds. But obviously osprey were losing ground. Mother Nature was balancing out the wrong way.

My second problem at Yellowstone Lake was also with birds — those on the Molly Islands. These are two low-lying sand spits in the upper end of the Southeast Arm of Yellowstone Lake, possibly ten acres in size, rising four feet out of the lake. They were the summertime scene of a normal and continually noisy *lebenstraum*, a competition between four species of ocean coastline birds which nested here. Each spring brought returning colonies — white pelican, California gulls, double-crested cormorant, and Caspian tern — winging in for thousands of miles to nest on this isolated secret place. It is easy to surmise that because these are sea coast birds this must have been a salt water sea at some earlier geologic time. But today it is a fresh water lake at 7,731 feet elevation. And the oceanic birds continue to return to nest.

Their meeting creates a free-for-all — gulls versus cormorants versus pelicans versus terns. It is a smelly, screaming, murderous crowd. California gulls were dominant because of their numbers and natural aggression. The pelicans were doing well because of their great size. But the cormorant and tern were having low nesting success, probably a normal situation. We would not interfere. We must respect "the process!"

But now it was the birds versus motor boats. There were many reports of the impact of boats on the Molly Islands rookery. A roar of huge boat motors nearby would frighten all the adult birds into flight, leaving nests and fledglings exposed. The brazen California gulls would return first and raid their neighbors' nests, destroying both eggs and young birds. In a natural balance of life, raiding is normal behavior. But the motor boat racket created a new dimension.

Also, the wake of speedboats would overwash the low shoreline. High winds and rain might also create this same kind of flooding, but birds somehow anticipated this and took protective action. They would brood over wet nests and eggs, which actually suffered little damage. Young birds could be sheltered or crowded to higher ground. But this natural protectiveness was lacking when the storm force was a destructive boat wake.

So my third problem was boats — the number of boats. Yellowstone Lake was isolated and superlative in beauty. It was wilderness. From Lake Ranger Station we looked east across twenty miles of the lake to the Continental Divide and on into 200 miles of wilderness. It was both enticing and frightening. The water was an inviting transportation route. It was also good fishing for the native cutthroat trout. This racially pure trout population had lived for millennia with the bears, the Indians, the osprey, the pelicans, and other birds. It had survived occasional natural famine and disease. But by 1958 the American fisherman had created a motorboat explosion on this fishing frontier.

At that time we had not judged that the fisherman's harvest was exceeding the annual die-off surplus. Later studies by Dr. Oliver Cope, our resident aquatic biologist, changed that belief. But we had also recognized the destruction of natural peace, serenity, and quiet. A native wilderness should be a natural experience whose challenges arise when people confront natural hazards such as wind, cold, storm, or the effects of elevation. But a new and destructive crisis for the birds now arose from the roar of motors, the profanity, the hustle, and the oil drip of a normal American fisherman with a motorboat.

Should the superintendent of Yellowstone National Park do something about this imbalance? I am a fly fisherman, so I appreciated the mystique of this kind of adventure. We were constructing marinas at

Bridge Bay and at Grant Village. Certainly I was not an enemy of either fishing or boating. But the number of boats seemed alarming. Three thousand boats a year — then four thousand — then almost five thousand. Soon to be six thousand? (Fortunately, no, but we didn't know that yet.) This was a lot of boats to haul a lot of miles to dunk in a wilderness lake. The trailer parking was a real problem. The awkward things used an incredible area just for storage, unless they could be hung up. No one had put any real pressure on us — this was just considered normal, traditional park usage. But I generated my own questions on that horseback trip with Omar and Stormy. "This is a wilderness lake, Garrison. Can you keep it that way? Or at least part of it?"

My last topic for review was my hopeful sense that we were just at the forefront of a surge in public awareness of environmental welfare. (And of course, we soon had a great breakthrough in conservation literature: *Silent Spring* [Rachel Carson, 1962], *The Quiet Crisis* [Stewart Udall, 1963], and *The Greening of America* [Charles A. Reich, 1970]. The later resurgence of Aldo Leopold's *A Sand Country Almanac*, published in 1946, was also part of the blooming.) I suddenly realized that three of my problems — osprey, the Molly Islands, and motorboats — were all varying aspects of the fourth problem, people versus wilderness and wildlife. I knew we had better prepare for some changes. Ecology was becoming our new watchword.

In the compromise between the ideals of park preservation and the pressures for more and more public use by more and more urban dwellers, the National Parks were again up against the same basic use-preservation conflict they had started with in 1916 and which I first met in 1932. I still believed that we must hang on for dear life to the irreplaceable beauty and wonder of nature. But I also knew we must protect it by adjusting to increased use. This meant building respect and political support. The conservation groups would be helpful, but in 1958 they had not become potent enough. I became firmly convinced that the preservation of wilderness must come from urban support. I became more interested in the national political process, which would ultimately test and endorse conservation as an issue. Could twelve-year-old Mary Brown, who lived in "the Jungle" at 12th and Spring Garden Streets in Philadelphia, endorse wilderness values? She did not know about them, yet their salvation lay in cities like hers and in the votes of her congressman. (He was an undertaker, yet surprisingly well-informed on issues of national land use and historic preservation.)

Omar screamed at me again. "Get out!" was his message. I wanted to, but first we had to find a way to live with the ever greater groups of people who would unthinkingly overrun it all unless we provided both awareness and alternatives.

I talked with Olaus Murie, a biologist and conservationist from Alaska and Jackson Hole. (At age seventy-two he went with Chief Ranger Otto Brown on a circumnavigation of the lake by canoe.) I talked with Howard Zanhiser of the Wilderness Society. I talked with Dave Brower, then with the Sierra Club, and with Tony Smith of the old National Parks Association, now the National Wilderness and Conservation Association. I talked with Bruce Kilgore, assigned by the Sierra Club to help influence community opinion. They were all concerned about these and similar aspects of the biological problems and the political and managerial binds we were confronting. I wished we could adopt the crusade recommendations of Olaus or Zannie or Dave or Tony, or even my own evaluations of what Steve Mather might do, but my honest conclusion was that my first step must be to propose zoning on motor boats on the arms of Yellowstone Lake. I could not endorse a program to ban all motor boats on the entire lake. I knew this would never be accepted, and probably fatally damage the general cause. The public was not ready for it. But I opted for a water wilderness on upper Yellowstone Lake. We would enjoy the recreation boating and fishing provided on most of the lake, but we would also create a water wilderness in the three arms, with limited access in rowboats or canoes.

And that's the way it started. I submitted the regulations. In 1959 I could do that. Then, on December 29, 1959, Fred Seaton, Republican Secretary of the Interior, approved my zoning proposals to ban motorboats in the upper ends of the arms of the lake. Note that date — December 29, 1959. This was the beginning of a big winter in Yellowstone. It was also a time of great political shift. Three more public hearings were held in August of 1960. There were endless meetings and discussions, and much opposition from the boating interests.

In January 1961 JFK came into the White House and Stewart Udall became Secretary of the Interior. John Carver from Pocatello, Idaho (formerly Senator Frank Church's management assistant), became the Assistant Secretary in charge of parks and wildlife. He thought the National Park management was nuts — we were overloaded with mystique.

Our new boating regulations were immediately suspended, and on February 3, 1961, the new Democratic junior Senator from Wyoming, Gayle McGee, held a hearing under the auspices of the Senate Appropriations Sub-committee in Cody, Wyoming. Were the Yellowstone boating regulations urgently needed? Was there public support for them? he asked. There was not, obviously, on this day in Cody! (Senator McGee later became a good friend, but this hearing was a tough one. The report was printed, but nothing happened.) I had done my homework, and the park staff was highly supportive and helpful. We replowed the same ground several times. The local press, as usual, was unfriendly. In fact, I realized that not only my job and my career were on the line, but with John Carver calling the signals, the wilderness program for Yellowstone Lake was in trouble. Secretary Udall was not a visible protagonist; he left the public announcements to John Carver.

However, we went at everything with a strong upbeat. We knew we would make it. The last public hearing was in Salt Lake City on July 17, 1961. Mr. Francis J. (Frank) Barry, Solicitor for the Department of the Interior, was the hearings officer. (Frank is now Professor of Environmental Law in the University of Oregon, and Vice-president of the Wilderness Society.)

Following this hearing, Don Brookes, the outdoor editor of the Salt Lake City *Tribune*, wrote simply that the only change from previous hearings was that the National Park Service had become increasingly persuasive in their presentation. Conversely, Hack Miller, outdoor writer for the *Deseret News*, was still persistently opposed to the whole process. Opposition to boating was akin to insulting the institution of motherhood!

However, Senator McGee soon announced a new set of Interior Department boating regulations for Yellowstone National Park, which he had largely written himself. Nearly all of the original proposal was endorsed, and the law was in place by late summer 1961. The Lewis

River channel between Lewis Lake and Shoshone Lake was closed to motorboats. So were Shoshone Lake and Heart Lake. We had a five-mile-an-hour zone and a motorless zone in Yellowstone Lake. The "white hats" had scored a resounding victory.

Before the 1961 hearing Frank Barry had wanted to look at the actual situation on the ground, and visited Yellowstone for a day and two nights. We camped at Shoshone Lake one night, then cruised Yellowstone Lake and anchored our patrolboat cruiser off Frank Island for our second night. It was the first time I had ever spent a night on a steel boat at anchor where the lap of the waves and surges against the anchor chain resounded hollowly all night long. It was like sleeping inside a base drum!

At daylight that second morning, Frank and I rowed ashore in our dinghy and walked in about one hundred yards. We were in a completely hushed and primitive environment. There was nothing to indicate that man had ever stood here before — no ax marks, no footprints, just a quiet, deep, spongy moss on the forest floor. We sat on a moss-draped log and conversed in whispers. I thought of John Muir's great dream: "Let nature's stillness and peace flow into you . . . ." It was humbling. We could hear the silence.

As we returned to the dinghy we found on the wave-washed beach the memorabilia of the boater and the fisherman — the indestructible bits of nylon line, a wad of tin foil, bits of paper and plastic, and a tin can. The moment of tranquility was lost.

But suddenly we were observers at one of nature's great confrontations. There was an osprey nest about four hundred yards from us along Frank Island. The silhouette of a silent young osprey's beak pointed skyward. The adult was circling high offshore. Suddenly it "stooped" into a great splash of water and emerged with a fourteen-inch cutthroat trout in its talons. Laboriously it began to climb for air space to reach the nest near us. The youngster was now a noisy observer. The trout was twisting frantically in opposition, but the bird's grip was firm.

Out of the sun came a thunderbolt — a golden eagle dive-bombed the osprey in an attack designed to jolt the fish loose. (The eagle is reported to be able to do this and actually recapture the fish in midair before it hits the water.) But the writhing fish twisted the osprey to one side and the eagle missed. Suddenly the eagle put on its own brakes and began to climb for more altitude.

Then we heard the third participant in the fray. A giant black raven was circling near us calling, and then hopping among the island trees, obviously ready to move in if the osprey dropped the fish on land.

Our sympathy was with the osprey — could it be Omar? — and the hungry youngster. The parent soon circled into the rim of the nest. The raven and the eagle disappeared. We had viewed a brief moment of raw wilderness battle and the roles of the various predators in their constant struggle for food and survival. We knew we still had one osprey nest in the park — and one eagle!

Just before we departed, a fast-planing cruiser rounded the west end of Frank Island. It suddenly began to circle wildly and criss-cross its own wake. Our binoculars revealed that the boat operator was using a $25,000, twenty-five-foot cruiser with a heavy motor to pursue a pod of molting and flightless ducks. We could not observe his results, but we could easily see his boat number. As our own cruiser began its journey to the lake dock, I could not help reflecting on the tragedy of this hapless boatman. We had his number, and Solicitor Barry had a new view of the problem.

Sixteen years later, in 1977, I joined Superintendent John Townsley (son of my former Yosemite Chief Ranger) and others for a wilderness discussion and overnight in the Trail Creek ranger cabin. This was canoe country! We had come by canoe, and would return the same way. The adjacent campground had a party of canoe visitors, four people in two canoes. I walked over to visit with them and discovered that the leader of the party was a Billings businessman who had been an officer of the Billings Chamber of Commerce. He was also an officer in the Billings Boat Club, vocal about club programs, but a friendly, pleasant, and forthright young fellow. I knew him fairly well. I mentioned my surprise at finding him at Trail Creek on a canoe expedition, and he gave me an embarrassed grin.

"This is a real lame apology, Lon," he said. "But during the lake zoning controversy there were several of us who wanted you to win. We could see what was happening about motorboats on the lake, and we didn't like it. But because of local politics and business we couldn't contradict the loud-mouths who were making all the noise. I'm not proud of my silence, but that was the reality of it and it was great that you hung tough.

"I'm here today with my uncle and two sons. I come up several times each summer in my canoe. I'd sure like to say "Thank You!" We think it's great!"

I did too. Sometimes you win one — and then find out about it. Oh Frabjous Day!

CHAPTER XIX
"A CONTINUED STORY"

As Director of Midwest Region in Omaha, Director of Northeast Region in Philadelphia, and Superintendent of Albright Training Academy in Grand Canyon, I was able, from 1964 to 1973, to implement goals and priorities that the National Park Service had set for itself.

In the short two years we were in Omaha, the St. Louis Arch, "the Gateway to the West," was completed. It stands as a successful cooperative venture of the city of St. Louis, the state of Missouri, and the United States Government. The dream of the architect, Aero Sarrinen, had come true.

Another task was development of state-wide support in Minnesota to enact legislation in Congress for Voyageurs National Park. The Voyageurs National Park Association was formed. Members came from all walks of life: "Judge" Ullyses Hella, Director of State Parks; Governor (and later Senator) Wendell Anderson; Judge Edwin Chapman; Congressman John Blatnik; and later James Overstar, who succeeded Blatnik. One businessman, Wayne Judy, almost lost his fishing tackle and boating business in International Falls because he supported the park.

The borning of a park is nearly always politically rough. The local people who have the most to gain over the years are generally against a new park (they prefer the status quo), and the protagonists are the nonresident visionaries, as were Yellowstone's Washburn Langford Doane party of 1870. (Acadia National Park in Maine and Isle Royale in Michigan came into the National Park Service easily without the corrosive memories that often don't disappear for at least two generations.)

I dealt with four great parks of our country in the Midwest Region: Rocky Mountain National Park, Glacier National Park, Grand Teton National Park, and Yellowstone National Park. There were historic sites like Fort Laramie and Custer Battlefield, and underway were the restoration of Bents Old Fort and the stabilization of Fort Larned. Pipestone National Historic Monument and Grand Portage National Monument were also in the region. In 1972 the old Midwest Region was divided into two regions — Rocky Mountain Region and Midwest Region, as a part of a general reorganization in the geographic jurisdiction of the regional offices.

Several recreation areas were in the region also: Yellowtail on the Big Horn River, Flaming Gorge on the Green River, and three on the Gunnison River. It was my first involvement in the planning and management of Recreation Areas.

George Bagley was the Deputy Director in Midwest Region during my tenure. He had been Chief Ranger at Yellowstone and Superintendent of Isle Royale National Park and Lake Mead Recreation Area. He had also worked in the Washington, D.C. office.

When I arrived in Omaha, Mrs. Lorraine Mintsmeyer was a part of the steno pool. She was eager to learn all the facts of the management of parks and the Midwest Region office. In a few years she became the Superintendent of Buffalo River, and later the first female Regional Director. She was an able, honest, and ingenious administrator, keeping the good of the parks foremost in her mind.

Duane Jacobs and I had rangered together in Yosemite. Omaha brought us together again. Jake and Fred Novak, a friend from my Glacier days, were both highly principled men, and a joy to work with. In Sequoia I had worked under Assistant Superintendent Dan Tobin. His son Jim and I were to meet again in Omaha. The coming together of old friends and acquaintances again and again, and the respect we felt for each other, probably prompted the title of Ronnie Lee's book, *The Park Service Family.*

Omaha was a good experience — friendly people, a challenging job, and a town large enough for good theater and art. My next assignment was in Philadelphia as Northeast Regional Director, upon the retirement of Ronnie Lee, the well-known historian.

Some of the staff members in Philadelphia suggested that as I travelled between Omaha and Philadelphia, I could visit the University of Ohio at Miami. There I might represent the Secretary of the Interior by taking part in a ceremony presenting a National Historic

Landmark plaque honoring the McGuffey *Readers*. These plaques had just been created by the Interior Department in a new program. The timing was advantageous, and the university desired to cap such a ceremony with an academic procession and an address by university President Vernon R. Alden. This opened new avenues of inquiry. Yes, the University of Ohio was indeed an early public university with proper bonafides as to dates and academic recognition. Yes, William Holmes McGuffey, the president of the university, had in the 1840s authored the series of McGuffey's *Eclectic Readers* — all twenty-four of them! Each of them was immediately sold to a publishing house for fifty dollars, so although the total printing was in the millions of copies, McGuffey himself profited only fifty dollars for each reader. It was a daring course of study of academic creativity, and Ohio had chosen to honor McGuffey and the academic office in which the readers were produced as a creative cultural achievement. This fit neatly into the new National Historic Landmark program which had only recently been authorized. So I stopped in Miami and presented the bronze plaque from the Department of Interior.

It was an inspiring ceremony — the first of many in which the National Park Service joined with the states in designating National Historic Landmarks. The Park Service was the action agency. Each state was invited to nominate and then establish its own group of localized historic places. The individual owners agreed to care for the sites properly. There were landmarks of history and landmarks of natural history. For the historically rich Northeast this program was especially rewarding.

My introduction to the Historic Landmarks came with my transfer to Philadelphia and my fortuitous proximity to some of Ohio's great historic places. I enjoyed the proud moments. My memory encompasses only a few choice gems: the point of the beginning of the public land survey in the United States on the Ohio River; the Albert Gallatin homestead in southeast Pennsylvania; the American Philosophical Society in Philadelphia; the first flat racing track in America at Goshen, New York; the Sleepy Hollow historical places along the Hudson River in New York; Franklin Roosevelt's summer home at Campobello, Nova Scotia; Dodge Home in Council Bluffs, Iowa; South Pass, Wyoming; the Chesapeake and Ohio Canal; Phillipse Manor; the Legends of Ichabod Crane; and the Quaker Meeting House in Flushing, New York.

There were several areas that defied classification as historical grounds. Or they were experimental units with unique ties, which required individual adjustments. One such creation was Fire Island National Seashore (one of the Barrier Islands south of Long Island), a challenge which Secretary of the Interior Stewart Udall referred to as a battle for "the winning of the East." Cape Cod was a new category — a National Park that encompassed five towns. St. Gaudens National Historic Site (near Conway, New Hampshire) was a tribute to the Hudson River school of sculptors and painters. Assateague Island included a charming, wild beach pony herd within the boundaries of the two proud states of Virginia and Maryland. President Eisenhower's Gettysburg farm was both cultural and historic. Campobello was on the Canadian shore, but related to FDR's family history.

The Northeast Region was an exemplar of the new dimension to which my ranger career had led — inevitable, logical, all legislatively proper. Most of these new dimensions were guided by citizens' advisory commissions. Strangely, Inger and I liked it, and often her growing dedication to the arts and crafts of America crossed the boundaries of both jobs. "Neat," youth might call it. "Delightful," was our own phraseology.

When I transferred to the job of Director of the Northeast Region, it was almost like an old party game of "musical chairs" or "the stage coach turned over." The staff had a new boss, a ranger, who was not a historian, but entirely a National Park man. I had a new crew, some of them uneasy about possible new seats. I still supervised about thirty National Park units, and only two of them were National Parks — Acadia in Maine and Isle Royale in Michigan. These two islands were lovely; they offered no new management problems. We did find that it was very expensive to cruise on the Isle Royale ship *The Ranger*. This 125-foot diesel motorboat was a "carry-all" for the park, with the curious distinction that since the park had only limited facilities for roads and trails, the Congress conveniently adjusted their appropriation by allotting an equivalent amount to construct and operate this beautiful, but costly, craft for passengers, wildlife management, freight hauling, research, and ranger patrols.

Most of the competent and knowledgeable field crews and regional staffs were attuned to my kind of management by objectives. The parks themselves were as anticipated. The field areas were superb, and included Independence National Historical Park, the Statue of Liberty, Gettysburg, Hopewell Village, Saratoga, Boston, Theodore Roosevelt's home, and Hyde Park. Our personal adjustment to these riches was smoothly done. My chapter about Hopewell Village reveals our love affair with Colonial history. There was much more.

The mid-1960s were turbulent years. Our young people were protesting the Viet Nam war. Black people gathered on the mall in Philadelphia in front of Independence Hall by the tens of thousands for a march on Washington; it was a peaceful gathering. We lived two blocks away on Locust Street. Independence Hall has always been a focal point for all those seeking freedom. Anniversaries of countries' natal days were celebrated with speeches and music. There was something going on at Independence Hall every day. Milford O. Anderson was the superintendent; he had set up very workable plans for managing a demonstration. He notified the press and the Chamber of Commerce when people were to assemble. Protesting groups had to be scheduled by the hour so that opposite viewpoints were not represented on the grounds at the same time. Ethnic groups also made the Hall theirs.

The Statue of Liberty became another symbol for protest, to a lesser degree simply because one could get there only by boat. Ellis Island continued to be an emotionally provoking piece of land. Almost everyone in this country has a relative, or knows someone, who came into this country as an immigrant and passed through Ellis Island. A group of black people led by a New York neurologist wanted to take over the island and use it as a rehabilitation center for drug addicts and as a work training center. Their plan was to invade and capture the island, but their boat stalled, and nothing came of the publicity.

We lived in Philadelphia in the 1768 home built by Mr. Rapoon, a breeches maker. This house had been restored with much tender loving care, and we treasured the "un-square" construction: "the Father, the Son, and the Holy Ghost" floor plan; the rose garden; and the compatibility with our Hopewell Village furnishings. The address was 410 Locust Street, adjacent to St. Mary's cemetery, which had been used as Dr. Rush's dissection laboratory as he worked with the beginnings of the Pennsylvania Hospital. So, "Hello, Ranger!"

The Philadelphia Council of the Boy Scouts of America suggested to me that I become a commissioner for their council. They were interested in enlivening their program for urban scout troops, not in "woodsy" tasks, but in activities for "block patrol." An urban block patrol was one city block square, and included "turf" problems. As there were only a few male residents in these enclaves, mothers served as scout masters or troop committee members.

What might we suggest for scouting activities? Window boxes for flowers, vacant lot clean-up, rat control contests, house number visibility contests, city park campouts, lessons in family and community courtesies, and reading about western scout lore. How much of this might we translate into boy scout formats?

Then, after five years of northeastern National Park leadership I was suddenly asked to consider a return to Grand Canyon as Superintendent of the Mather-Albright Training Academy. I had also been asked by several universities to join their graduate faculties, and I found contemplation of that kind of work with young people who were pursuing park careers, to be inviting. I wanted to try a book about my adventures, and Inger, who has always had a happy faculty for being involved in the tasks at hand, would have been happy to retire in the Philadelphia cultural milieu, but the environmental allure of continuing park identity and leadership was impelling. "Here we go again! Move number fourteen."

By mid-summer the formalities were complete. I was Superintendent of the Ranger Training Academy, and my roving ranger days came to a halt.

Our next move was to Texas A&M University. "But why Texas A&M?" I am asked with some astonishment, on occasion. Actually, the population of graduate students is such that my opportunity to have some academic influence was higher at Texas A&M than seemed probable elsewhere.

So we did it. Albright and then the University.

CHAPTER XX

EPILOGUE: THE SPIRIT OF THE RIVER

In September 1975 I attended the tri-ennial session of the International Union for the Conservation of Nature (IUCN), held that year in Kinshassa, the capitol city of Zaire, West Africa. I had been a long-time personal member of IUCN because I was interested in its conservancy programs. But this was the first time I had attended a meeting. I had just retired from the United States National Park Service, and this meeting promised to be a rewarding conservation review.

An afternoon discussion was led by Dr. E. P. Assibey, Ecological Science Advisor to the government of Ghana, on a proposed electrical power project. His topic was "The Spirit of the River."

He talked with his people about the physical factors of the dam, such as elevation differentials and latent energy, the flood pool, the quantity and the quality of water, and finally the dam construction, the economics, and the machinery needed to generate the power. He ended with a discussion of the construction clutter that would ensue. However, he could not answer inquiries about the Spirit of the River. And, as 85 percent of the local population lived in rural communities along the stream, this had become an important emotional issue.

The river was a major force in the people's lives. It dominated their landscape. It controlled their agriculture and their economy. It was part of their culture and their mores. And its friendly Spirit had nurtured the traditions and transitions of many generations. Their weather fluctuations and their harvests depended upon support of the Spirit. How might a dam alter it? Would it displease this powerful ally? It was worrisome.

I have thought of this situation often in discussions about an American lake or dam across a stream. We speak of the latent foot-pounds of energy, the water quality, the number of bathers served, the biomass or the tons of fish protein produced, the oxygen generated from the

[299]

ecosystem, or even its beauty. But we have seldom remembered the water Spirit — the ethereal wist or memory trace of our own cultural heritage.

Look at this inspirational factor in a number of active situations. Begin with the "Spirits" of the Grand Canyon of the Colorado River. In the grinding of the boulders during flood stage from a side stream; in the roar and vibration, the growling and the might of Lava Falls Rapids; in the lovely dancing water patterns near Deer Creek Falls Rapids; in the pleasant laughter of Bright Angel Creek — there are several river Spirits. Are they annoyed with man's interference with their daily patterns and routines? The John Wesley Powell Expedition of 1876 dubbed the muddy and alkaline Fremont River just above the Grand Canyon "the Dirty Devil," and, by contrast, the sweet water of the next major tributary was "just like a Bright and Shining Angel!" The names and the personifications persist.

There is a mystique with each of the natural and scenic special jewels of America, and of the beautiful and inspirational places of the world. I have experienced many of these in America's National Parks. Think of the Grand Canyon again, eternal and occasionally rim-full of clouds; then the great westerly face of The Sierra del Carmen in Big Bend at sunset; or a mid-summer visit to Trail Ridge Road in Rocky Mountain National Park and a stroll onto the edges of the tundra. This may quickly bring you to your knees as you view the glory of nature around your feet in the miniatures of grasses, flowers, and shrubs — a great bounty of floral micro-beauty. Smell the lushness and sudden eruption of spring freshness in the southwestern desert, or follow the blazing glimpses of a cactus blossom, the misty cloud of blue ceniza flowers in response to brief desert showers. Each of these carries a quiet and sacred mystique. View the lunar rainbow at the foot of Yosemite Falls as the soft mist drifts quietly around you. The Spirit of Yosemite Falls enthralls you with its ethereal Lethe.

I ride on horseback to the very top of the trail through Donahue Pass on the eastern boundary of Yosemite National Park and stop abruptly. Suddenly, I see to the far edge of the world in the eastern distance, across an endless jumble of wild mountain tops. Standing as tall as I can before the Lord, I am humbled and bareheaded and silent. I have met Creation.

An old lady at the Grand Canyon murmurs to her companion, "I feel that I must whisper!"

A visitor to the Liberty Bell drops to her knees and quite obviously offers a quiet prayer, rises, kisses the bell, and walks out. Why does this seem a natural place for her to offer her devotions?

The joy and inspiration, the uplift of beauty, the song of wonder. This is the essence of the great places of nature or history in the world. Spirits dwell in all of them, and for me they are kindly Spirits of environmental completeness and the grace of nature.

We do not often speak of the evanescent or the inspirational, but they are a very real part of our total resource heritage, where a dream becomes a reality rather readily. I found that the beautiful, clear Current River in the Missouri Ozarks gave an absolute impression of purity and unfettered flow as the limpid, clear water swirled joyfully over sandbars — a sensation satisfying to behold and experience. Similarly, I found the rustle of incoming tide with its liquid water beauty at Trunk Bay in the Virgin Islands equally unforgettable. These are among our jewels!

Do we treasure them? Can we find ways in our eager land management formulas to rediscover their intangible ideals, to structure organization that will care for them, to articulate the formal political language needed in statements of purpose, environment, objectives, standards, master plans, and legislation? Can we truly communicate from our own unlifted spirits and hearts? Can we express our concerns for the Spirit of the Colorado River or the Spirit of the Grizzly Giant Tree, or of Old Faithful Geyser? Or are we locked irretrievably into an economic measure, and can only ask, "What good are they?"

I had a stunning experience during the full eruption of Old Faithful Geyser at 2:00 A.M. in mid-February 1959. In the moonlight at twenty below zero, a lonesome coyote sang an obligatto in rhythm with my own shivering spine. As Yellowstone National Park Superintendent, I was attending a cold weather seminar at Old Faithful with Dr. Vincent Shafer of the State University of New York. After a stimulating evening of conversation, was unable to sleep. So I crawled out of my comfortable Woods Robe sleeping bag and into typical Alaskan or Yellowstone mid-winter garb. Over my woolen underwear I pulled a Hudson Bay wool shirt and pants, thick socks and shoe pacs, fur cap and mittens, and finally a great parka. I crunched my way through four inches of noisy snow to the Old Faithful boardwalk. The geyser was somnolent, and only a silent wisp of steam marked it at all.

This was a memorable night. Moonlight below a black sky jewelled with star brilliance. In many parts of the northland the statement is made that the moonlight is often bright enough to illuminate a newspaper. I do not know why it must be a newspaper, but I have no doubt at all that at least I could have read the headlines under the Old Faithful moon. My fur cap with huge earflaps wrapped my face warmly. The tiny plume of steam from my own exhaltations, and the bite of frost in my nostrils and the catch in my throat kept me alert to the problems of survival under these circumstances at twenty below.

But suddenly there was a puff of steam from Old Faithful — a hiss, a gurgle, and again quiet; I was to witness a noisy and spectacular eruption under these lonely circumstances, while the friendly coyote announced his territorial salute. There was another kind of atavistic chill in my gut.

Another gurgle — a rumble — a soft splashing, and again silence. But the premonitory display continued with more jets of steam and higher and higher splashing of water, until with a great roar the steam column burst free into a shaft of white water going up and up until a vagrant breeze caught the top of the rising plume and flung it away to the south in a shower of white ice crystals.

A pause, and then a spurt of renewed ejaculation to greater heights and crescendo and excitement. A great splashing of falling water amid a rolling cloud of steam — I am uptight and tense with it, fists clenched into the big mittens, jaw and belly muscles taut.

At full eruption the column began to waver, the jet sagged, and my own tensions subsided as the spent column suddenly receded into a blur of light vapor. Another surge — a spasm — a great splashing of water, but the roar had climaxed. The geyser halted with diminishing splashes, followed by the gurgle of running water hurrying across the frozen ground to join the Firehole River enroute to sea level and the Gulf of Mexico.

What a violence of birth! What a beginning to a journey of thousands of miles and a drop of thousands of feet in elevation! This new water might be intercepted and stolen away in West Yellowstone or

Three Forks or Great Falls or Minot for irrigation or domestic use, or even for sewer system flushing — but this phase of the hydrological cycle was complete, and the water hastened along to meet its next appointment.

This was my perception of Old Faithful. In the moonlight adventure in mid-winter, I followed my own guidelines and enjoyed the scenery by looking at it with my sensibilities and sensitivities at full pitch. This is part of the looking. And the Spirit of Old Faithful was about that night, and it was mighty and real and moving, and I said "Thank you, Mr. Old Faithful — you keep a tidy shop!"

Some years later, in another aspect of mystique, I presented a Registered National Historical Landmark Plaque for an ancient structure called The Friends' Meeting House in Flushing, on Long Island, New York. This rustic, unpainted, and sturdy structure, built about 1685, had served the local congregation of Quakers for almost 250 years, and was still the spiritual center of their church lives. Many generations of Friends had worshipped there; it had also been a community center for airing political controversy, for sharing observations on economic events, a center for cultural discussions, and a point for intellectual understandings.

As I stood there, humble indeed in my temerity in seeking to glorify this building beyond its own character and significance, it came to me suddenly that the river Spirit was here! And as this church marked a continuum of mankind's cultural, intellectual, and religious history, so many of our great and wild natural areas are repositories of nature's wisdom and lore and lessons, in the unbroken chain of natural law which has controlled their events since the beginning of their own time. So the mixture of natural history and human history in our National Park system seems completely natural and logical.

In a very real, but too often unrecognized sense, our National Parks are indeed great historic storybooks of the geology, the environment, and the processes and forces which have shaped both the land, and the people, who have lived on and with them. But they are more; they are the homes of the Spirits of man and of the river.

This is the message I was impelled to present to the Quaker congregation, as I shared my own deep personal philosophy of the satisfaction that comes from working with history and nature. The programs of the National Parks are our faith and heritage, our trust, and my task.

It was appropriate that my own historic divination was in an ecclesiastical, or churchyard, environment, just as it was in a Monastery Churchyard in Tibet fifty years ago that botanists rediscovered the Dawn Redwood — the *Meta-Sequoia* — long considered extinct. Dr. Ralph Chaney, a paleobotanist in the University of California, realized that in the enclosed spiritual compound this relic of natural history had fortunately been preserved over the centuries. Those beautiful and strange trees were old friends — the *Meta-Sequoia*! And since that time I have noted in many churchyards and rural cemeteries the historical natural islands often preserved. Rural or urban, such sanctuaries are often the only natural green spots or wildflower gardens in the community. I had learned this as a teenage bird hunter. Although I never dared the sacrilege of hunting there, country churchyards frequently provided shelter for quail, pheasants, doves, and other game birds.

Often these were historical plant islands. So, quietly near or within the pulpit, as at the Friends' Meeting House, we might enjoy such natural glory, and at the same time faintly sense the reverberations of the thunder of faith, freedom, and spiritual pronouncements. Our forefathers developed an euphemism in "the Harmony of the Spheres" to account for the celestial pattern, the miracles enacted daily in the simple acts of sunrise and sunset, the land, and its response in beauty and crops. It persists. The Spirit of the River and the Harmony of the Spheres are companions. We must pause momentarily in honor of this awareness. I stand taller in the home of the Spirit of the River. It is my home also.

APPENDIX

"Camper Activities in Yosemite Valley"
Study of 1937–1938

originally published in
Vol. XVIII, *Yosemite Nature Notes*, No. 6, June 1939

An analysis of the travel into Yosemite National Park during 1938 showed that 41 percent were one-day visitors, 33 percent stayed at the Park Operator's units, and 26 percent stayed in the free public campgrounds. However, when the length of stay of all three groups was considered, a totally different picture developed. Out of the 1,233,500 visitor days in Yosemite Valley between May 1 and September 30, the campers in free campgrounds with their longer average stay, accounted for 59 percent of the total days' use; those who stayed at the Park Operator's units accounted for 28 percent, while the one-day trippers dropped to 13 percent. Thus, it would seem that in any study of the problem of overcrowding in Yosemite Valley, it would have a direct bearing if we could determine the appeals that brought in the close to 20,000 campers and led them to stay an average of nearly seven days apiece. With this thought in mind, during the summers of 1937 and 1938, questionnaires were distributed to the campers to try to determine camper interests. If a direct question were asked — "Why do you want to camp in Yosemite Valley?" — many of the visitors would be unable to formulate a truthful and satisfactory reply. They quite honestly didn't know exactly why they came. Rather, an indirect approach was used — to find out what the campers did and then assume that these things were the ones that interested them the most.

No effort was made to contact all of the campers. In 1938 the questionnaire covered only 1572 cases — about 2 percent of the campers. To obtain this many samples, 2140 papers were distributed, giving us a return of 74 percent, which is very high for this type of survey. It is a good indication of public cooperation.

In distributing the questionnaires, a carefully prepared schedule was followed which took account of three variables as determined from the 1937 statistics. First, the percentage of the total population in the different camps, thus allowing for any differences in the quality of population. Second, the week of the camping season, in case there should be any difference in the class of campers at different times during the summer. Third, the day of the week, to distinguish between the mid-week and weekend visitors, and sample them both alike.

When a test of this type is used more than once, the correlation between the results of different samplings, or between the samplings of different years, is a fairly reliable index to the adequacy of the sampling and the reliability of the results. Using this criterion, the correlation of .968 between the 1937 and 1938

[305]

results would indicate that this test has measured fairly accurately the activities of the Yosemite Valley campers.

Prior to the listing of the general activities, some questions were included on which information was wanted. Question One asked:

"For cooking do you use (   ) Gasoline Stove   (   ) Campfire   (   ) Both?"

The results show that 57 percent of all campers used gasoline stoves exclusively, 16 percent a campfire, and 23 percent both. Miscellaneous and no answer, 4 percent. The interesting thing on this tabulation is that 60 percent of the campers at least had gasoline stoves with them. This figure was exactly the same in the 1937 questionnaire. Of course, the shortage of firewood in Yosemite Valley may have something to do with the number of people coming here who bring stoves with them, and this percentage might not be applicable to other campgrounds in other areas.

Part two of the same question asked:

"Do you have a campfire of your own in the evening? (   ) Yes   (   ) No."

Fifty-two percent indicated that they had an evening campfire, 42 percent did not, and 6 percent did not answer the question. Certainly this is an interesting item. It probably illustrates more clearly than any other one the extreme changes there have been in camping habits in the past twenty years. Formerly, the communal spirit of sitting round an evening campfire, talking, singing, and telling stories, was considered one of the prime advantages of going camping. However, the present condition is right in line with modern social trends which do not give much emphasis to self entertainment in the evening, or any other time. Obviously if 42 percent do not have evening campfires, this same 42 percent must not stay "at home" in the evening. And, if they do not stay in their own camp, they must go to some of the entertainments provided: talks, programs, dances, and shows. And, there are some advantages to this. It reduces the number of fires and the consequent scattering of ashes which are detrimental to tree growth. Also it provides an opportunity to expose these visitors to some of our National Park Service educational efforts.

These figures are particularly interesting in connection with planning any campground layouts. Obviously each camp will not need a cooking type of fireplace. Possibly the best equipment would be a fire layout that could be used either for cooking or an open fire in the evening, with fires confined to these places only.

Question Two:

"Have you ever camped before in Yosemite Valley? (   ) Yes   (   ) No. How many times?"

On the 1938 questionnaire, 54 percent had camped here before as compared with 51 percent in 1937. In 1938, 43 percent had not camped here before, and 48 percent in 1937. The balance did not answer the question. Average number of times was 3.67 for the 1938 group, and 3.36 for the 1937 group. One interpretation of these figures would be that the percentage of our "permanent" camp population is increasing slightly and along with that is a normal increase in the average number of visits. Apparently those who come in time after time must be satisfied. Figures from the 1937 questionnaire indicate that 11 percent of all campers had never been camping before. Reasoning from this, it would seem logical that the acceptance of overcrowding, and the casual toleration of camp surroundings far removed from the normal forest environment they supposedly come to seek, is at least in part a responsibility of the Park Service. The people don't know any better, merely taking what is offered. If many of them were forced to move to a really isolated spot, it would scare them out. Observation further bears this out. In the fall, when camps become scattered, many people move just to be near to other camps.

Also, if this observed increase of the percentage of repeaters is a true increase and not a minor fluctuation due to inadequate sampling, we may expect an increase of campers year by year, assuming that the number of newcomers remains about constant. This makes a study of what they do and why they come of even more interest to the park administration.

Question Three asked for an indication of age group. Results were: No answer, 2 percent; over 50, 16 percent. 31–50, 46 percent; 26–30, 13 percent; 21–25, 13 percent; 15–20, 10 percent. One reason for getting this data was to determine if the younger part of the campground population — age fifteen to twenty — was really as high a percentage as it seemed, or if they were mainly conspicuous by reason of their greater activity, noise, and spectacular dress. A Forest Service questionnaire used in 1937 gave only 7 percent for this group. It would have seemed reasonable to assume that this figure was off by at least 15 percent. However, our figures indicate that the juveniles are really only a minor part of the camp population picture. By comparison, the 1930 U.S. census figures give 9.5 percent as the number in this age group.

Question Four:

"In choosing a campground, do you prefer one that is (   ) 1, busy and near the center of things, or   (   ) 2, quiet, several miles from a recreational center?"

On this question the answers were about even, with a slight majority preferring the busy campgrounds. The results in 1937 were the same. There does not seem to be much room for doubt that the Yosemite Valley campgrounds are "Busy and near the center of things" rather than "Quiet, several miles from a recreational center"; and under those circumstances the most obvious conclusion is that about half of the campers do not know what a really isolated campground is like. There have been a number of contributing factors to this situation. Many visitors date their camping experience to the construction of good roads to the mountains, bringing crowds that overloaded the existing campgrounds. And, as new campgrounds were opened, even if there were room for only very few campsites, these were put right beside each other for greater ease of administration. So, again, if many of the visitors think they are in a really quiet and isolated spot when they camp in Yosemite Valley, the responsibility for this misapprehension is not theirs. There has been no opportunity to learn anything different.

Further along this line, the campers in camps twelve and eleven furnish the majority of those voting for a "quiet" campground. Relatively speaking, camps 11 and 12 are more quiet than camp fourteen, yet they are still short of an ideally isolated camp. Thus, we have campers coming in here because it is a busy place with many things to do located in one area, while others come in sincere in the belief that because they go across the river or the road to camps eleven and twelve, they are in a quiet place. It provides considerable insight into the mental processes of the campers to learn this.

Question Five:

This question listed fifteen campgrounds in Yosemite National Park outside the valley, and along automobile roads, and asked if any of the campers had at any time used these campgrounds. Twenty percent checked one or more of the outlying camps. The most popular of these camps in the order named were: Tuolumne Meadows, Mariposa Grove, Tenaya Lake, Glacier Point, Wawona, White Wolf, and Yosemite Creek.

Part two of the same question asked reasons for camping in the valley this time if the camper had checked the first part of the question. Eight reasons were given for checking with write-ins requested. Of the eight listed, the three most outstanding were: more diversified recreation for all the family, more conveniences, and a more extensive naturalist program. Following were: better recreation provided for children, more company, dances, bears less bothersome than in outlying camps, and better advertised. The write-ins were sporadic, totaling only twenty-five. Of these, seven wrote in "I like it," evidently a vague, nostalgic sort of feeling towards the place.

These results tend to prove what was suspected — that the lure of the Yosemite Valley campgrounds is mainly in the things to do and the conveniences provided. Good roads, piped water, and modern comfort stations seem to outweigh the call of the wild in most campers' minds. The easiest thing to do is the one that gets done. Consequently, the easiest place to drive, and the one where there is the least thinking to do about recreation, is the one that is used. This throws some light on the problem of encouraging the use of the outlying camps. To accomplish much along these lines it will probably be necessary to make these camps seem as attractive as Yosemite Valley. This attraction would not be limited to the provision of all the physical details of a well-equipped camp, but would include things to do — drives, hikes, and programs. After all, one of Yosemite's chief charms is that it is almost an ideal camping place for families. There are recreations geared to every age group. If the outlying camps are to compete with the valley attractions, either these same attractions must be installed in reasonable amount, or the valley entertainment curtailed.

Question Six:

This question listed twenty-three activities and asked for check marks to indicate in which of them the visitor participated while in the valley. Since the correlation between this list in 1938 and the one in 1937 is .968, the 1937 list is omitted, and only the 1938 rating given here. "Museum Visits" came first in visitor participation with 80 percent. This was followed by "Hikes With Own Party," 75 percent; "Drives to Scenic Points," 71 percent; "Bear Feeding and Talks," 69 percent; "Just Resting," 62 percent; "Camp 14 Program," 57 percent; "Visit Museum Garden," 55 percent; "Campfire Program, Own Campground," 53 percent; "Visit Indian Demonstration," 51 percent, and "Swimming in the River," 50 percent.

Following these first eleven items, there was a definite break in the percentages. Fishing interested 21 percent, as did dances. Twenty percent read in the Museum library. The same number — 17 percent — went bicycling and attended nature hikes. Sixteen percent joined the auto caravan, and 13 percent swam in the Lodge or Curry Pool. Ten percent went to movies, and 5 percent on horseback trips. Three percent played tennis, and 1 percent took tours by bus. Only five played golf — less than one-half of 1 percent.

When these items were listed by campgrounds, the average correlation between the camps was .955. This is so high that it is safe to assume that there is no great difference among the various campgrounds as to the amount, extent, or priority of participation in the various activities. While the visitors in camp eleven voted 81 percent in favor of a quiet campground, they then took part in nearly as many activities as those in camp seven who voted 65 percent in favor of a busy camp. Also, there was no appreciable difference in the quality of the activities they liked. This further bears out the idea that the majority of those who state that they favor a "quiet" campground really don't know what they mean.

The average number of activities per person was 8.03. On the basis of age groups, the number of activities showed a steady increase from 7.40 for those over fifty, to 8.83 for those fifteen to twenty. There was no significant difference among the various campgrounds as to the number of activities.

Question Seven:

This question asked for double-checking of the three items in which there was the most frequent participation. It represents the repeat value of any activity. Obviously a visitor might like to go fishing every day while one auto caravan might satisfy him — not that he has seen it all, but he has seen all that interests him. Thus, there is a qualitative difference that might normally be expected to show up in these tabulations. Also, a length of stay has considerable bearing on the results of this question, but inasmuch as there were some campers who stayed the full thirty days and double-checked four or five items, as well as those who stayed only one or two days and double-checked none at all, it was felt that this factor would about average up the data as a whole. The percentages given represent the number of those participating in an activity who then double-checked it, and have no direct relation to the total number checking an item:

"Hikes with Own Party," 45 percent; "Fishing," 45 percent; "Swimming in River," 44 percent; "Drives to Scenic Points," 41 percent; "Camp 14 Program," 39 percent; "Naturalist Conducted Hikes," 37 percent; "Campfire Programs, Own Campground," 36 percent; "Dances," 35 percent; "Just Resting," 34 percent; "Curry Program," "Horseback Trips," and "Tennis," 23 percent. The rest tapered on down to "Visits to Indian Demonstration," with 6 percent.

In applying these figures, it would seem reasonable that the activities having a high repeat value should be those stressed in any development of outstanding campgrounds planned to relieve the load in Yosemite Valley. Trails for hikes, heavy planting of fish nearby, a good swimming pool in a lake or stream, drives, and a campfire program area.

Of this list, fishing seems to be the item which is most likely to misinterpretation. Observation indicates that usually the man of the family is the one who goes fishing while the rest of the group takes in other activities. Thus, since father is presumably the boss and must be consulted in choosing a vacation site, fishing would play a far more important part in the general picture than might be indicated by the number fishing.

Further, in planning developments elsewhere, care must be taken to include items having an appeal to the whole family. Of this list, the educational opportunities for children offered would be quite important. There are few incentives more powerful in influencing parents than that of offering educational advantages for children.

Written comments were asked for on every page. Thirty-nine percent wrote a comment of some type. Nearly half of these implied general approval by some phrase such as "Swell," "O.K.," "Perfect!," or "Well pleased." The rest of the comments were divided among criticisms of sanitation, roads, Yosemite Park and Curry Company operations, praise for rangers and ranger-naturalists, and a general miscellany of odds and ends. Here, as in most of the items on the questionnaires, the public cooperation in filling them out was highly satisfactory.

From special tabulations the following data are taken: (1) Of all campers, 40 percent had children of school age. (2) There was an average participation of 50 percent in the "Indigenous" activities; 46 percent in the "Educational" activities; and 18 percent in the "Exotic" types of activity. These figures were exactly the same on the 1937 study. (3) If only one activity was joined, "Just Resting" was the most frequently indicated. If two were marked, "Hikes with Own Party" were added. If three activities were checked, there was time for "Museum Visits," or "Drives to Scenic Points." If four activities were indicated, "Visits to the area below the Old Village to see the bears and hear the talks" were added to the list.

In conclusion, probably one of the most interesting results of this study was the amount of camper cooperation received. Most of the campers are substantial, reasonable individuals with a feeling of love and respect for Yosemite. The manner of presentation of any problem to them will largely determine the response, as they start with a very friendly attitude towards the Park Service and would be glad to be of help in supporting moves that seem reasonable. In other words, it might well be possible to increase the quality of use in Yosemite Valley by a well thought out, aggressive, educational campaign. Certainly some of the problems now facing the National Park Service, both in the campgrounds and in other areas, might be ameliorated by presenting them and a proposed solution to the people who create them.

Certainly campers are human beings with human, understandable ways of thought and action. It is interesting to know what they consider worth doing on their visits to Yosemite Valley, and still more interesting to get some insight into their mental reactions to the conditions they meet while here.